ROSARIO CANDELA & THE NEW YORK APARTMENT 1927–1937

David Netto

ROSARIO CANDELA & THE NEW YORK APARTMENT

1927–1937

Foreword by Aerin Lauder

Essays by Paul Goldberger and Peter Pennoyer

Designed by Takaaki Matsumoto

New York · Paris · London · Milan

TABLE OF CONTENTS

FOREWORD

Aerin Lauder

There are few architects who have shaped the Manhattan skyline quite like Rosario Candela, a maestro of the early twentieth century who revolutionized prewar apartment living on the Upper East Side and beyond. Like so many native New Yorkers, I knew his buildings long before I knew his name. Growing up, I would often pass his famous projects along Fifth and Park Avenues, looking up at their signature setbacks and water towers, each one an unforgettable presence on the city skyline. But I've also had the great pleasure of calling his buildings home, experiencing their extraordinary architecture firsthand both as an adult and a child. Now as then, I am captivated by the genius of his work, from the beauty and restraint of his classical facades to the complexity of his layouts. Stepping across his checkerboard marble floors, surrounded by original molding, you just feel time stand still.

I can think of no one better to revisit and celebrate the architect's legacy than my dear friend David Netto, a star designer who came of age on the Upper East Side immersed in Candela's lore. Though we were peers as children, David and I only got to know one another later in life, as our professional paths crisscrossed over the past decade. Still I have long been a fan of his wonderful interiors, which draw upon the past while forgoing cookie-cutter nostalgia. His sense of ease and refinement is so special, from the elegance with which he layers a room down to the way he presents himself, in classic preppy perfection. Like Candela before him, David is now reinventing tradition for the present moment, redefining what it means to live well.

Candela may have been coy when it came to his ideas, famously hiding his drafting table behind velvet ropes as a student (or so the legend goes). But David is generous with his wisdom and wit. Whether co-hosting a preview of the Hubert de Givenchy auction with me at Christie's in Paris or sharing the stage for our panel at the Antiques & Garden Show of Nashville, David always makes everyone around him laugh and learn.

That deep knowledge and benevolent spirit are David's gifts, and he bestows them upon us in this remarkable book alongside essays by two other consummate New Yorkers, architecture critic Paul Goldberger and architect Peter Pennoyer, both talents I tremendously admire. Together their voices bring new research and fresh perspective to Candela's work as they graciously unpack the fundamentals of his buildings. Floor plans, facades, fenestration—these elements and more come alive through their words. No matter if you are a new student of Candela's innovations or already an aficionado of his pioneering buildings, the chapters that follow offer an unparalleled look into a timeless world. And we are so fortunate to have these three marvelous scholars as our guides.

PUZZLE BOXES AND CITIES IN THE SKY

David Netto

Nerds

It would be impossible to dream the dreams we have of New York without the architecture of Rosario Candela.

Candela's apartment houses are the means by which we know the great residential neighborhoods of the Upper East Side and Sutton Place—the built environment by which they signify. They are the crown jewels of Park and Fifth Avenues. His legacy and somewhat mysterious genius as a designer have been examined with a growing momentum, beginning with the first mention of him, which I am aware of, in Paul Goldberger's *The City Observed* (1979). In a few words, Paul captured the importance of their silhouettes in the visual landscape of New York, describing the towers of 770 and 778 Park Avenue as "great gateways to 73rd Street"—or, if viewed from the east, to Central Park. Coming across this citation of Candela in the New York skyline was a validation of my instincts as a young architectural historian; I had been walking by these buildings on my way to Buckley, the school I attended until tenth grade, on 73rd Street between Park and Lexington. As I made my way down certain blocks day after day, I found myself only looking up.

I knew why—because I was a nerd. But in one sentence, Paul's observations made me realize there was something more to this. He gave expression to what I had noticed, that there was indeed something resembling another city up there, one I later came to call Candela's "Second City." The action started above the twelfth floor, at the point many of his buildings set back from the lot line and start to terrace their way up to an enclosed water tower, and to my mind this fantasy town in the sky was much more exciting than the real city at street level down below. Like a Dead End Kid, but wearing a tie and a backpack, I looked up, mesmerized, and thought about the life that must be going on in apartments like those. As it turns out, I was right about all of it. But other than that one sentence by my fellow contributor to this book there was nothing else to read, and nowhere to learn more. I had to find

The poignant relationship between luxury and the squalor at its feet is explored in the movie *Dead End* (1937).

another way to learn about buildings than from books, and that came in the form of reading plans.

So even though my introduction to Candela's work was from the outside, as I learned more I realized that was not even half of the story. Because his architecture and the nature of his gifts as a designer can only be understood by appreciating the interconnectedness between the massing of his buildings and the mystery behind their facades (is that a water tower, or the most romantic room in the city?)—to come to know them from the inside, by studying their plans, which reveal all. But finding these plans took time, and the view from the street was a good place to start, because nothing can arouse curiosity more than looking at the facade of a building one wants to get to know. It made me a passionate investigator. The patterns of windows and the spaces they masked were a riddle I very much wanted to solve; the terraces and their relationship to the layouts inside, a mystery I wanted to get to the bottom of. Most specifically, what became of the typical apartments that stacked up to form the base of the building as they morphed into setbacks above the eleventh or twelfth floor? Were those apartments better, each one unique, or were they somehow still like the ones beneath? The answers finally came (as many of them do) at Columbia University's Avery Architectural and Fine Arts Library, where in 1987, while researching a paper at Sarah Lawrence, I discovered their set of *The Select Register of Apartment House Plans.*

We learn more from the floor plans than the exteriors because, like most and maybe all great architects, Candela designed with logical underpinnings and rigor equal to his aesthetics. Using this metric he was the most gifted apartment house planner there has ever been. He possessed extraordinary powers of spatial organization, using them to conceive room arrangements that follow a certain formula to create what we might call the "off-the-foyer" layout. This method of laying out apartments around a central reception space that acts as a "fourth room" in the ensemble of living room, dining room, and

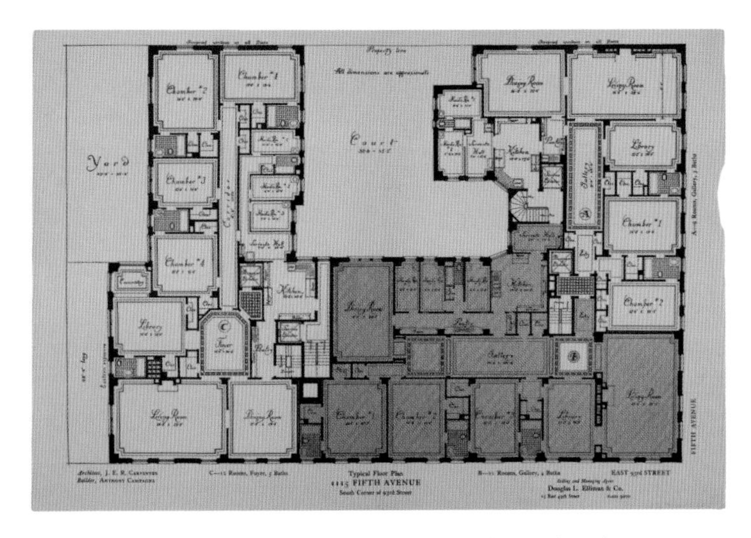

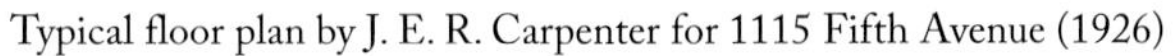

Typical floor plan by J. E. R. Carpenter for 1115 Fifth Avenue (1926)

William Frederick Friedman, Army Signal Corps cryptographer

library was not Candela's invention; it was developed by his peer, the architect J. E. R. Carpenter. But Candela perfected it.

Before Carpenter, a New York apartment might have had no hierarchy between front- and back-of-the-house spaces. Or there might have been a corridor running the length of the apartment, off which all rooms opened. You might have had to cross this corridor to get from the kitchen to the dining room, inadvertently looking as you did so into the open door of someone's bedroom. Like Carpenter's floor plans, which in 1912 crystallized his ideas for superior apartment planning in the design for 635 Park Avenue, Candela's also adhere to certain consistent principles for dividing the apartment into discrete areas for entertaining, service, and private life. But Candela was the superior planner, refining Carpenter's principles ingeniously by resolving things like the means of getting from the kitchen to the living room without having to pass through the dining room, so that drinks could be cleared or a fire lit for after dinner.

These abilities—or at least those emanating from the same area of the brain—also found expression in Candela's parallel life as a cryptographer. In the 1930s and 1940s, he wrote two books on the subject, and taught three courses on cryptanalytics at Hunter College during World War II. Problem-solving in an obstacle-ridden environment came naturally to him.

The most unusual thing about Candela, however, is his duality as a designer. While a gifted architect might typically excel at devising either brilliant plans or handsome elevations—one thing or the other—Candela was not only the best apartment planner, he was also one of the great romantic givers of form to New York. His sensuous instinct for external expression is reinforced by the sensitive detail of his buildings at street level, but more dramatically by their massing into terraced setbacks in the higher stories—ironically, in response to a constraint, the New York zoning regulation of 1916. The series of buildings representing Candela's best-known work are where he developed, beginning in 1927, the now-familiar (but at the time totally

Hollywood by Candela. In *Follow the Fleet* (1936), Fred Astaire and Ginger Rogers perform the finale to Irving Berlin's "Let's Face the Music and Dance" against a set inspired by the roofscapes of 770 and 778 Park Avenue.

Hearst Castle, designed to resemble a Spanish hill town in much the same way Candela's terraced setbacks evoke their Sicilian counterparts

William Randolph Hearst found in Julia Morgan an unlikely medium to express his most extravagant architectural fantasies.

innovative) residential form: the terraced setback crowned with a penthouse water tower. Deployed in commercial office towers in the Financial District, this device had not been used for a residential building before Candela did so on the easternmost section of 960 Fifth Avenue, which contained rental apartments using the separate side street address 3 East 77th Street.

The towers of 770 and 778 Park, which inspired Paul Goldberger to invoke and identify an architect no one knew, and those of 834 and 1040 Fifth Avenue, which inspired Robert A. M. Stern to revitalize high-end limestone-clad apartment houses as a building type with his own designs, are—in contrast to their rigorous internal planning—dreamlike. Think of the famous sequence in the 1936 film *Follow the Fleet* where Fred Astaire and Ginger Rogers dance on a terrace in front of a lantern-like illuminated tower: this penthouse set is directly inspired by Candela's Park Avenue skyline.

Where such decadence sprang from is anybody's guess. Candela himself was a rather severe, crew-cut family man, not prone to Hollywood theatrics or excess in his personal style. It is hard to think of a greater contrast between personality and product: Julia Morgan and her work for William Randolph Hearst at San Simeon come to mind. But from this outwardly modest architect came visual drama that gave rise to a mythical idea of living well in New York City. Candela's buildings define the image and character of the Upper East Side in our era as much as they did on the day they were completed—to no less a degree than the great stone office skyscrapers of Wall Street, or Emery Roth's sheer towers on Central Park West.

Planner, Innovative Form-Giver, Urbanist

The first mention of Rosario Candela in an analytic vein was Paul Goldberger's, as I mentioned. Andrew Alpern's monograph *The New York Apartment Houses of Rosario Candela and James Carpenter* (2002), on which Christopher Gray and I collaborated, provided a catalogue raisonné of Candela's body of about

Rendering of 960 Fifth Avenue showing fictional tripartite facade and loggia as originally proposed (1926)

Lobby of 960 Fifth Avenue as decorated by Dorothy Draper

seventy-five buildings; Michael Gross's genre-busting *740 Park: The Story of the World's Richest Apartment Building* (2006) delivered the riveting social history, basically a biography of an apartment building. But the great book Candela's work richly justifies has yet to be written. Perhaps it is this book, as I hope, which will close that gap.

The idea for a book decoding Candela's genius, focusing expressly on the buildings that count, was born on an early summer evening on the steps of the Museum of the City of New York in 2018, after a panel discussion arranged to launch the exhibition *Elegance in the Sky: The Architecture of Rosario Candela.* Peter Pennoyer had designed the exhibition, and he and Paul Goldberger had just spoken on a panel that also included Elizabeth Stribling, who knows the apartments well from having sold so many of them. The talk had been most interesting, and attendance was standing room only, with people all the way up the stairs. The most memorable feature of that show was a visual tool that broke new ground in explaining the ingenuity of Candela's architecture: Peter and his office produced a film dissecting the sectional diversity of 960 Fifth Avenue, where the windows of each apartment lit up individually as the units with wildly different ceiling heights were discussed by a narrator. It was an MRI of the building, so to speak, investigating it in tranches and illuminating with total clarity the features that make 960, in my opinion, Candela's most interesting project.

How are we to describe these buildings? They belong to a specific building type, which is the New York steel-frame and masonry-clad high-rise apartment house. But why are Candela's worthy of special consideration? A good number, in fact, are not so special—Candela was capable of serviceable, attractive work on a budget, and most of his commissions before 1926 fall into this category, with the conspicuous exception of 1 Sutton Place South. (It is worth mentioning here that the dates we use throughout this book are the dates Candela filed the building plans with the city, not the dates of completion.)

Central Park Casino (1934). The sheer walls of 1 East 72nd Street and 907 Fifth Avenue are visible directly behind, with the newer setbacks and towers of 778 and 770 Park Avenue silhouetted in the distance.

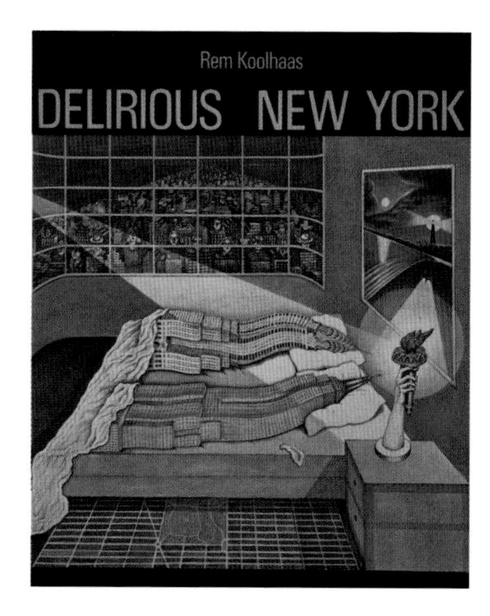

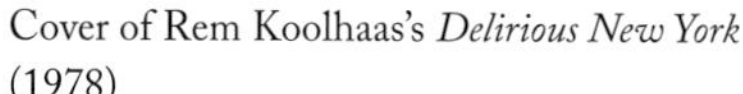

Cover of Rem Koolhaas's *Delirious New York* (1978)

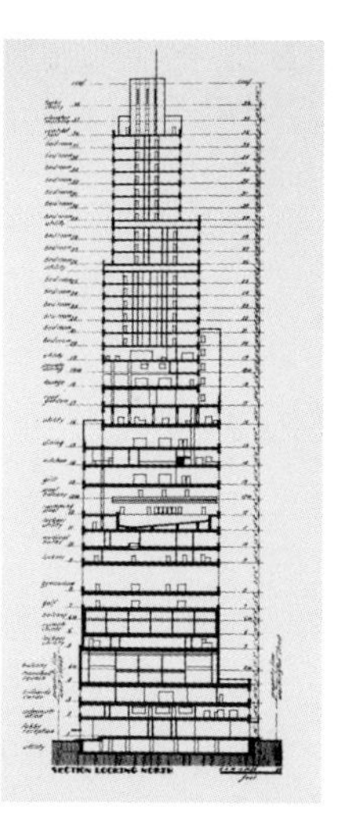

Section drawing of the Downtown Athletic Club, Starrett & Van Vleck (1926)

But the handful that *are* masterpieces are important works of architecture because they transcend their own typology and exist in a super-category by themselves. Chief among these is 960 Fifth Avenue. The three-dimensional puzzle box of its plans and ceiling heights is unique in American architectural history, with the advent of the setback aspect on the side street—Candela's first use of this device—ensuring the building's significance externally as well. Rem Koolhaas's identification of the "free section" in his description of the Downtown Athletic Club published in *Delirious New York* (1978) could be applied as appropriately to an analysis of this building—and indeed it should be, because there is no other way to interpret the design. Again, there is only one 960, largely because of the unusual circumstances of its birth as a co-op in which prospective tenants could specify and purchase blocks of vertical, as well as horizontal, square footage.

The buildings at 720, 740, 770, and 778 Park Avenue, all with the exception of 740 designed as rental apartments, are notable because they represent—just three years after Candela's completion of 3 East 77th Street—the apotheosis of his setback and water tower strategy in combination with plans of exceptional skill, if not sectional differentiation. There are two outliers: 1220 Park Avenue, often overlooked because of its location north of Carnegie Hill at 95th Street, but nevertheless a superior work where he applied the same formula as these buildings in terms of plans and massing, and 19 East 72nd Street, Candela's only post-crash design which espouses all his principles as luxuriously—or nearly, anyway—as his pre-1929 buildings. It is also of special interest with respect to the involvement of associate architect Mott B. Schmidt, a very unlikely designer considering the modernist exterior vocabulary found here and at Candela's 740 Park Avenue—and even less so, the plans.

There is a subcategory of buildings Candela designed on thirty-by-one-hundred-foot townhouse lots such as 2 East 70th Street and 990 Fifth Avenue. These are worth a closer look because of what they teach us about his planning

720 Park Avenue

Installation view, *Elegance in the Sky: The Architecture of Rosario Candela*, May 17–October 28, 2018, Museum of the City of New York

Massing studies by Hugh Ferriss explore the possibilities of high-rise construction for commercial buildings following the 1916 zoning law.

principles. In such confined, awkward sites, devised to hold a five-story house, what was important to him? What does an apartment with a footprint like this have in common with its much more generously proportioned cousins on Park Avenue? For one thing, the sequence of living room, dining room, and library is intentionally strung out across the longest possible distance, to provide the illusion of greater space.

If James Carpenter's greatest innovation was his formula for the planning of apartments, Candela's was his development of the terraced setback. This can be seen in its apotheosis on buildings such as 770 and 778 Park Avenue, both designed in early 1929. It is remarkable that Candela's most significant contribution to the cityscape, and the signature architectural asset of these apartment houses, came about in response to an obstacle: the New York City 1916 Zoning Resolution. This regulation came about to keep streets from being cast permanently in shadow, after the sheer walls of the 1915 Equitable Building at 120 Broadway did precisely that. It required that a building constructed higher than one-and-one-half times the width of the street it faced be set back from the lot line at a point higher than what was typically the eleventh or twelfth floor.

Most of Carpenter's apartment houses were constructed at a time when penthouse living had not yet caught on, and rooftop space was conventionally used for servants' quarters. These buildings followed the example of an extruded Renaissance palazzo with a prominent roof cornice set by McKim, Mead & White's 998 Fifth Avenue of 1910. However, by the time Candela reached the height of his powers in the late 1920s, the marketability of penthouses could no longer be ignored. Borrowing from the dramatic effect of Wall Street's skyscraper district, and in response to developers' need to achieve greater profitability through height, Candela developed the prototype for the New York setback penthouse, crowned with a roof tower. This combination of features put his architecture in the movies and embedded his buildings in the

998 Fifth Avenue, designed by McKim, Mead & White (1910)

public imagination. Without them, it is safe to say, the Museum of the City of New York exhibition would not have been titled *Elegance in the Sky*.

We know Candela's buildings represent a certain kind of urban luxury. But in what way, apart from that, do they constitute important architecture? Anytime I look at a building and think about the question of its importance (something quite apart from its likability or its beauty), I find it is helpful to ask two things: On what and how many levels does it signify? (Antoni Gaudí, for example, is not everyone's favorite designer—but even if one doesn't like his work, one has to respect its originality). And what would be missing if that building had just never happened? How much has it elevated, or perhaps even redefined its context? (Now try to imagine, whatever your opinion of him, Barcelona without Gaudí. It's a trick question; you can't.) And, with the passage and perspective of time, his architecture more than ever has the power to visually define the region of its birth and the image we have in our imagination of that city.

Turning our attention back to the New World, Lower Manhattan without the stone skyscrapers of the Financial District would be an unimaginable non-landmark; the very definition of arrival in New York City is the sight of it from the Statue of Liberty. These buildings have been well-documented and collectively classified, regarded now as ultimate manifestations of the architectural experiment that began in nineteenth-century Chicago when two inventions—steel-frame construction and the elevator—made tall buildings possible and opened the door to the modern city. No one today questions them as crown jewels of American architecture.

Any architecture that has the power to shape a city, or our perception of its part of a city, is important. And if any buildings have done that on Park Avenue or Fifth Avenue—made you blink, looking up, and then just as I did as a child, find yourself thinking about them long after you have moved on—there's a very good chance they were designed by Rosario Candela.

Dr. Satterwhite Pays $450,000, Record Price, For 20-Room 5th Av. Cooperative Apartment

---

Dr. Preston Pope Satterwhite, for many years socially prominent in New York, purchased a cooperative apartment on Fifth Avenue yesterday at a figure that is said to be the highest ever paid.

The apartment consists of twenty rooms in the cooperative structure 960 Fifth Avenue, which Anthony Campagna is to erect on the site of the late Senator Clark's mansion at the northeast corner of Fifth Avenue and Seventy-Seventh Street. The price was reported to be $450,000, although confirmation of this figure was unobtainable from either the brokers or Douglas L. Elliman & Co., Inc., agents for Mr. Campagna.

The previous high price record for a cooperative apartment was paid by Mrs. William K. Vanderbilt II when she purchased for about $185,000 a maisonette of twenty-seven rooms, covering three floors in the cooperative building on the north-west corner of Park Avenue and Sixty-seventh Street.

Even two years ago apartments that sold for $150,000 were almost unheard of. Since then, three apartments in cooperative buildings on Fifth Avenue have been sold at this price or even more, while at least four apartments in the Park Avenue section, including that of Mrs. Vanderbilt, and on side streets have been sold at prices in excess of this figure.

Dr. Satterwhite, who, in addition to a town house, maintains estates at Palm Beach and Great Neck, will occupy the tenth and a large part of the eleventh floors of the structure that will replace the famous Clark mansion.

According to Douglas L. Elliman & Co., Inc., the new apartment house will be ready for occupancy early next year. The building, which has been designed by Warren & Wetmore and Rosario Candela, with Mrs. George Draper as consultant, although physically one structure, will in reality be two buildings. It will be known as 960 Fifth Avenue.

New York Times, Wednesday, June 22, 1927

So read the front-page article announcing the first of many price records apartments in buildings designed by Rosario Candela were to break. The text also provides a vivid window into the feverish economic circumstances of New York in the 1920s—the time of Gatsby and Mayor Jimmy Walker, when there was nothing to do but watch the money roll in and buildings punch ever higher into the sky. Shoeshine boys traded stock tips, and music by Eddy Duchin and his orchestra wafted up into the night from the Central Park Casino. If you listened carefully, you might just hear the sound of the *Aquitania*'s horn as she set sail at midnight, trailing confetti and streamers in her wake. What could stop it? And why would it ever end?

The Roaring Twenties, the era Candela dreamed and drew for, in reality spanned less than a five-year moment in time. But his buildings and their apartments have lived on for a century, and will certainly live another hundred years (actually, in perpetuity, or as long as steel clad in masonry can be made to last—a method of construction about which Eugène Viollet-le-Duc was so leery that he called it "the wolf in sheep's clothing"). The 1981 designation of New York's Upper East Side Historic District, which protected huge swaths of the city and nearly all of Candela's best buildings, has seen to that. The *Times* article shows that the best of these were newsworthy before they were even finished—not just as notable architecture and ornaments to the city's streetscape, but because of who they attracted to *live* in them. This social and economic aspect of their history is a big part of our story, essential to an understanding of how successful they have been as architecture with an intended purpose. Let's talk for a moment about who Candela's clients were at the time and are today, and the use they have made of the buildings he designed for them. Essentially, the social aspect.

How Candela's buildings have been used is interesting to consider, because adjectives like "elegant," "posh," and so forth only go so far. To do a forensic study of who lived where, and what they paid for the privilege, is to hold up a mirror to the social history of New York City. As the *New York Times* article on the Satterwhite apartment does in microcosm. Who was Preston Pope Satterwhite? Nobody much remembers now, and his name is rarely mentioned except in connection with 960. The lion's share of Satterwhite's suite, incidentally, is now home to the author of our foreword (after it went unoccupied for many years, Candela himself subdivided it in 1947). Satterwhite was married to Florence Brokaw, an heiress by birth but also the widow of a Standard Oil executive. The scale of their life and entertaining exploits in Palm Beach and on the North Shore of Long Island were chronicled lavishly in the press. The decoration of this apartment was Hearstian: a neo-Renaissance and Gothic affair that mirrored the style of their Addison Mizner house in Palm Beach, a late robber baron style enjoying its last gasp at the end of the 1920s that would soon be passé. (Dorothy Draper was already at work downstairs in the lobby.) Much of the contents of the thirty-by-sixty-foot living room—including tapestries that the room seems to have been designed specifically to accommodate—were bequeathed by Satterwhite to the Speed Art Museum in Louisville, Kentucky, and may be seen there today. This was the grandest room ever constructed in a New York apartment (though not the biggest apartment by room count, which at fifty-four rooms on three floors goes to Marjorie Merriweather Post at 1107 Fifth Avenue). The Satterwhite apartment is an anomaly in Candela's oeuvre, unique for its baronial scale and unconventional layout, for the price record it set as a spec design, and for the snapshot looking through its spaces offers us of a moment in time in the history of American decorative arts. This apartment also provided 960 with its external visual

Dining room for Anne Bass at 960 Fifth Avenue, interior design by Mark Hampton (1985)

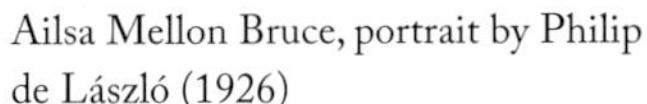

Ailsa Mellon Bruce, portrait by Philip de László (1926)

Consuelo Vanderbilt Balsan, photograph by Louise Dahl-Wolfe (c. 1953)

identity in the form of the triple-arched, double-height tenth floor loggia anchoring the Fifth Avenue facade.

Upstairs on the twelfth floor, the sprawling simplex with thirteen-foot ceilings throughout has had considerably more staying power. Despite being one of Candela's largest and grandest layouts, this apartment survived the Depression unscathed and has never been broken up. It has also, to speak generally, always been considered the best apartment in New York, consistently setting price records and lived in and coveted by people of superior means. After paying $350,000 for the apartment on December 1, 1929, Horace Havemeyer erected a private exterior freight elevator to minimize the impact of his renovations beginning in 1930; Ailsa Mellon Bruce, Paul Mellon's sister, called the apartment home until her death in 1969 after which it sold for a then record $900,000. In 1985, the apartment was bought by Sid and Anne Bass of Fort Worth, Texas, who renovated it with Mark Hampton in a striking Georgian-minimalist style and filled the rooms with masterpieces by Monet, Rothko, Agnes Martin, and Balthus. The apartment was not photographed liberally, but with all the talk about its stripped-down style and contents of sensational value, it became one of the most influential projects of its time, and what pictures trickled out of it became very influential, not least to me. It is probably Mark Hampton's most timeless and admired, not to mention singular, work. He never did another thing like it.

The exceptional duplex penthouse at 2 East 67th Street was for a time the home of Consuelo Vanderbilt Balsan, who counted Marble House and Blenheim Palace as backdrops for an extraordinarily glittering (if not always happy) life. Once a vast duplex with a window in the stairway, it marks Candela's only use of the device of a loggia embedded in a facade apart from at 960, here in the form of the three arched windows of the library. The apartment today is home to a cosmetics executive and collector. Or rather, *apartments*. The duplex was broken up in 1954. The present owner acquired the two floors at separate

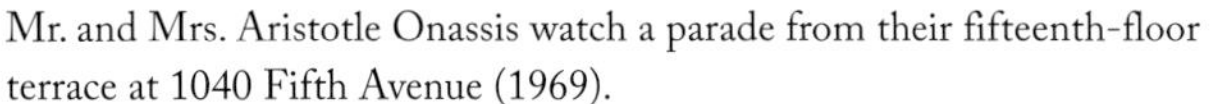

Mr. and Mrs. Aristotle Onassis watch a parade from their fifteenth-floor terrace at 1040 Fifth Avenue (1969).

Jackie O emerging from 1040 Fifth (1971)

times but decided not to reconnect them, instead using the penthouse floor as a sort of hermitage—a cottage in the sky, all the more romantic to access by elevator. These rooms have been home to one of the great collections of Cubist and modern art ever assembled in New York, most of which has now made its way up Fifth Avenue to the Metropolitan Museum of Art as part of a monumental bequest by its owner. Whether she ever knew his name or not, Mme. Balsan was a Candela fan, in that she was a repeat client. After her time at 2 East 67th Street she moved to 1 Sutton Place South, living there until her death in 1964. Born at Blenheim to an American mother, Winston Churchill had a lifelong and very close friendship with his cousin by marriage and visited her at home whenever he was in New York.

The most famous owner of any Candela apartment without a doubt has been Jacqueline Kennedy Onassis. She bought the fifteenth floor of 1040 Fifth Avenue as a widow in July 1964 from Mr. and Mrs. Lowell Weicker, who moved upstairs to the penthouse. The apartment had been found for her by her friend Jayne Wrightsman, and the purchase price was $200,000. It would remain her New York home for life. One of the most balanced and satisfying of Candela's layouts, generous if not grand—with a certain amount of quirkiness and romance to the plan that comes from being a setback—this is a Candela apartment that has everything. Terraces, views, three fireplaces, five bedrooms. Mrs. Onassis was passionate about decorating and the interiors evolved over the years, with Billy Baldwin's help in the beginning and latterly the assistance of Keith Irvine. A certain amount of bohemianism was in evidence, with an easel set up in the Louis XV–paneled living room overlooking Central Park that the owner, a watercolorist all her life, actually used.

Folklore concerning Jackie and her time at 1040 is a rich and tapestried series of anecdotes, some widely known, some not. Photographer Ron Galella's antics in the street have been well chronicled, but one especially amusing incident occurred when Mrs. Kennedy first moved to the building,

High style in the porte cochere of 10 Gracie Square (Van Wart & Wein, 1930) as seen in *Vogue* (1935)

In the rarefied world of New York's luxury apartment buildings, doormen—the keepers of the gates—who see it all have been subject to the wit of *New Yorker* cartoonists.

and everyone was still quite flustered by her presence there. One evening, a distinguished older couple arrived in black tie for dinner with Mr. and Mrs. Charles Whitehouse (parents of the present senator from Rhode Island), who at that time lived in apartment 10/11C. The doorman—in a Freudian moment upon hearing the words "White House" and perhaps confused by their attire—sent them mistakenly to the fifteenth floor. Mrs. Kennedy answered the door in a cardigan, barefoot and amused.

A few blocks south and to the east, in the early 1980s Gianni and Marella Agnelli bought two adjacent apartments at 770 Park Avenue. The CEO of Fiat and his wife were already Candela fans, having previously owned 16A at 720 Park Avenue. Mrs. Agnelli, a contender for the distinction of having the best taste in the world, combined the two D-line duplexes into what she wanted and sold off the remaining small but charming penthouse space to Mr. and Mrs. Ward Carey. The Agnelli apartment is an echo of what Winthrop Rockefeller had done earlier at 770 in his "enhancement" of 17A, combining three bedrooms from another apartment and adding features like a bay window, to the new dining room and windows forming a loggia that runs the length of a sixty-foot terrace on Park Avenue. The downstairs was decorated by Renzo Mongiardino with Peter Marino as architect. Marino also decorated the upstairs. No photographs taken during the time the Agnellis lived there were published, but pictures emerged in the Sotheby's catalog of the contents in 2005 that revealed the apartment to be a singularly successful New World outpost of Mongiardino's artistic—and always original—take on a truly formal way of life. Like his early work for Marella Agnelli's sister-in-law Countess Brandolini at Villa Vistorta, Mongiardino conjured up a bohemian sort of opulence.

The renovation included an addition to a small but very privileged club: Candela apartments that include double-height arched windows in a stair. Originally there were two: 11/12A at 834 Fifth Avenue, and in a special

Swans of New York. Marella Agnelli, portrait by Richard Avedon (1953), at 770 Park Avenue, and C. Z. Guest, photograph by Cecil Beaton, at 1 Sutton Place South (1952)

apartment on the fifteenth and sixteenth floors of 19 East 72nd Street that had been directly inspired by the owner's admiration for the duplex at 834 Fifth. Four decades after the architect's death, Agnelli makes it a posthumous three, indistinguishable from what Candela might have designed himself (undoubtedly inspired by these examples, Peter Pennoyer has also deftly quoted this detail in his own work on the east facade of the new building at 1045 Madison Avenue). While the Agnelli apartment was sold in 2003 for $25 million, the lessons and philosophy of its décor ("There was always a certain kind of sisal on the floor, and beautiful books everywhere, and the unmistakable Rigaud candle," her niece Priscilla Rattazzi has recalled) live on in photographs by Eric Boman. And in a quote attributed to Marella Agnelli, never intended for print—upon seeing Mercedes Bass's new apartment after a multiyear renovation was undertaken at mammoth expense, the success of its owner's mission to bring the gilded and emerald-green velvet taste of Hubert de Givenchy to 4 East 66th Street was appraised thusly: "It will take her another forty years to understand wicker."

Here are some sketches from the notable lives of Social Register families and well-to-do occupants who have lived in a few of the most special Candela apartments from 1927 to the present day. Campfire stories, if you will, about the New York social and design history they made there. Money and a privileged style of life are the context in which Candela is most often mentioned, because everyone loves to talk about fancy real estate—but also because these are the things that made his architecture possible. But the posh aspects of his story can also be a distraction from serious consideration of the buildings: as with an expensive contemporary art collection, glitter and the recurring theme of material value make critical analysis harder, threatening to overtake the conversation and obscure the original concepts, to become all we perceive.

Into the social history of each building is woven, however, the indelible evidence of its success. Take Brooke Astor, widowed in 1959, who could

Peggy Bedford, photograph by Slim Aarons (1958), at 71 East 71st Street (740 Park Avenue)

have chosen to live anywhere. She moved to 778 Park Avenue and began her fabled reign as New York's leading philanthropist from the sixteenth floor, working out of what Sister Parish and Albert Hadley affectionately termed the "Money Room." Laurance Rockefeller bought 834 Fifth Avenue in its entirety in 1944 to secure continued occupancy of his penthouse apartment—and then, at a time of his own choosing, oversaw the conversion of the building to a co-op. His father, John D. Rockefeller Jr., did the same at 740 Park, a transaction chronicled definitively by Michael Gross in his book. Wallace Harrison, de facto architect for the Rockefeller family, lived at 834 as well. In addition to John D., Laurance's brother Winthrop also called a Candela building home, living at 770 Park Avenue in an expanded combination of apartments on the sixteenth floor, which still exists today. I mention all this not to drop a name, but to point out that distinguished tenants have always been part of the life of these buildings, in good and bad times, and everything that came between.

Parallel to the social history we have just glanced upon, there is the economic history. What was the performance, or staying power of a price record set in 1927? After 1929, all bets were off, and the Depression cancelled most peoples' plans either to erect luxurious apartment buildings or live in them. "It was an inopportune time for people to move into fancy buildings," Michael Gross quotes James T. Lee's granddaughter LeeLee Brown as saying. "They were jumping out of windows!" Price declines are not as easy to track as records, since they rarely make the news, but one yardstick of how bad things got was that in 1939, both of Emery Roth's masterpieces, the Beresford and the San Remo, were sold for $25,000 plus the assumption of their mortgages. By the mid-1930s many Candela buildings had been repossessed by the banks that funded their construction, lingering as semi-occupied ghost ships until larger units could be broken up and offered at more reasonable rents, or "whale" tenants like John D. Rockefeller, Jr., and Laurance Rockefeller bought them in order to keep their own apartments. Candela's buildings were always in fashionable use, but beginning in 1930 and over the next few decades, they were perceived not as assets, but white elephants.

When did things turn around? Despite fits and starts, for over thirty years nothing much happened to restore prices to what they had been. Until the mid-1960s, when a buoyant stock market elevated real estate prices and redeemed, to some extent, the original offering prices of the late 1920s—not accounting for inflation. All the ground gained in this surge was given back during the fiscal crisis of 1974, when confidence in New York plunged and for a couple of years took real estate with it. During this time, you could have had any Candela apartment in the city for $200,000; one of the largest and most desirable duplexes at 720 Park Avenue, known as 12/12A, had been built for US Ambassador to France Jesse Isidor Straus, of Macy's (and *Titanic*) fame. After the death of his wife, Irma, in 1970, Straus's estate attempted to dispose of the apartment to no avail. With no buyer in sight, the duplex was broken up into two single-floor units in 1972.

So, consider this: a Candela apartment that cost $150,000 in 1928 did not sell for anything like that again until after 1960 (again, disregarding inflation). It took the span of forty years, from 1929 to 1969, for values at the time of construction to return to what they once had been. Then, in an air pocket moment, 1974, it dipped in value again. The next big leg up was from 1981 to 1982, when Reagan administration policies jump-started the stock market and with it the national economy, luxury real estate very much included. Apartments began crossing the million-dollar mark at that time and have never looked back.

The last decade or so has seen a wave of luxury apartment design in the form of glass curtain walls, sky needles, and neo-traditional masonry-clad buildings in a style mimicking that of their distinguished ancestors. Are any of them the equal of Candela's great works of the 1920s? New York is a small town, and I don't want to step on any toes. Apart from representing different opinions on *how* to live in New York, these new buildings are nearly all condominiums anyway, in contrast to Candela's co-ops.

With the jumps in price has also came a shift in perception: instead of being seen as an indulgence, real estate had become an asset class. And there it has stayed. Anyone with the foresight to recognize that shift, or the composure and wherewithal to sit tight, pay the maintenance, and hang on to what they had, has been very glad since 1981 if they found themselves in an apartment by Rosario Candela. And what of the top of the top? Superlative terms aside, markets think clearly and offer less subjective data. If we seek an example of the enduring power of Candela's work beyond its beauty, we only need to look at its value: in five distinct eras in the history of the US economy and that of New York City, spanning the date of construction to the present day (the years 1927, 1970, 1982, 2000, 2014, and 2015), the price records for a New York co-op apartment were all set in buildings designed by Rosario Candela.

These are: the Satterwhite apartment at 960 Fifth Avenue on the tenth and part of the eleventh floors ($450,000 in 1927); Ailsa Mellon Bruce's apartment, again at 960 Fifth Avenue, on the twelfth floor ($900,000 in 1970); the sale by bombshell divorcée Gregg Dodge to John DeLorean of 9/10A at 834 Fifth Avenue ($2 million in 1982); the Saul Steinberg, formerly John D. Rockefeller Jr., 15/16A apartment at 740 Park Avenue ($30 million in 2000); the Edgar Bronfman apartment (penthouse of 960 Fifth Avenue), sold to Nassef Sawiris for $70 million in 2014; and 11/12A, again at 834 Fifth Avenue, which passed from Woody Johnson to surprise buyer Len Blavatnik ($77.5 million in 2015).

THE ARCHITECTURE OF CERTAINTY

Paul Goldberger

Let us begin by getting an uncomfortable truth out of the way: Rosario Candela was a remarkable architect who designed quite a number of ordinary buildings. He was also perhaps the greatest designer of apartment houses who has ever lived, and some of his works rank among the most distinguished apartment buildings ever constructed, not only in New York but anywhere. But he was also a journeyman, an architect who worked for commercial developers, and he made the compromises they asked of him. I mention this at the outset neither to diminish him nor to make the obvious point that not everything a master produces is a masterwork. The real lesson his career offers us is more subtle—that perhaps he was a great architect not despite his being a journeyman, but because of it.

Architecture is inevitably the product of a complicated and often contradictory set of factors: practical concerns of internal layouts, economic realities of paying for land and construction, structural needs, and zoning requirements. In the case of an urban apartment house, all of this equals a set of demands that are unusually intricate, not to say byzantine. It was Candela's gift to be able to mix all these things together, solving every problem and responding to every external pressure, and still end up with a compelling piece of architecture. He was exceptionally good at making it look as if he had not compromised, in other words, at making you think that his designs really had been generated out of some larger aesthetic vision, when they were at least as much a matter of disciplined, rigorous, and thoughtful problem-solving.

To put it that way sounds bloodless, almost clinical, and in Candela's hands it was anything but. The best architecture is only rarely the demonstration of a pure aesthetic concept; the greatest architects are the ones who can solve problems and fulfill practical needs and at the same time create something beautiful, even majestic, that transcends the mundane and inspires exhilaration. That was the essence of Candela: that out of an internal jigsaw puzzle of dozens of different kinds of interlocking rooms and an exterior

Rendering of 834 Fifth Avenue showing building as originally planned for a mid-block site

constricted by a tight urban site and a daunting set of zoning rules he could still conjure a piece of art. Candela's greatest buildings, most of which were constructed in the late 1920s and early 1930s, like 834 Fifth Avenue, 1040 Fifth Avenue, 740 Park Avenue, 770 Park Avenue, and 778 Park Avenue, are at once formidable, stylish and serene; they embody the essence of New York between the wars.

Plenty of other architects designed luxury apartment buildings, but Candela's are so revered that knowledgeable real estate brokers have always referred to them simply by their street numbers, as if they were speaking in code: when someone says "there is a great twelve-room apartment on the market at 1040" the initiated all know that it is within Candela's palatial building at the corner of 85th Street and Fifth Avenue. Other buildings on other streets may also be numbered 740, but when the cognoscenti hear that number, they think of only one place, 740 Park Avenue.

They have an aura. That is the word, really, for Candela, at least so far as his most important buildings are concerned. They exude not just wealth and grandeur, but certainty. It is an architecture of self-assurance, not an architecture of doubt or an architecture of striving. Candela never appears to be trying too hard. Like a gifted violinist or a great athlete, he makes it all seem easy and natural. It is a way in which the rich once lived; you can picture characters from John P. Marquand novels living in Candela buildings in the same way that characters from Edith Wharton novels lived in the Fifth Avenue mansions that were torn down to make way for them. Candela's most celebrated buildings—a list to which we should add 1 Sutton Place South, 19 East 72nd Street, and 960 Fifth Avenue—were built for the quiet rich, for the New York bankers and industrialists who lived grandly but whose names were unknown to most of the public. This is not the transparent architecture of the age of celebrity. It is the opaque architecture of the age of privacy.

That is what first struck me when, back in the early years of my tenure as the architecture critic of the *New York Times*, I found Candela's name attached to so many older buildings that I admired. Who was this architect? I had never heard of him. He was not in any of the architectural history books that I had read. He was not mentioned in any of the lectures I had attended in college. His buildings were more traditional than modern, but he was not one of those famous historicist architects, like John Russell Pope or Cass Gilbert, who became a part of twentieth-century American architectural history by virtue of the significant and distinguished public buildings that they produced. Candela seemed mainly to have operated in New York and not to have built much other than apartment houses. But what a group of apartment houses. They were the best of the best, the ones that defined urban living during the decades when New York seemed to set much of the style of the twentieth century. (Notably, one of the only buildings Candela designed outside of New York is the splendid apartment house at 1500 Lake Shore Drive in Chicago, which makes claim

1040 Fifth Avenue

to bringing Candela's New York style to Chicago.) And so I began to write about Candela, and to try to rescue him from anonymity, helped by the late Christopher Gray, who shared my passion for Candela's work, even though he admitted to reserving his greatest admiration for Gaetan Ajello, the architect who preceded Candela as an immigrant from Italy and hired him when he first arrived in New York, starting his American career.

Like his mentor Ajello, Candela began by designing buildings for developers who were building for the middle class and gradually worked his way up the social hierarchy, often along with developer clients, many of whom, like the Paternos and the Campagnas, were also of Italian descent and were making the same rapid climb up the American economic ladder. What I find particularly intriguing about Candela's oeuvre is that it is not a simple matter of two kinds of architecture, the plain and the fancy. He didn't start out doing banal buildings for clients with low budgets and then move on to do beautiful ones for clients who wanted to spend more. His work was more of a continuum, with almost every gradation from solid, bourgeois convention to oligarchical extravagance, and throughout his career he designed a range of different kinds of apartments for different kinds of tenants, often at the same time. And his middle-class buildings on West End Avenue represented aspiration as brilliantly as his upper-class buildings on Fifth Avenue represented arrival. You can see him adding a flourish or two to enliven a simple building, just as he is demonstrating restraint in his grander ones. Many of his finest buildings have the simplest, one-over-one double-hung windows, large because the rooms are large, but plain in design as if to shame the insecure fussiness of other buildings with the confidence of their grandeur.

Indeed, not the least of the reasons I have always found Candela's work appealing is how consistently he shies away from flamboyance, particularly where it might be most expected. Buildings like 740, 778, 834, and 1040 are relatively cool and reserved; they represent understatement, not pretension. Of course they are elegant and in no way plain, but they are never over-the-top. There is plenty of historical ornament in Candela, and like all the great American eclectic architects of the twentieth century he wove all kinds of historical references into his work, often with an astonishing degree of compositional skill. But whether he is borrowing from Robert Adam or Christopher Wren or the Italian Renaissance, you feel Candela's inherent sense of restraint. It may have been encouraged by the stripped-down classical aesthetic that was beginning to edge out his preferred neo-Georgian style in the late 1920s and early 1930s, the period when most of what we could call "High Candela," his most sumptuous buildings, were designed and built. But throughout his career he always knew where to stop. He was incapable of excess, whether he was designing the residences that were setting the standard for opulent urban living or crafting comfortable apartments to give upper-middle-class Manhattan life a taste of flair.

Robert A. M. Stern's roofscape at 15 Central Park West with scooped buttress and loggias is an homage to 1040 Fifth Avenue.

Peter Pennoyer's The Benson, with windowed stair à la Candela

But restraint doesn't quite sum him up, either, because for all their reserve and for all their refinement there is also a consistently romantic, not to say emotional, aspect to his buildings. They delight, especially those that, like 770 and 778 Park Avenue, take advantage of the setback requirements of the 1929 multiple dwelling law to become veritable hill towns of playful shapes in their upper floors. David Netto long ago described Candela's major designs as having a "voluptuousness," and it is true: there is something lyrical about the facade details, limited though the amount of decoration may be, and you feel that the mass of these buildings is somehow more expansive, more solid, more impenetrable, and yet more alluring than the structures that are their neighbors.

Candela's buildings are inventive. It is not an accident that Robert A. M. Stern, the most prolific channeler of Candela's spirit in our time, has used so many elements of Candela's work in his own, sometimes quite literally, as in the high, buttress-like wall with an open quarter arc that dances along the top of his 15 Central Park West apartment tower, an inventive detail taken literally from the pinnacle of Candela's 1040 Fifth Avenue. Peter Pennoyer, another gifted designer of modern-day New York apartments, has studied Candela with equal care. Candela's buildings, like Stern's and Pennoyer's today, belong in the city; we perceive them not only as objects in themselves but even more as part of a larger assemblage, part of a street and part of a neighborhood, and they enrich the urban context. There is not a single one of them that shouts, and there is not a single one of them that can be imagined as being on a different site than the one on which it was built. Candela did not deal in formulas. He did not use the same designs over and over again, as many architects working for commercial developers did, although when he had the good fortune to build two buildings across the street from each other, as he did at 770 and 778 Park Avenue, which face each other across East 73rd Street, he did not hesitate to make them a pair, giving each an ornate tower so that together, the two buildings form a gracious urban gateway, pointing the way to Central Park two blocks west.

But even here, Candela did not duplicate. The buildings are just similar enough to speak to each other across East 73rd Street, but they are not identical. On the south side, 770 is larger, which is to say deeper, with a site that runs farther back from Park Avenue, and a small courtyard enclosed by an Italianate loggia topped by stone urns facing the street and separating what are, in effect, two wings. By contrast, 778 to the north rises as a single mass on the corner of Park, culminating in the exclamation point of its tower. The more you look at the two buildings, the more you see that they are not the same: 770's facade is somewhat flatter, and the unusual loggia along 73rd Street is one of the few major pieces of decoration. The building has an unusual window pattern that reflects the different room layouts of duplex apartments, giving its corner a kind of proto-modernist geometric energy. But the details of the facade, when Candela allowed himself to indulge in ornament, are primarily Italianate, and the setback top, with portions of the roofs covered in red terra-cotta tile, has a pleasing irregularity to it. By contrast, 778, designed at the same time—1929—and finished in 1931, a year later than its neighbor, is more rigid and more proper, with a more lavishly decorated but notably more traditional facade, and the inspiration of the ornament here is English, not Italian. The limestone base is three stories high at 770 and four stories high at 778; 770's massing flows uninterrupted from its thirteen-story base to the terraced setbacks of its upper floors, while 778's massing includes a twelve-story base topped by a cornice, making a decisive break between the traditional, boxy base and the terraced setbacks of its upper floors.

The differences would seem trivial, but they are enough to turn these two buildings, taken together, into a kind of fugue of urbanism, in which Candela takes a theme, the limestone and brick apartment house topped by setbacks, and plays with it, showing us how much differentiation there can be in buildings that are fundamentally the same, and how interesting the streetscape can be when an architectural theme is varied to just the right extent. He could have made them twins, at least so far as their front sections facing Park Avenue were concerned, but that would have been dull; he could also have made them completely different, but then they would not have spoken to each other in the wonderful way that they do.

Candela understood urbanism. You can see that also in his work along the East River, where he designed six superb buildings, 1 and 14 Sutton Place South; 4, 25, and 30 Sutton Place; and 447 East 57th Street, each of which responds to a different kind of site in a different way. Number 4 is a slender tower of duplexes, tightly organized, its actively composed facade teasing at symmetry but avoiding it in favor of a livelier rhythm, whereas 1 Sutton Place South sprawls across a full-block site, with its magnificent triple entry portal and lobby overlooking a riverfront garden: all is formality. There is a more casual kind of urbanism in a nearby project that was never realized,

770 Park Avenue

4 Sutton Place, the southernmost of Candela's buildings that form a composition there

an Italianate waterfront fantasy Candela conceived in 1929 for the site between 48th and 49th Streets now occupied by the United Nations Plaza apartments. Candela's design, which was to have been called Water Gate, prefigured many of the elements, like a yacht mooring, that William Bottomley was to include a couple of years later in his majestic River House, one of the few buildings in the area to rank with Candela's. But the unbuilt Candela version is more a whimsical composition, addressing the East River with splendid, asymmetrical massing and a private riverfront piazza.

Much of Candela's strength as a designer was in knowing when to turn the design intensity up a notch or two, and when to turn it down. The lively pair of buildings at 770 and 778 Park Avenue face an earlier project of Candela's, 765–775 Park Avenue, which he had finished in 1927 directly across the street from 770 and diagonally across from 778. The earlier building spans a full block; it is a rectangular mass that has all of Candela's understated details but none of the formal inventiveness of 770 and 778, and it provides a quiet, measured counterpoint to the livelier massing of its two later neighbors. All three of these buildings suggest great propriety, but the emotions are more under wraps at 765–775. But when the 1929 multiple dwellings law offered the opportunity to create a stepped-back profile, Candela responded with a pair of designs that have great panache, yet which sacrifice none of the dignity of the earlier building across the street.

The remarkable pair of buildings at 770 and 778 Park Avenue was completed shortly after another Candela building just a couple of blocks to the south, 720 Park Avenue, his first effort at exploring a series of setbacks atop a blocky base. It lacks the splendid towers of 770 and 778 Park, but it is otherwise a close sibling, with a similarly restrained but elegantly detailed base that breaks out into a series of lively setbacks at the top, a chunk of Italian hill town in the sky. To one of the few contemporary critics who reviewed Candela, George S. Chappell, who wrote for the *New Yorker* under

Water Gate apartments, the unbuilt prequel to River House

WATER GATE
·COOPERATORS·
CONSTRUCTION·CO:
Inc
·OWNER·
CROSS·&·CROSS
ROSARIO·CANDELA
ASSOCIATE·ARCHTS
G·MAGUOLO·1928·

the pseudonym T-Square, however, it was all a jumbled mess, a building that displayed incoherence more than compositional imagination. Chappell is little remembered today, and his critique is of note mainly because there was so little writing about Candela's buildings when they were new; like the residents for whom they were built, they generally avoided public notice.

In between 720 and 770 stands 740 Park Avenue, one of Candela's masterpieces, completed at the same time as 770 and sheathed entirely in limestone. It is New York's Gibraltar, not only because of the financial wherewithal of most of its residents, but because of the way in which the limestone facades make the building feel so solid that you would think that a bomb set off in one apartment could not be heard in the next. There are hints of Art Deco here, but they are tame, for nothing would have been worse than to have the gentry of Park Avenue think they were being given the style of Central Park West or the Grand Concourse. The front door is magnificent: it is cut through a marble slab topped by finials, and it contains lettering that announces the address with Roman affectation as 740 PARK AVENVE. (There is also a secondary entrance around the corner with the address of 71 East 71st Street, and true to the tradition of understatement, this side-street entry leads to many of the largest and finest apartments.)

Candela designed both 720 and 740 Park in association with other architects, the firm of Cross & Cross at 720 and Arthur Loomis Harmon at 740. He often formed such temporary alliances—he would work with Cross & Cross again at 1 Sutton Place South and at 4 and 25 Sutton Place, with Warren & Wetmore at 960 Fifth Avenue, and with Mott Schmidt at 19 East 72nd Street—which raises the obvious question of how much of these buildings should be credited to Candela, and how much should be credited to his partners. There are no archives to provide a definitive answer to this question, but it is hard not to believe that these associations were driven more by practical matters than the need for design support. Candela did not have a huge office, and in the late 1920s, as his reputation as the architect of the city's most desirable apartment buildings was growing, he received what amounted to a torrent of commissions, and likely needed help beyond what adding more draftsmen to his staff could provide. That 720 Park Avenue is not notably different from 770 and 778, both of which are credited solely to Candela, and 740 Park has much in common with the sumptuous Candela buildings at 834 and 1040 Fifth Avenue, both of which were also fully by Candela, suggests that the contributions of his associated firms to the actual designs were minimal—and that the other firms may have been engaged more for the prestige of their established names than for any design elements they might have provided.

The one possible exception to this is 960 Fifth Avenue, a Candela tour de force in limestone that is something of an outlier here, since it is not quite like any other building. It is, in effect, two buildings, the main one that fronts

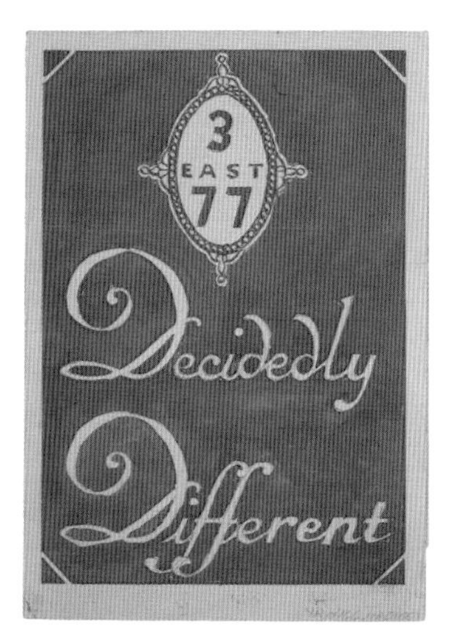

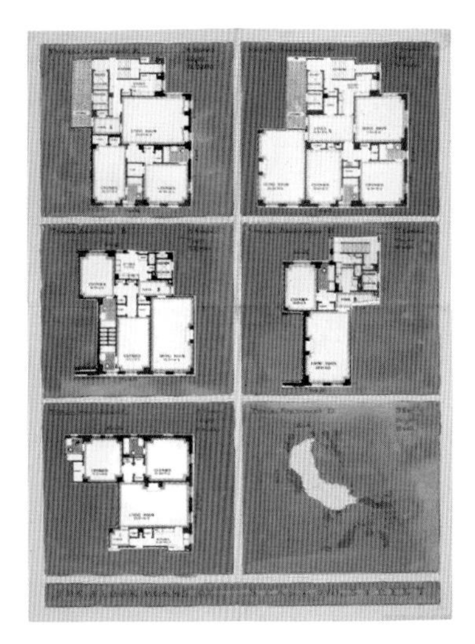

Marketing brochures tried out a variety of graphics and phrases (and in the case of 3 East 77th Street, alliteration) to express the uniqueness of a building and capture public attention.

on Fifth Avenue that contains some of the most lavish apartments Candela ever designed, and a wing of smaller apartments at 3 East 77th Street, as well as a private restaurant, called the Georgian Suite, at 1A East 77th Street. The frontal section on Fifth Avenue has a cornice of carved garlands and caryatids that is more like a bas-relief than a true projecting cornice. It has some resemblance to the ornamentation that decorates the central portion of the facade of 770, but this is far larger and grander in scale, stretching across the entire top of the building. And then, above this explosion of ornament, the facade simply ends, with the clean line of a modern box; the front of 960 manages to be at once a lavish expression of tradition and a kind of proto-modernism.

Even more remarkable is the uneven pattern of windows above the fifth floor, reflecting the dramatically different interiors of the apartments, many of which were duplexes and some of which contain one-and-a-half or two-story spaces. But here, too, Candela's instinct toward balancing emotion with restraint prevailed. The facade is divided horizontally into three main portions: an even and ordered base; an intensely varied, active, and asymmetrical mid-section; and a top floor in which the pattern of identical windows, evenly spaced, returns to meet the sky. This facade is a sandwich in which richly expressive variation is the meat, and Candela's moderation is the bread. And even the mid-section is topped by a central composition of three arched windows, two rectangular ones, pilasters, urns, and balustrades, as if to anchor the facade in symmetry and mitigate the visual impact of the different types and sizes of windows all around it.

The unusual facade of the 960 building is explained, in part, by the building's unusual history. It was built by Anthony and Michael Campagna, loyal clients who developed several of Candela's major buildings, but in this case the Campagnas sold much of the building to tenants as raw space before construction began, allowing them to specify many aspects of the layout within. Making the different parts of the building fit together efficiently and coherently was Candela's strong suit; 960 Fifth has a section of magnificent complexity made up largely of one-of-a-kind apartments that are interlocked with non-matching units above and below, an architectural Rubik's Cube. Yet somehow out of this Candela was able to produce floor plans as sumptuous and as natural as those in his less intricate buildings.

Whatever contribution Warren & Wetmore, the eminent Beaux-Arts firm best known as the primary architect of a building completed fifteen years before, Grand Central Terminal, made to 960 Fifth Avenue is impossible to know. Not long before 960, Warren & Wetmore had designed 1020 Fifth Avenue, a discreet, refined building in which almost every apartment was given an unusual one-and-a-half story living room, and the success of 1020 may have led Anthony Campagna to believe that Warren & Wetmore were specialists in creating apartment houses of spatial complexity. But it is doubtful that they were charged with designing the apartment layouts themselves or fitting them together. This was Candela's great strength. He saw the making of the internal arrangement of a building as an intellectual puzzle, and his conceptual skills and ability to think in clear, abstract spatial terms would eventually bring him to a second career during World War II as a cryptographer for American intelligence. Along with J. E. R. Carpenter and Emery Roth, his only two peers in the design of luxury apartments in the years between the two world wars, Candela developed the notion of laying out the rooms of an apartment around a central foyer, a gracious arrangement beside which the linear string of rooms along narrow corridors that constituted luxury apartment layouts in the years before World War I seemed crude and primitive. The foyer in a Candela apartment—or a Carpenter or Roth apartment, for that matter—was more than a circulation space. It was the heart of the apartment, the arrival space, the piazza within the palazzo, as it were, as well as the neutral zone that allowed privacy and separation between public rooms, private rooms, and service spaces. Candela, even more than his peers, almost always figured out a way in which each of these sections could be distinct yet flow easily from one to the other.

The floor plans of Candela's most luxurious buildings are a study in hedonism, or at least in fantasizing about a certain kind of elegant and urbane life in which the formal, ordered grandeur of a great house was transferred seamlessly into a slice of space in the sky. Almost every large Candela apartment opens into an expansive gallery foyer, which in turn leads to a large rectangular living room, in the best instances at a corner of the building and set with its long end parallel to the street to maximize light and views. Often the dining room is at the opposite end of the foyer, since Candela understood the importance of the processional in architecture and how the movement from living room sofa to dining table and back again could be an entire experience in itself. The bedrooms are in a separate wing, usually hidden behind a door off the foyer, and the kitchen, pantry, and service spaces are tightly arrayed beyond the dining room. Duplexes, sometimes deftly interlocked with simplexes, generally have grand, often curving, staircases set within the central foyer, and there are usually separate service stairs leading to an upstairs service wing above the kitchen.

None of these elements are unique to Candela; other architects designed grand apartments with formal galleries at their heart and public rooms and bedroom wings coming off them and service wings tucked in the back, but Candela almost always did it better. He had a way of making public rooms feel important and private rooms feel intimate; the proportions are almost always elegant, the spaces flow easily and naturally from one into the other, and the servants are always close by but out of sight. The best "High Candela" floor plans not only have service spaces that connect discreetly to bedrooms and public rooms, some of them also have secondary routes into the living rooms to allow servants to clean up after cocktails without passing through the dining room.

These are places for formal, dignified, and contented life, in other words, places that imply a perfection and a serenity that never exists in the real world. But what is domestic architecture, in the end, but a vision of an ideal life, something that architecture can never guarantee, but at its best can nurture and cultivate? Candela had a vision of domestic grandeur that did not merely reflect the elegance and style of New York between the two world wars but helped to bring it into being. He did this not only by knowing how rich people wanted to live, but also by giving them an architecture of dignity and high ambition, an architecture that, at its best, can stand with the civic, public, and cultural buildings of the same period—with the clubs of Delano & Aldrich, with the museums of John Russell Pope and Guy Lowell, with the public buildings of Cass Gilbert and Carrère & Hastings, and with the campuses of James Gamble Rogers. By this measure Candela's grandest buildings are also, in the end, not so different from his more modest ones, since everything he designed, from the sumptuous palaces of limestone on Fifth and Park Avenues to the smaller piles of brick on West End Avenue, is aspirational. It is all a vision of New York life not as it is, but as we have always imagined it, and Candela's architecture made it as real as it would ever be.

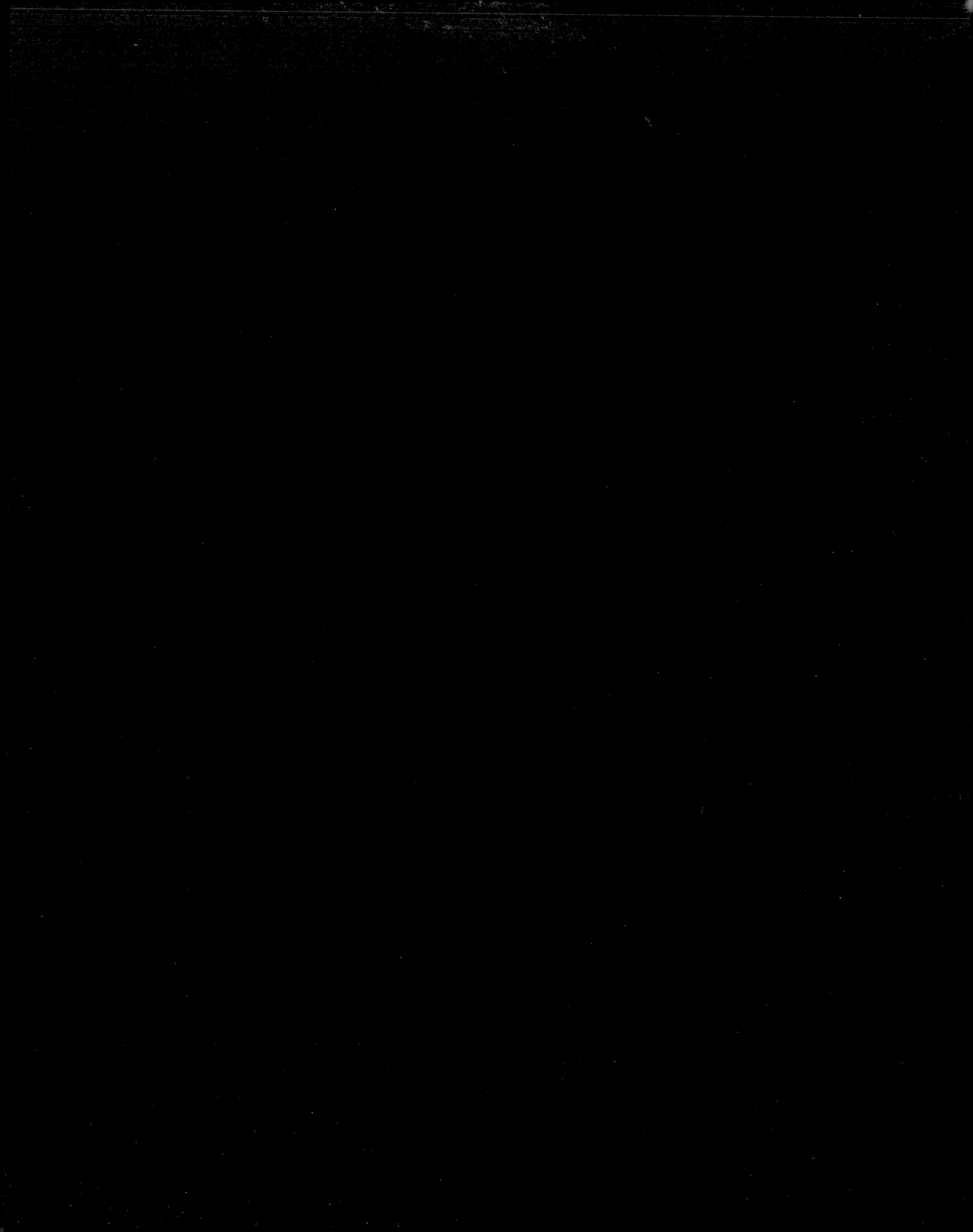

CODEBREAKING IN LIMESTONE

Peter Pennoyer

As a young New Yorker, I first experienced Rosario Candela's legacy through the glimmering, glamorous abodes of certain well-heeled friends. Like many who set foot in these apartments for the first time, I was impressed by the scale, elegance, and beauty of the public rooms—which were always visible from the entrance—and equally intrigued by the apparent absence of kitchens or staff rooms, undoubtedly tucked away somewhere.

My introduction to Candela—and to the idea that apartment plans were worth studying—was through the publication of Andrew Alpern's 1975 *Apartments for the Affluent: A Historical Survey of Buildings in New York*. Poring over the book's drawings was an obsession that I later discovered was shared by other architects of my generation, whose well-worn copies are still in use. Candela's buildings had been reviewed in newspapers and journals in his time, and given the stature of the tenants, even the purchase of individual apartments and their owner's disputes were newsworthy. *The American Architect and Building News* commented on many new apartment houses, while the *New Yorker* ran a column about apartment houses signed either Duplex or Penthouse.

After the Great Depression, however, Candela disappeared from the architectural press as New York descended into a decades-long real estate lull. Apartments that had commanded the top prices ever recorded languished on the market. Duplexes and larger apartments were subdivided. Architects were then mesmerized by modernism and had little interest in the historically inspired designs that lined Park Avenue.

Alpern's book renewed the focus on apartment plans. Since then, other astute historians and critics, including Elizabeth Hawes, Christopher Gray, Robert A. M. Stern, Gregory Gilmartin, Thomas Mellins, and my co-authors David Netto and Paul Goldberger, have examined Candela's work. In a city of constant change, many observed that the qualities of Candela's planning held essential lessons of continued relevance.

View from lobby to interior garden at 19 East 72nd Street. Along with 1040 Fifth Avenue, this late work of Candela's (1937) with its spartan limestone detailing has inspired Robert A. M. Stern's buildings beginning with 15 Central Park West.

Very few Candela-designed buildings have been demolished. Rather, New Yorkers are constantly improving these apartments by renovating and redecorating. Since 1992, my firm's role in renovating many apartments on the Upper East Side has given me clues about what makes Candela's planning and interior architecture work so well. More recently, some designers—including my own firm—have followed the lead of Robert A. M. Stern Architects by designing new apartment buildings inspired by Candela's work.

Rosario Candela is an important name not only in apartment building design. He also has the odd distinction—for an architect whose practice flourished one hundred years ago—of having created what we now call a brand. His built legacy is some eighty-five apartment buildings in New York City, a drop in the pond of the city's thousands of buildings. Among his designs, however, those he created in the core of his career from 1927 to 1937 are still considered the best of apartment house architecture. The standard he set means that his name is better recognized than that of any other residential architect in New York City. His genius in planning apartments is still legible today and is the reason for the often-repeated claim: "It's a Candela." His core skill was consolidating the best qualities of a freestanding house into an elegant and livable apartment.

Candela's story puts him outside of the early twentieth-century architectural profession's mainstream, but rapid social and economic change brought him the opportunities to prove his skills in the marketplace. The son of a plasterer from Sicily, Candela arrived in New York in 1910 knowing barely a few words of English. Architecture in that era was a gentleman's profession, and we have no clear picture of how he gained admission to the Columbia School of Architecture. Commissions for many architects came from social and family connections. For instance, Stanford White and his partners had traveled in the same circles as their clients and shared the same passion for bringing European culture to America. White would look up from his orchestra seat at the old opera house to greet his clients in their subscription boxes.

Though Candela had no subscription to the opera and no connection to that social world, his skills would be in demand as America's economy surged. Despite periodical financial crises and World War I, New York was on an upward trajectory from when Candela arrived at Ellis Island until 1932. The power of the economy and the burgeoning population caused an intense and concentrated focus on redevelopment in real estate. Each decade brought new ideals for how the wealthy should live, and this evolution spurred almost continual waves of demolition and new construction. The architectural expression of this period, while varied in style, staked a claim on European cultural heritage as the basis of the American Renaissance.

This movement encompassed both enriched Beaux-Arts landmarks and more sedate, academically correct interpretations of precedents from the Old World. A sense of appropriateness, balance, and reserve began to eclipse the excesses of eclecticism of post–Civil War America's roaring decades.

The Clark mansion, completed in 1911, was demolished to make way for 960 Fifth Avenue.

The Tiffany house—actually a complex of houses—at 72nd and Madison, by McKim, Mead & White (1883), demolished in 1936

The almost continuous row of castles and palazzos on Fifth Avenue was being cleared, block by block. In 1927 New Yorkers witnessed the demolition of the 121-room Clark mansion—the grandest, most excessive French mansion on the avenue—to make way for 960 Fifth Avenue, an apartment house that would be one of Candela's great achievements.

New York society was turning from the modern French style with its exuberant, voluptuous fusion of sculpture and architecture, toward quieter modes. J. P. Morgan, who had been the main patron for Whitney Warren's flamboyant 1900 New York Yacht Club, rejected Warren's Beaux-Arts design for his library and turned instead to Charles Follen McKim, who created a poised, masterful, classical villa, inspired by the subtle interpretation of Renaissance precedents.

The shift on Fifth Avenue from chateaux to apartment houses was emblematic of a fundamental change in the social and economic circumstances of New York City, best described by Stern and his co-authors as the Era of Convenience. Between Candela's 1915 graduation from the Columbia School of Architecture through the construction of his last grand apartment house at 19 East 72nd Street in 1937, Candela and his contemporaries condensed the unbridled programs of the great mansions into more practical forms. On the one hand, land prices in the best districts made the freestanding house or mansion unattainable; on the other, even the richest New Yorkers were reducing their household staffs. The butler no longer surveyed a staff of ten, if he had a job at all. Many functions that had been held important in a mansion were edited out of the program entirely. The seamstress's room was no longer required. But all the attributes of living in a house had to be brought forward, as plausibly as possible, into an entirely new building type.

The interior character of the mansions on Fifth Avenue also came to be seen as overblown. Tapestries, brocades, velvets, and carved paneling clogged the parlors and ballrooms of the greatest New York houses of the late

The Trellis Room at the original Colony Club, decorated by Elsie de Wolfe

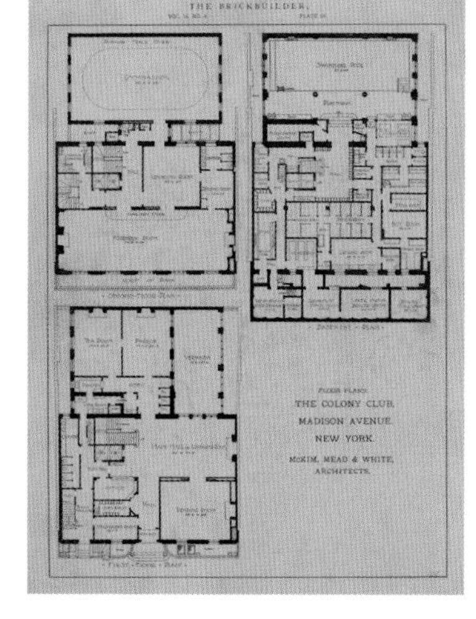

Plans of the Colony Club

nineteenth and early twentieth centuries. Windows were cloaked in layers of draperies. A parlor with just one beam of sunlight reaching through a crack in the curtains into the darkness would be praised as having the "Rembrandt light." Many of these houses were decorated by French firms such as Jules Allard et Fils and Alavoine et Cie., which supplied complete rooms down to artwork and suits of armor.

Though these firms continued to serve New York clients, a new, lighter hand in interior design arrived with the establishment—by Elsie de Wolfe in 1913—of one of the first decorating practices in the country. De Wolfe's first project was the Stanford White–designed Colony Club (1915). The light, simple, colonial revival rooms with their understated furnishings presaged a new approach to domestic interior design. Some, for instance William Randolph Hearst, brought their dark, baronial, cigar-smoked interior taste to new apartments, but de Wolfe and her peers led the way to a less elaborate and more feminine approach. Candela leaves no record of his exact views on decoration, but his planning makes it clear that he understood the importance of light, proportion, and the clear arrangement of rooms.

The ground had been broken for Candela by architects who preceded him in making apartment living appeal to wealthy New Yorkers. It was McKim, Mead & White's new generation of partners that broke through the resistance to apartment living with 998 Fifth Avenue, an imposing palazzo filled with fifteen-room suites. Most notably, the architect J. E. R. Carpenter established the arrangement and hierarchy of program that set the standard for apartment planning. Carpenter's 635 Park Avenue (1912) was the first building to create separate areas most effectively for service, sleeping, and entertaining. In Carpenter's plan each apartment's elevator lobby opened through a vestibule to a formal, circular entrance foyer that connected, on axis, to the drawing room. The three zones were strategically placed so that the family could enjoy the living room, dining room, and library while completely insulated from

NO. 635 PARK AVENUE

Southeast Corner Sixty-sixth Street

This new thirteen-story apartment building of the highest type of modern architecture is located in the heart of the most exclusive apartment house neighborhood of the city.

Apartments are arranged in suites of fourteen and sixteen rooms and four baths. All windows open to the outside, as there are no interior courts, insuring exceptional light and ventilation for every room.

The building contains every known convenience for housekeeping, including best porcelain plumbing fixtures, wall safes, garbage closets, laundries and dryers in basement, complete telephone system, filtered water, passenger and service elevators, etc.

No 635 Park Ave.

TYPICAL FLOOR PLAN

635 Park Avenue, by J. E. R. Carpenter (1912)

907 Fifth Avenue (1915)

the kitchen and staff rooms. The family bedrooms, while accessed from a hall connected to the initial entry vestibule, were separated from both the public rooms and the service areas. Carpenter's largest apartment house at 907 Fifth Avenue (1915) featured galleries that were larger than the drawing rooms and dining rooms beyond.

Carpenter codified an approach to planning that made his buildings the standard for luxury apartment development. With the standard set by Carpenter, the way was cleared for Candela. Following his graduation from Columbia in 1915 he worked in the offices of Gaetan Ajello and Frederick Sterner. In 1920, just thirty years old, Candela established his own practice. Though he didn't have society connections, he became the favorite architect of developers Anthony Campagna and Michael Paterno, fellow Sicilian-born immigrants. During his first five years of practice, he designed eighteen buildings, almost all on Manhattan's west side, a market that catered to the professional and middle classes. These apartments were smaller than the palatial plans on the best avenues of the east side but nonetheless included staff rooms and many other functions of the more luxurious end of the market. A typical apartment in Candela's first years had a compact service area tucked behind the bedroom hall that diminished the privacy of the bedrooms. Although these apartments were well-received, they were not at the level that he would achieve when Campagna and Paterno set their sights on the prime avenues of the Upper East Side.

The west side buildings, and indeed all apartment houses before 1910, had more elaborate, complicated interior architecture than the core apartments we cover in this book. Apartment planning was just emerging from a decade where the requirements for an appropriate plan were in flux. From studio apartments to early cooperatives to French Flats, the shape and plan of the New York City apartment was an ever-evolving proposition that included eccentric notions like Warren & Wetmore's plans for a building on West End

Hotel Marguery at 270 Park Avenue, developed by Joseph Paterno. When completed in 1917 it was the largest apartment building in the world.

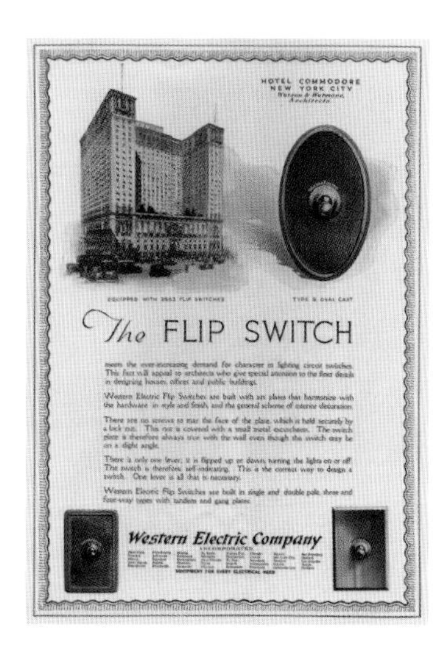

Advertisements for technology often boasted of their use in new hotel and apartment buildings.

Avenue, where each apartment featured a ballroom-sized entertaining room with beds relegated to drawers hidden within the paneling.

The market also saw the influence of the École des Beaux-Arts, which—thanks to Richard Morris Hunt—was considered the most celebrated architecture school for the American profession. However, not all lessons from Paris made sense in New York City. Chester Aldrich, fresh from his studies in Paris, designed 925 Park Avenue with an open fire stair wrapping around a birdcage elevator. This forced the service elevator and the kitchens to the Park Avenue facing front of the building, an inversion of the hierarchy that Carpenter and Candela would never allow in their plans.

Candela took Carpenter's model and refined the planning while juggling the complexities imposed by the shape of the building. The interruptions to the plan of structure and systems and the diversity of plan types would lead to sectional variations. Candela's planning manifests a set of rules that inform every apartment. The most recognizable trait of his planning was that a Candela apartment appears to have been designed from the inside out. In most apartments a substantial gallery or foyer leads to the main entertaining or public rooms. Views to these rooms are either axial or diagonal, but in either case the relationship of the public rooms is clear to a stranger while the connections to other parts are less obvious. The bedroom wing is often connected to the formal rooms through an ample hall, discreetly situated off the foyer. The connection to the service areas, including the kitchen, pantry, laundry, and staff bedrooms, is further obscured.

Candela has often been cited as the master of apartment planning. His diversity of floor plans and combinations within the confines of a constant floor plate encompassed most of the apartment houses except at the uppermost stories. Within one building, for instance 960 Fifth Avenue, there are simplex, duplex, and triplex units. Adding to the complexity, double-height rooms appear in the largest apartments and an entirely different scale and arrangement is provided for the rental unit wing of the building. The heart of the puzzle is how all these volumes fit into one uniform block while following the vertical alignments of the window bays of the facades.

Nesting a variety of units into one volume is a challenge, and multistory buildings also present structural, core, and mechanical systems that complicate that task. Each beam, column, stair, duct, pipe, and flue was located to satisfy the technical requirements of the design. In many areas these locations limited the options for programming. The structure itself presented challenges. Steel columns and beams supporting concrete slabs provided an efficient frame, however, the structural grid was irregular, as loads transferred from setback floors at the top of the building to the lower floors.

Other systems further added to the complexity. For example, Candela's plans included more bathrooms than were thought necessary just one generation before. The plumbing, especially drains, occupy vertical chases—slot-like shafts—that must align through various apartment types and, where alignment is impossible, piping runs back to the chases, often above ceilings or within walls. Further complicating the arrangement of rooms, other vertical features interrupted the floor, including boiler flues and air ducts that served to ventilate rooms without windows such as elevator halls and bathrooms. Because each fireplace required an individual flue, a thirty-apartment building with three fireplaces per apartment would require myriad flues culminating in sixty to ninety flues at the roof.

The principal vertical feature of every apartment house is the core, which contains fire stairs and elevators. In his larger buildings, Candela created two or more cores. Most often, he oriented one core—equipped with passenger elevators—toward the front or principal facade. The position and orientation of this element set the entrance sequence for every apartment in that line. Within each apartment, the private elevator lobby is the entrance to the unit. In most Candela plans, the elevator lobby, which is generally quite compressed, leads directly to the entrance gallery, which in turn introduces the public rooms, sleeping areas, and service areas in descending order of prominence.

The core serves both to orient the front of the apartment and, in some cases, to help obscure the service areas. Candela's placement of the core, an element that is experienced as background—almost invisible—determined the sequence from the public lobby on the street level to the apartment gallery. By controlling this path, Candela succeeded in reinforcing the perception that each unit has a clear and correct relationship with the building as an object on the avenue. Rather than a path of turns and offsets, as was common in many other apartment buildings of the era, Candela assumed that the entrance to the apartment was a clear sequence that started on the sidewalk and maintained an order that transcended the cramped volume of the elevator.

Within the service zone of each unit, Candela exploited the need for a service elevator to sequester the kitchen, pantry, and staff rooms from the entertaining and sleeping areas. This ensured that staff would be able to come and go discreetly and independently. As was common, Candela typically placed the principal entrance to the service core at the basement level to preserve floor area on the ground floor for apartments, doctors' offices, and other uses. In an arrangement that is no longer seen as convenient or considerate of staff, the service lobby was often accessed by an external stair to the basement.

While every apartment designer had to grapple with these structural and systematic givens, Candela exceeded his peers in suppressing these elements within the interior architecture of his apartments. In many apartments, steel beams, which followed the engineer's plans for structural efficiency, were encased in plaster and advertised as a feature of the interior architecture. To Candela these beams were no more than structure and had no place in his interiors. While these structural beams appear in his kitchen or staff areas, in the main rooms, Candela specified an additional uninterrupted plaster ceiling under the beams. Taking the same approach on the exterior walls of his plans, Candela specified an interior plaster facing inboard to create a void that hides the steel columns and vertical piping from view. In essence, instead of adding finish plaster to the inside of structural steel and concrete, Candela was building a finished room within the structure.

Compared with other buildings of the era, Candela's managed to regularize the shape of the rooms within his apartments. By hiding the frame of the building, a Candela room is not compromised by the protrusions of structure beyond the finished wall. The resolution of the form of each room meant that Candela's moldings—uninterrupted by the irregularities of the underlying structure—reinforce the proportions of each room. The extra ceiling and internal finish partitions increased the thickness of the walls and the floors and added to the sense that his apartment houses were robust and even comparable to the solid, substantial construction of the mansions that had lined Fifth Avenue a generation before.

Candela perfected the quality of his interior architecture by resolving the functional complexities of the building and obscuring its structure. Having established well-proportioned rooms as the building blocks, he showed real genius in his arrangement of overall floor plans.

He demonstrated this planning skill at 775 Park Avenue, his first large apartment house for developer Michael Paterno and one of four designs completed in 1927. In this block-wide building, private maisonette units connect directly to the street and to the public lobbies. Typical of Candela's maisonette apartments, these units approximate the atmosphere of a private mansion at the ground floor while expanding substantially above. For instance, the entry to the largest, corner maisonette leads to a generous foyer that serves as the landing of the private stair. This foyer is centered between the library and the reception room. Together, these rooms, including closets and a powder room tucked into the sides, occupy a rectangle of roughly the same size as a townhouse on a nearby side street. But within this relatively compressed plan, Candela creates an impressive enfilade of rooms that spans seventy feet from the library fireplace on the north to a south-facing window in the far end of the reception room.

At the upper (second) floor of the maisonette, Candela expanded the plan substantially beyond the townhouse-like dimensions of the floor below. The stair from the street lands at the center of a larger foyer, which is centered on a wide opening to the main living room. Family or guests who arrive through the public lobby emerge from a private elevator lobby that opens to the end of the foyer. The dining room and living room are aligned at one end of the floor with the bedrooms and service areas arranged discreetly on the avenue-facing and courtyard-facing sides of the plan, respectively.

Within one apartment, Candela deployed many of the strategies that make his plans so compelling. Rather than simply stacking floors, he offset an upper duplex floor above another unit below. He used the internal stair to move the eye not just vertically, but toward the center of the larger floor. He also dropped the floor in the living room to achieve the higher ceiling that this major room requires, thereby lowering the ceiling to a level that is appropriate for the smaller reception room below. With three other maisonette units, and many simplex and duplex apartments, Candela devised a variety of intriguing plans at 775 Park Avenue. Within this one building, a variety of apartments provided an extraordinary range of size, orientation, and layout. Candela had what the market wanted.

Although most Candela apartment houses include a complicated mix of unit types, smaller sites made more conventional stacked planning inevitable. At 990 Fifth Avenue, which Candela designed with Warren & Wetmore, the twenty-seven-foot width facing Fifth Avenue constrained the design. Here, Candela arranged the core, including the fire stair and service elevator, at the northeast corner of the plan, with the passenger elevator also on the north but at the center of the floor plate. This separation of service and public core functions was a typical approach to sequestering the kitchen and staff rooms on a narrow lot. Instead of using a courtyard—impossible in such a narrow plan—Candela arranged the cores, closets, and fireplaces along the shared property line at the north known as the "lot line." This organization left the full width of the plan at the Central Park–facing side for the living room, and in duplex units, for the master bedroom above. By alternating floor heights Candela provided eleven-foot ceilings on living room floors and nine-foot ceilings on the bedroom floors.

At 2 East 70th Street, which Candela designed with Walker & Gillette, the narrow lot was even longer than at 990 Fifth. Candela's solution was to split the building internally to create large, Central Park–facing simplex apartments with smaller duplex and triplex units occupying about one third of the eastern end of each floor. By locating a graceful but compact curved stair at the center of the smaller apartments, Candela approximated the charm of a small townhouse

WURTS BROS

with living rooms and dining rooms in enfilade facing the Frick Collection to the north and courtyard windows to the south. To reduce the volume of separate fire stairs for the east and west apartment lines, Candela tucked a shared stair that is accessed discreetly through closets from the east between the apartments.

Shoehorning fire stairs into the plan was one of the tools Candela deployed in these plans. Most Candela-designed apartments captured the requirements of a luxury apartment in the 1920s by consolidating the service functions—kitchen, laundry, and staff rooms—into a relatively tight area to free up as much volume as possible for entertaining and sleeping rooms. Staff rooms shared bathrooms but usually were fitted with individual sinks. In larger apartments, kitchens were centered on large, cast-iron gas ranges and buffered from the dining room by a pantry. The pantry also offered a connection to the main foyer and beyond a servant's hall.

While service spaces, being located on the rear of the buildings with direct connection to the service core, were almost always stacked, Candela had more leeway locating entertaining rooms and bedrooms. At 1 Sutton Place South, which Candela designed with the architects Cross & Cross, the U-shaped, block-wide building was divided into three sections with large simplex apartments at the ends bracketing duplex units at the middle. In every apartment, the living rooms are positioned with their long wall facing east toward the view of the East River and the building's garden below.

The procession from Sutton Place to the East River–facing entertaining rooms is carefully choreographed. Cars enter the building through an arched porte cochere carved out of the west facade. The lobby spans the entire center section, aligning with a garden terrace that is embraced by the north and south wings. A more intimate, residential scale resumes at the ends of the lobby where elevators serve each of the apartment lines. Within each apartment, the elevator lobby leads to a smaller vestibule that connects to each apartment's foyer, further connecting the symmetry established by the entrances to the living room and dining room facing the river. This sequence, from grand public space to more compressed rooms (including the elevator) to the generous scale of each apartment's public rooms is emblematic of Candela's deft planning.

In some of his most sophisticated designs, Candela sorted and ordered several disparate programs with the same authority. For example, 960 Fifth includes maisonette apartments, simplex and duplex units, and unique apartments with double-height rooms. In a continuous section on the side street, Candela designed floors of much smaller rental units over an extensive suite of entertaining rooms reserved for the residents. In the main section of the building, shifted plans and double-height spaces result in interlocking apartment volumes. The typical duplex is organized around a thirty-five-foot-long gallery that connects the entertaining rooms and is centered on an ample elliptical stair. At the bedroom floor above, a six-foot-wide hall allows a band of space for dressing closets and creates a vestibule for each of the largest bedrooms.

990 Fifth Avenue

Josef Hoffmann's Austrian Pavilion at the *Exposition internationale des arts décoratifs et industriels modernes*, Paris (1925)

The complexity of the program of 960 Fifth was driven by the number of designers. Warren & Wetmore were likely engaged for the facades; Cross & Cross represented the owners' interests; and Dorothy Draper, practicing as the Architectural Clearing House, designed the interiors of the public spaces. Purchasers of units were allowed to modify the apartment plans as the building was under construction. Only an architect of Candela's genius for planning could have coped with so many voices and delivered a perfectly arranged building in fifteen months.

Among Candela's most challenging assignments must have been 834 Fifth Avenue, which was planned as a mid-block symmetrical building until land under an additional townhouse was added to the footprint. A renovation of one of the duplex units supervised by my firm revealed the side-by-side structure where the apartment was expanded into the newly available real estate. This building is notable for its vast apartments, and while the service spaces are squeezed into courtyard-facing rooms, the principal rooms are impressively scaled, and some of the duplex stairs engage outside walls.

The last of Candela's great apartment houses, 19 East 72nd Street, completed in 1937 with Mott Schmidt, was a development fueled by the vapors of wealth created before the crash of 1929. The base of the facade is a close copy of the ogee profiles on Josef Hoffmann's Austrian Pavilion at the 1925 *Exposition internationale des arts décoratifs et industriels modernes*, and the lobby is a study in modern classicism. But despite the post-crash atmosphere and the ascendancy of the modernist paradigm in design, Candela's ingenious planning of the apartments remains true to his original principles. The clear and compelling procession from the street into the apartment leads from public to private space in an elegant sequence that is both urbane and comfortably residential. Rosario Candela, who had been a star of the Roaring Twenties when apartment house architects were setting the standards for elegant living, had a genius that has not been eclipsed by time or changing fashions. He set a standard that is still valid today.

Entrance to 19 East 72nd Street (1936), with three story channeled rustication at base, modeled upon Hoffmann's design

19

1 SUTTON PLACE SOUTH, 1925

Mainly owing to its block-long site overlooking the East River, this first of Candela's "important" buildings has features ranging from unusual to unique.

The entrance through a graceful triple-arched porte cochere is an event, and an ornament to the street. Passing through it to the lobby and garden led to a marina for arrival and departure by commuter yacht, until the construction of the East River Drive (now FDR Drive) put paid to this amenity in 1939. The twin water towers servicing the two wings of the U-shaped plan are contained in a pair of tempietti more restrained in scale than Emery Roth's would be, but still expressive. The organization of the facade into an extruded Italian palazzo of three belt courses above a limestone base is deft and successful, anticipating similar massing at Candela's block-long 775 Park Avenue of the following year. But the poetry of 1 Sutton is in the site-driven details.

The building was built by the Phipps family on Phipps land, which had formerly contained slaughterhouses and tenements. This development represented the second stage of the invention of Sutton Place out of whole cloth that began in 1920 with the block of townhouses to the north, specifically Mott Schmidt's houses for Anne Vanderbilt and her neighbor Anne Morgan. With those as anchor tenants the desirability of the area was assured, and luxury apartment house development followed. The transition period when both squalid slum and opulent towers existed side by side occurred in this exact spot, the source of the imagery in the film *Dead End* (1937).

Comprised of thirty-three apartments (some now subdivided), 1 Sutton is crowned by a sprawling penthouse. In 1964 Winston Guest encountered financial distress because of his disastrous investment in the airline Aerovias and put his own apartment—half of the roofscape of 1 Sutton—on the

Of all Candela's buildings, this one may offer the most "sense of place" upon arrival, removing one from the street via porte cochere to the private world of a river garden.

market. Janet Hooker, Walter Annenberg's sister, explained she would buy it, but only if she could have the adjacent unit once occupied by his mother as well (Amy Phipps Guest had died in 1959). In that transaction lies the explanation for how the very odd plan came to be assembled for the full-floor penthouse, which still exists today.

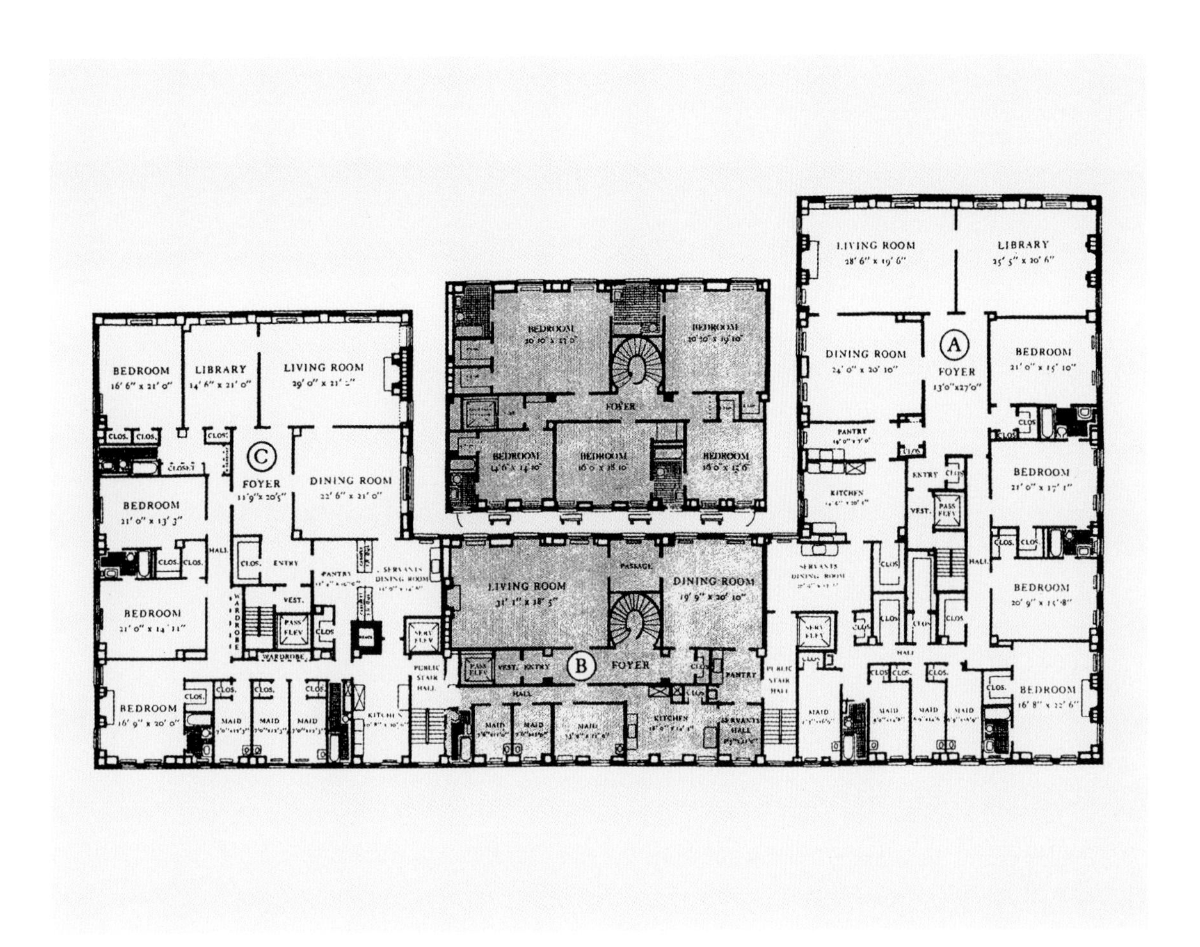

A typical floor plan consists of two simplexes and a B-line duplex.

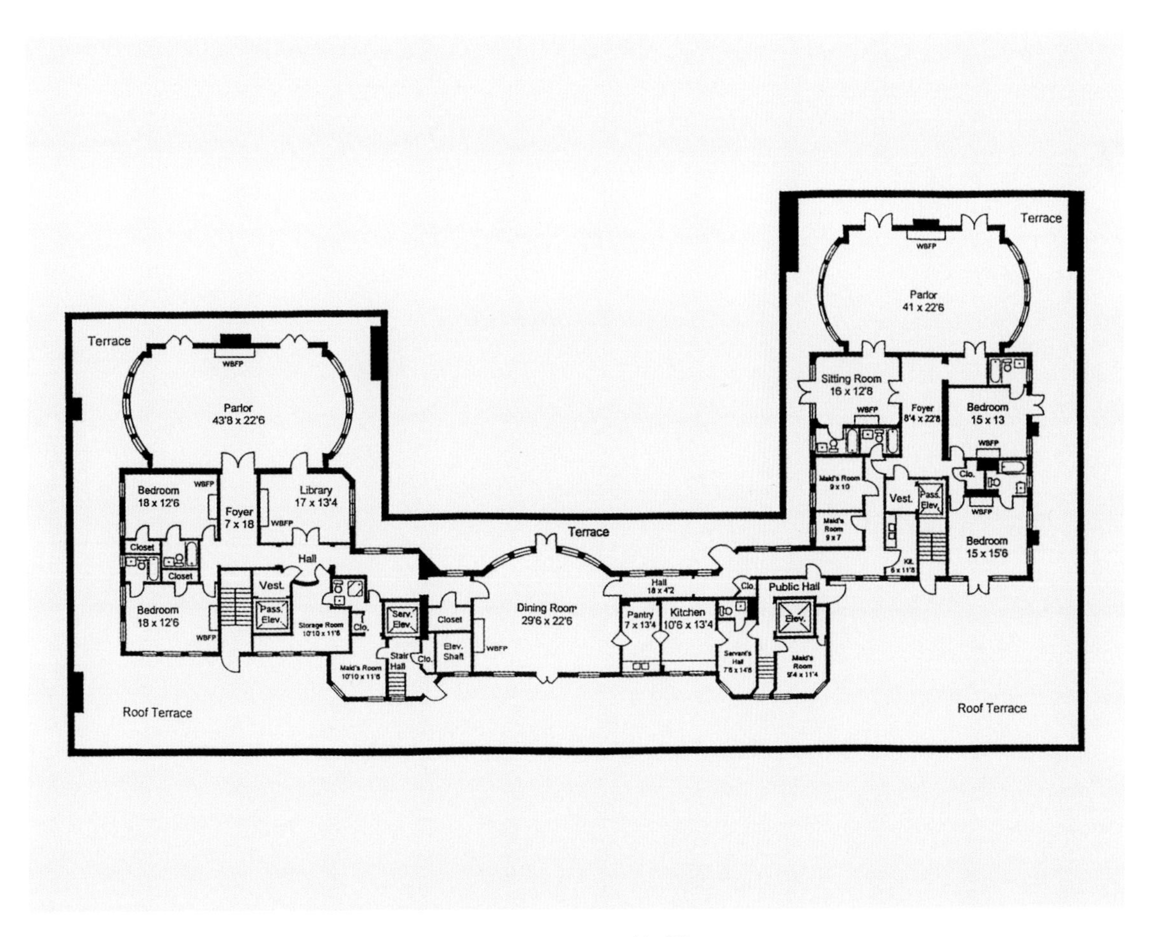

Penthouse plan as renovated in 2002. The original two apartments owned by Winston Guest and his mother were combined somewhat awkwardly by Janet Hooker around 1967.

Bill Blass's apartment at 1 Sutton Place was the ultimate expression of his philosophy of interior design, in which neoclassical furniture and stark white architecture added up to something modern—and did more than any other interior of its time to give antiques a *future*.

The living room of the Blass apartment, not conducive to conversation but one of the handsomest rooms in New York. The seventeenth-century drawing of a ship was later replaced by a Picasso.

The bedroom, somewhat Jeffersonian in character, occupied what was formerly the huge library of a Phipps apartment. Blass found the table at Ciancimino in London.

775 PARK AVENUE, 1926

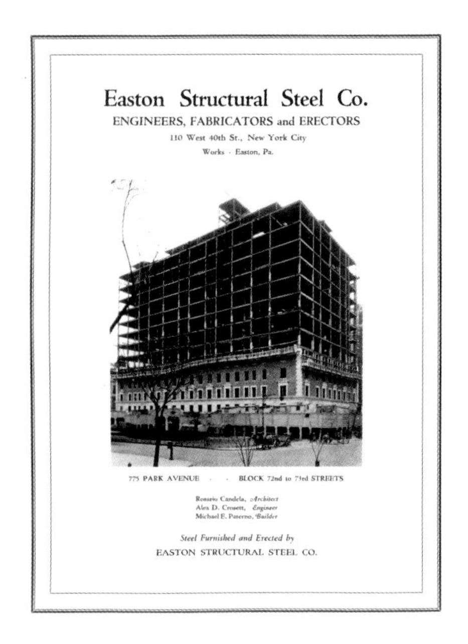

Following close on the heels of 1 Sutton Place South, 775 may be seen as its Upper East Side sibling—comparable because of their "extruded palazzo" massing, unusual full-block sites, and Georgian/Italian baroque exteriors executed in brick and limestone. The developer was Michael Paterno, with Dorothy Draper (then billed as Mrs. George Draper) as consultant on plans and decorations.

The substitution of Park Avenue for the East River means the plans behave quite differently; main rooms here are oriented toward Park Avenue and the main facade, rather than the river views in back as at 1 Sutton. But the buildings are closely related in appearance, even topping out at the lot line at the same height—thirteen stories, with the penthouse above obscured behind a substantial limestone cornice.

Candela's 775 is one of the few "good buildings" on the east side of Park Avenue, an oft-whispered New York real estate trope that (without any obvious explanation except perhaps the lack of morning sunlight on that side) happens to be true. In similar New York real estate parlance 775 has always been a "family" rather than a "society" building—notable, however, in that one of the great collections of modern art in the city is housed here.

In addition to five penthouses, there are four duplex maisonettes ranging from eleven to fifteen rooms, each with its own street entrance and separate address.

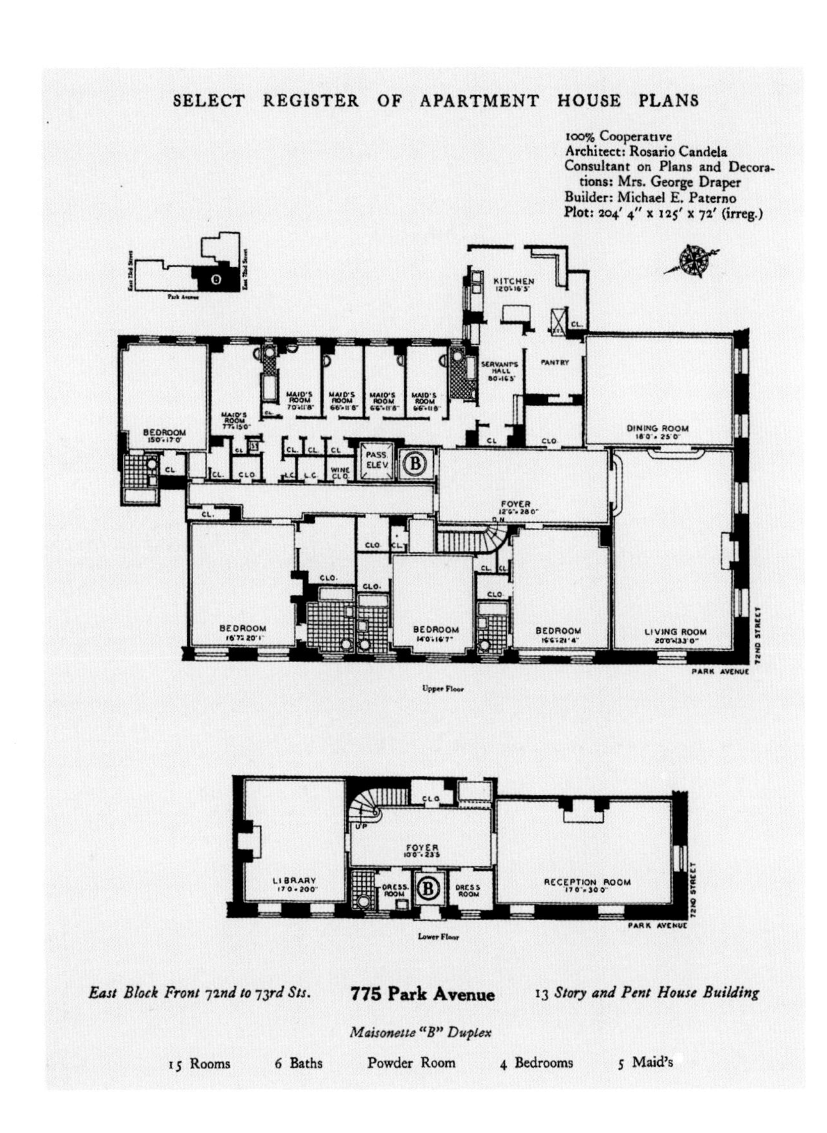

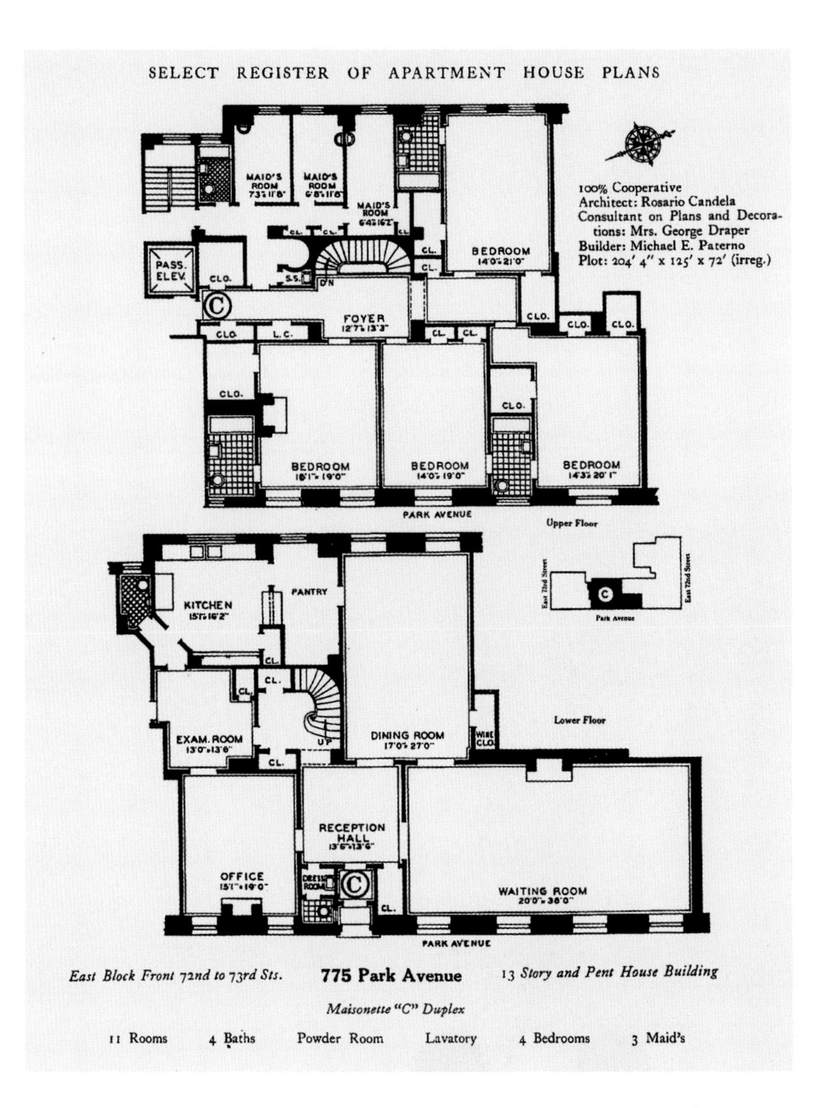

Southwest corner maisonette, at left. The C-line center unit is—unusually—offered here with room labels showing potential use as a doctor's office.

Lobby, as originally decorated in the Georgian style favored by Dorothy Draper

990 FIFTH AVENUE, 1926

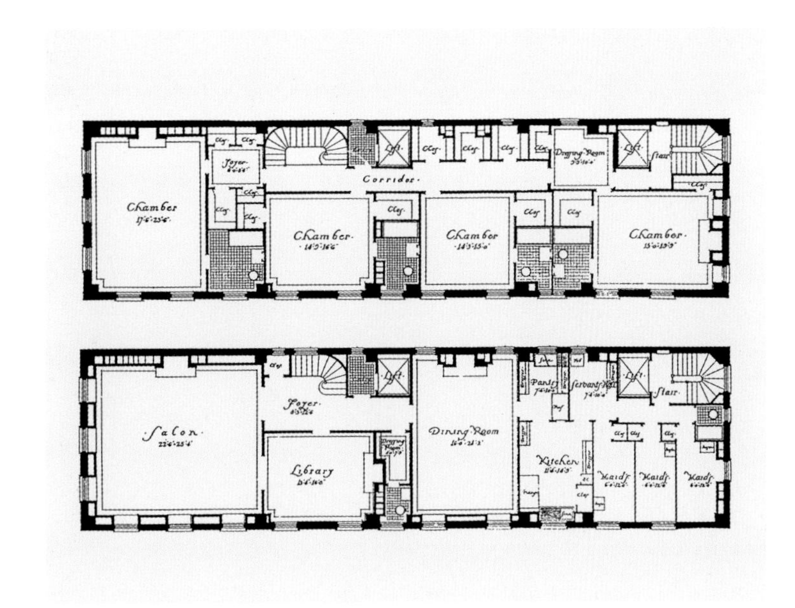

The building that replaced the imposing chateau built for F. W. Woolworth by C. P. H. Gilbert (it lasted only twenty-five years), 990 Fifth Avenue has a generosity of scale that makes the apartments here something that can truly come close to being called townhouses in the sky. There are only five typical duplex units and a triplex penthouse; the thirteen-room duplexes have five fireplaces. This is the first of the Candela apartment buildings to replace a mansion on a thirty-by-one-hundred-foot townhouse lot, and the most opulent in terms of its layout.

Residents over the years have included Pat and Peter Lawford, Sam and Judy Peabody, and Russell and Annie-Laurie Aitken (mother of Sunny von Bulow, who grew up in the building). The backdrop to the story in Christine Coulson's novel *One Woman Show* is set at 990, where principal character Kitty Whitaker lives until her death.

In contrast to its neighbor 950 Fifth Avenue a few blocks down at 76th Street, 990's facade has never had the nonelective surgery to combine openings into a single enlarged window popular in the 1970s, before the establishment of the Upper East Side Historic District; it retains its original three-across window design from top to bottom on the Fifth Avenue facade. The closest thing to an "intervention" here has been Robert A. M. Stern's renovation for Andy Capasso in the postmodern style (1980–82)—which included a double-height glass brick window on the lot line wall to the north, behind the stair connecting the tenth and eleventh floors, part of which is still visible.

2 EAST 67TH STREET, 1927

This site at 67th Street and Fifth Avenue is a case study in the short life of Fifth Avenue mansions, and the transitioning of domestic arrangements from townhouse to apartment living.

Judge Elbert Gary's house at 856 Fifth Avenue stood for only fifteen years; his widow, having sold it shortly before his death in 1927 to developer Michael Paterno, then bought an apartment in the new building. This was the new New York, squarely in the Jazz Age: it took less than fifteen years to get from C. P. H. Gilbert's erection of one of the finest houses on the avenue to this line in the July 15, 1927, edition of the *New York Times*: "Anybody who will take away the marble spiral staircase in the mansion which was the home of Elbert H. Gary, at Fifth Avenue and Sixty-seventh Street, can have it for $1, Edward R. Walsh, President of the house wrecking company which is to start demolishing the residence on Monday, said yesterday." The stair had originally cost $150,000.

What resulted is a sparingly detailed limestone stack of nine simplex units atop two duplex maisonettes, one of the handsomest and most quietly sumptuous of all Candela's buildings. Number 2, also known in its offering materials by the original Gary house address of 856 Fifth Avenue, has the very unusual feature (for a Candela building) of large steel casement windows, oversized and low to the floor to maximize park views. As with the contemporaneous project at 960 Fifth Avenue—the two buildings were filed nineteen days apart in August 1927—Warren & Wetmore are the associated architects here. The two facades are in many respects related, with similar rustication at the base and detailing of the cornice and water tower, along with the unusually theatrical device of a loggia anchoring the Fifth Avenue facades.

Elbert H. Gary House undergoing demolition, having stood for fewer than fifteen years (July, 1927)

The loggia belongs to an exceptional penthouse, originally a duplex of eighteen rooms containing one of Candela's largest stairs. This apartment was at one point the home of Consuelo Vanderbilt Balsan (a double Candela client, here and later at 1 Sutton Place South), but in 1954 was broken up into two separate apartments. Today's owner has both floors—but has declined to reconnect them, preferring instead the romance of using the upper level with its wrap terraces as a discrete "country house" in town. Combined or otherwise, this remains a contender for the title of most desirable apartment in the city.

SELECT REGISTER OF APARTMENT HOUSE PLANS

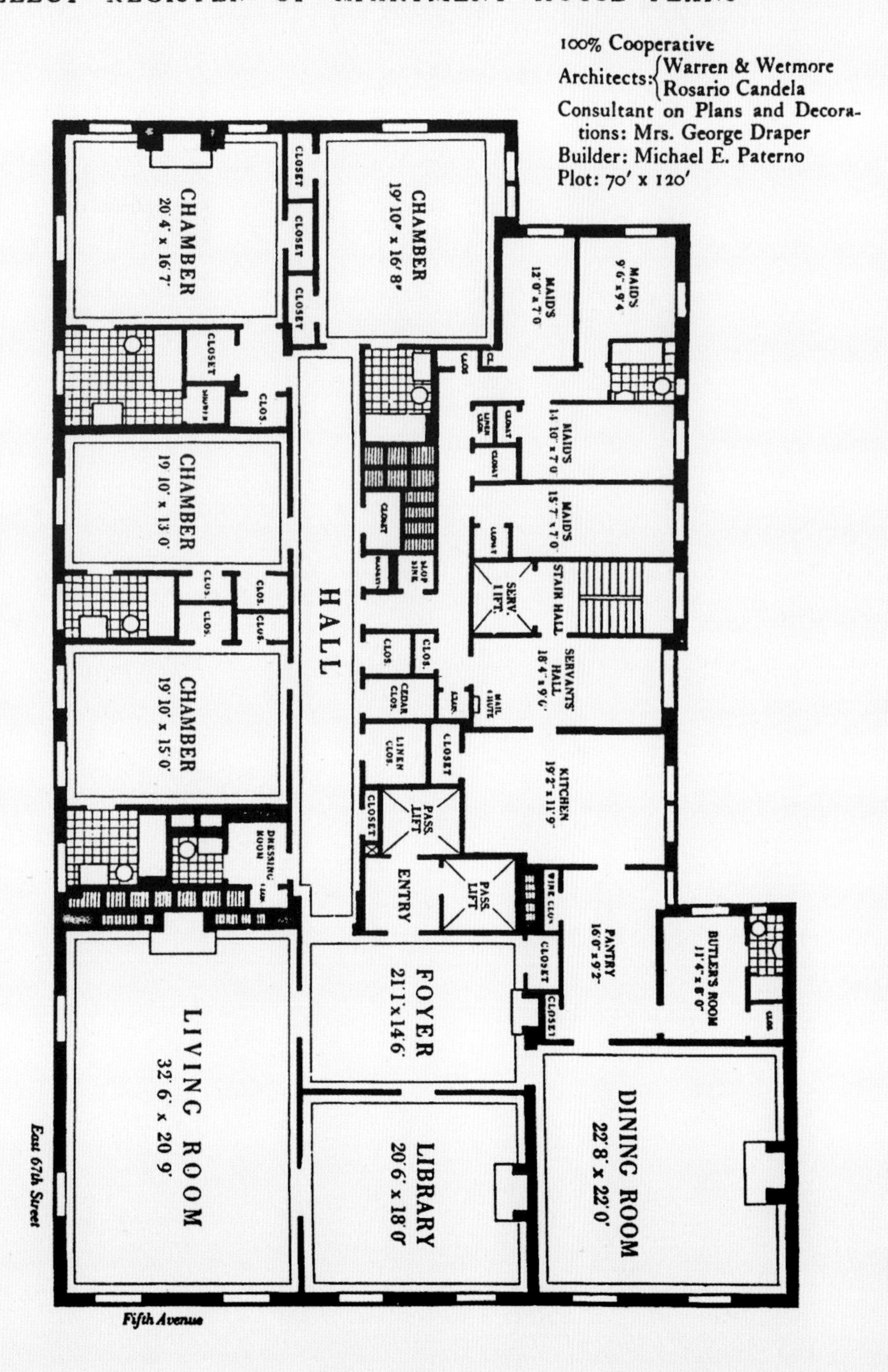

S. E. Corner 67th Street **856 Fifth Avenue** 13 *Story and Pent House Building*

14 Rooms 6 Baths 4 Master's 4 Servants'

Typical floor plans contain five fireplaces, with the unusual feature of one in the entrance hall.

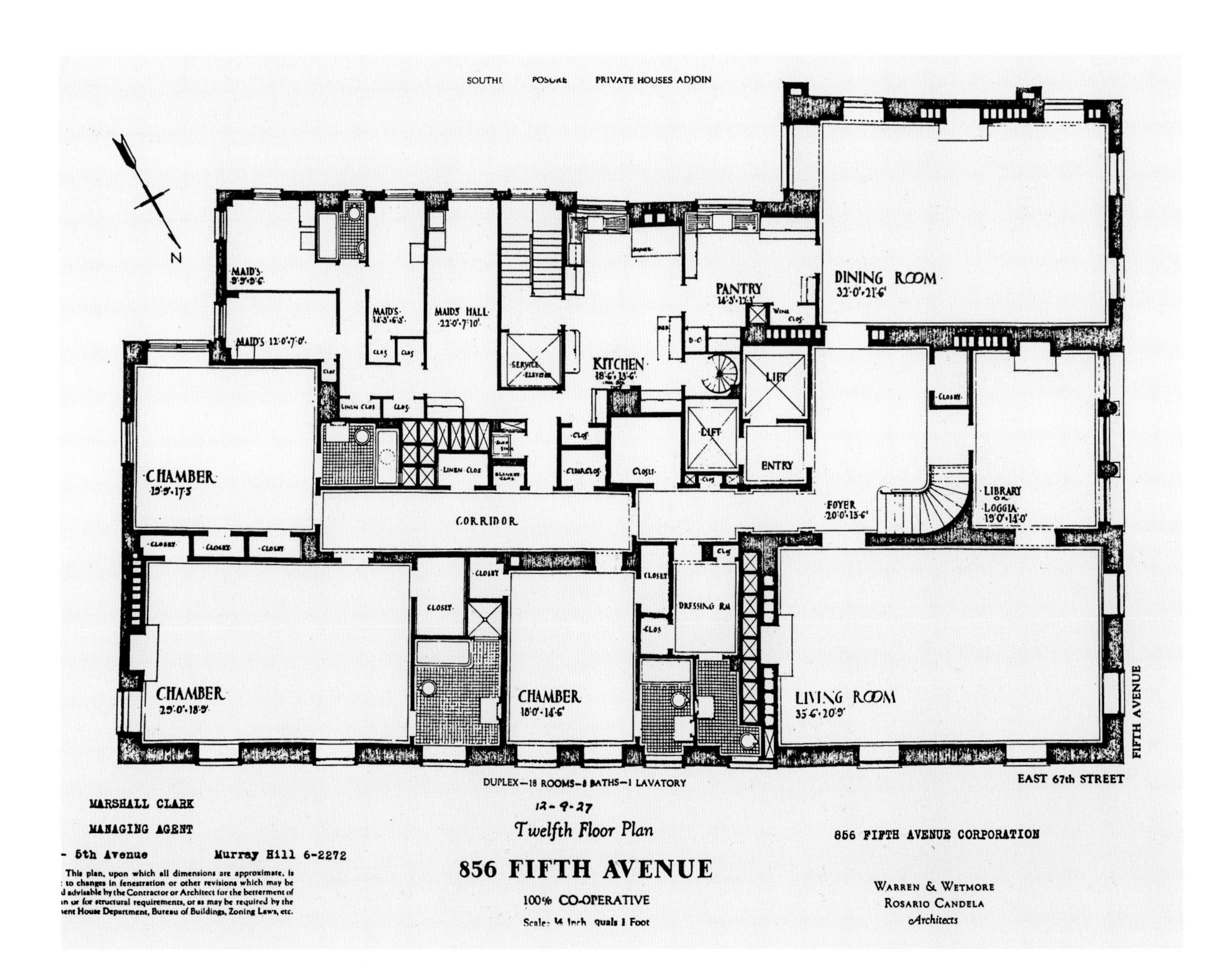

Twelfth floor and penthouse plan. Subdivided into two units in 1954, this was and remains—united again but without its stair—one of Candela's most lavish apartments.

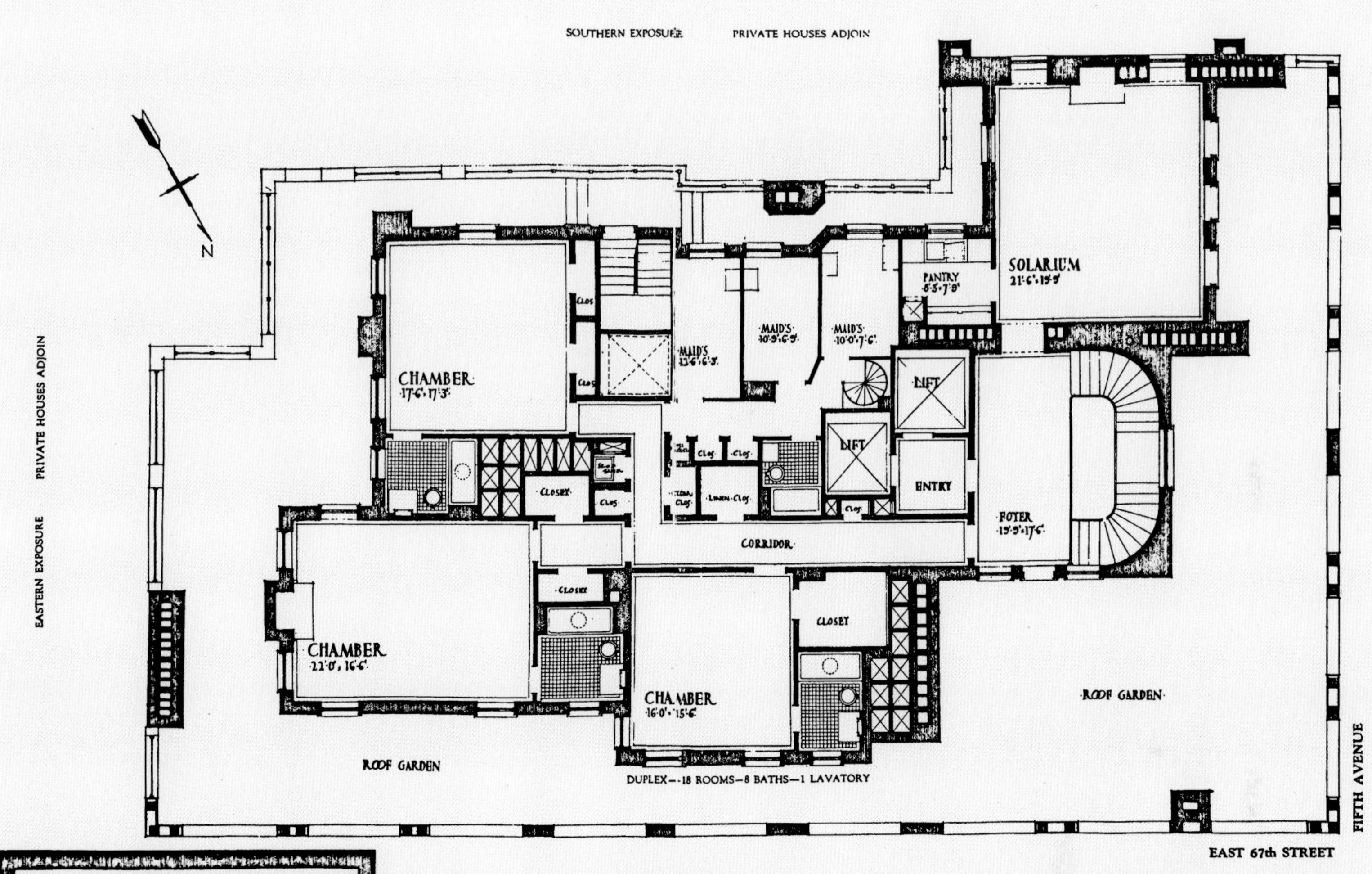

SUBMITTED BY
Douglas Gibbons & Co. INC.
REAL ESTATE AND INSURANCE
VOlunteer 5-4600 73 E. 57th Street

Pent House Plan

856 FIFTH AVENUE

This was made into a seperate apt.

WARREN & WETMORE
ROSARIO CANDELA
Architects

Two views of the living room in the apartment of
Thomas Cochrane (1929)

The room with three arched windows labeled "loggia" in the plan is now a library, with Louis XV boiserie likely installed by Consuelo Vanderbilt Balsan.

Overleaf: In the penthouse, looking southwest from what was once the second floor stair landing toward the solarium.

2 EAST 70TH STREET, 1927

The second of the Candela buildings occupying thirty-by-one-hundred-foot townhouse lots, 2 East 70th Street replaces the short-lived Ledyard Blair house by Carrère & Hastings of 1917. During the barely ten years of its existence, the Blair house formed a sort of southern wall to the garden of Henry Clay Frick's mansion by the same architects to the north. Candela handles this context as sensitively as possible, given that what he is replacing it with is a fourteen-story building; many of his gestures on the facade of 2 East 70th Street are similar to the preceding house. The choice of exterior design vocabulary, in a French style unusual for Candela (who favored English and Italian precedents), was obviously influenced by the neighbor to the north as well.

Unlike its predecessor 990 Fifth Avenue, which contains very generous duplex units of two full floors each, the typical floor plan here consists of one compact two-bedroom unit (three if the library is sacrificed) facing Fifth Avenue and a duplex of similar scale and slightly smaller room count to the east. Thanks to the proximity of the Frick and its lowness, all the apartments, even those that are exclusively north-facing, enjoy favorable park views.

The use of French casement windows for the living rooms of the A-line apartments and dining rooms of the B-line apartments is also unusual for a Candela building, lending a further continental touch to the Louis XVI refinement of the limestone facade. Six-over-nine double-hung windows in the other public rooms mean elegant lower openings with charming wrought iron railings and maximal views. It was clear in 1927 that the Frick mansion, then still a private house occupied by Frick's widow, Adelaide, was not going anywhere—it would become the museum we know it as today.

Ledyard Blair house by Carrère & Hastings, 1917

View north from 2 East 70th Street overlooking the Frick Collection. Candela's 19 East 72nd Street is visible at right, which places this photograph after 1937.

The intimate scale of these apartments is on the small side for a family; the building skews toward older couples or Europeans looking for a pied-à-terre. Perhaps the most visible tenant of 2 East 70th Street was Joan Crawford (the "tear down that bitch of a bearing wall" line is set in the penthouse duplex she and Alfred Steele renovated extensively in 1957). Other distinguished residents have included Ted Forstmann in the same apartment, Jules and Doris Stein, and Oscar and Françoise de la Renta. A prominent Italian fashion designer maintains a New York apartment here, the rooms decorated in high style by Jacques Grange and shown in color on these pages.

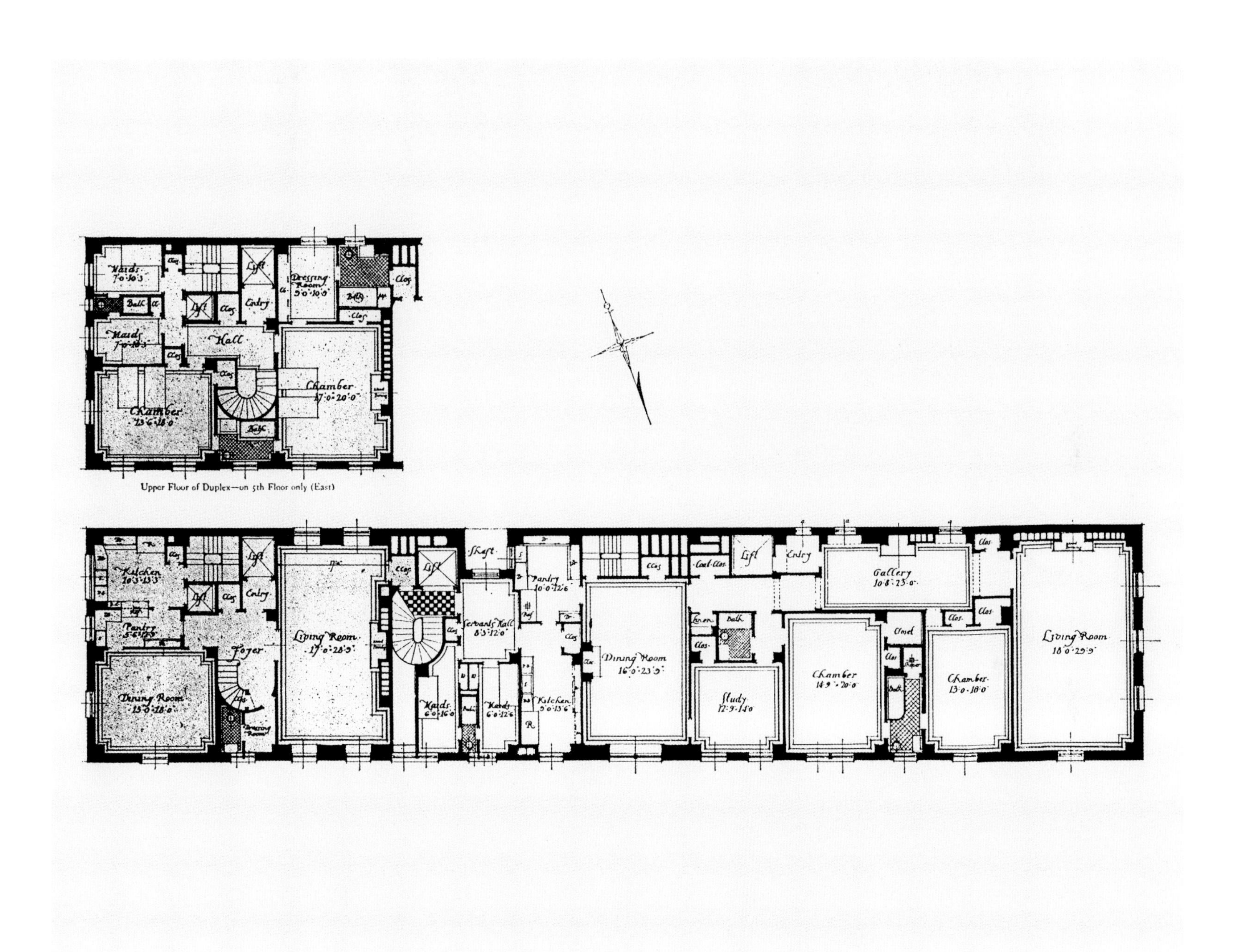

Typical floor plan with compact but very elegant duplex and simplex apartments, altogether occupying a space that would have held three rooms in the Blair house

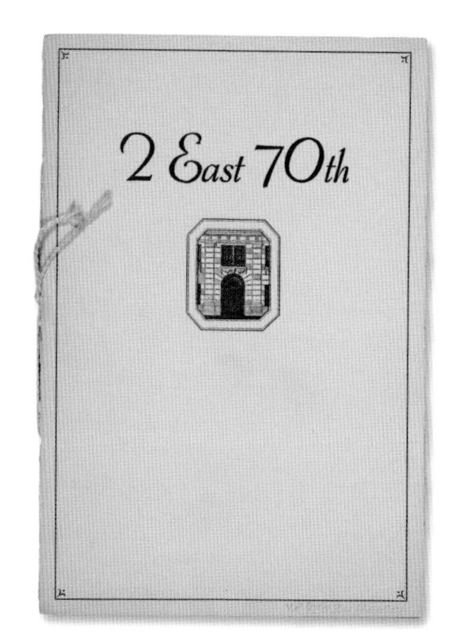

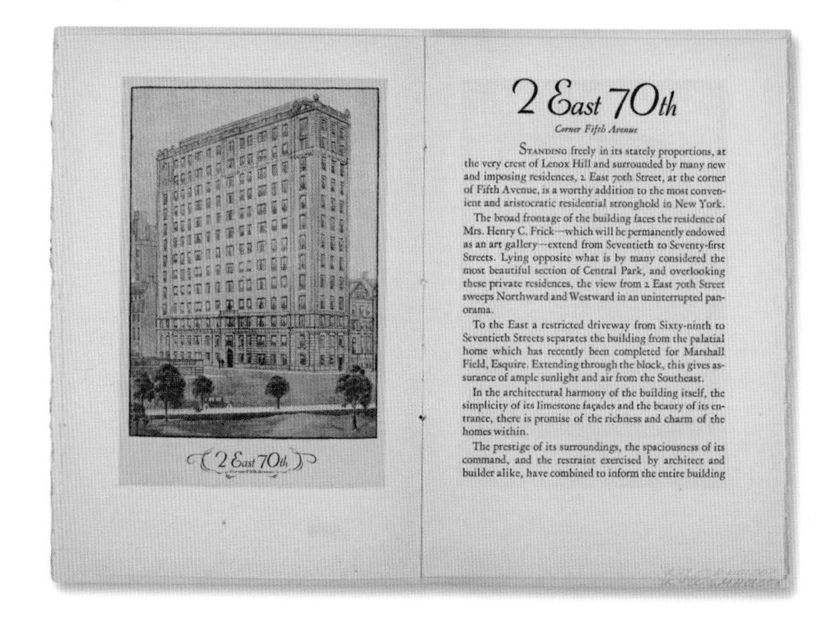

2 East 70th

Corner Fifth Avenue

STANDING freely in its stately proportions, at the very crest of Lenox Hill and surrounded by many new and imposing residences, 2 East 70th Street, at the corner of Fifth Avenue, is a worthy addition to the most convenient and aristocratic residential stronghold in New York.

The broad frontage of the building faces the residence of Mrs. Henry C. Frick—which will be permanently endowed as an art gallery—extend from Seventieth to Seventy-first Streets. Lying opposite what is by many considered the most beautiful section of Central Park, and overlooking these private residences, the view from 2 East 70th Street sweeps Northward and Westward in an uninterrupted panorama.

To the East a restricted driveway from Sixty-ninth to Seventieth Streets separates the building from the palatial home which has recently been completed for Marshall Field, Esquire. Extending through the block, this gives assurance of ample sunlight and air from the Southeast.

In the architectural harmony of the building itself, the simplicity of its limestone façades and the beauty of its entrance, there is promise of the richness and charm of the homes within.

The prestige of its surroundings, the spaciousness of its command, and the restraint exercised by architect and builder alike, have combined to inform the entire building

Overlooking the formal beauty of the Frick gardens and the natural grandeur of Central Park, the environment and view are unsurpassed

ing place of extraordinary restfulness. On this floor there are also two chambers, 14′6″ x 17′3″ and 13′6″ x 14′4″, each with two large windows and its private bath.

Balancing the rest of the apartment is the servants' portion. Entered from a separate lift which opens into the servants hall there are here rooms for four maids, a splendid kitchen and roomy pantry.

Maisonette

ON the Fifth Avenue side of the building a private entrance, with its separate number on the Avenue, leads to a delightful Maisonette which occupies much of the first and second floors. This is a complete house of thirteen rooms, with five baths and extra lavatory. The entrance foyer gives onto a commodious gallery from which a circular stairway leads to a similar gallery above.

To the left of the foyer and gallery, on the first floor, lie a beautifully proportioned reception room, 17′6″ x 21′, and a chamber 14′6″x 19′, which has two windows and a private bath.

On the second floor is a spacious living room, 18′ x 31′, and a library, 13′ x 19′9″, both of which have generous wood-burning fireplaces. Then come two comfortable chambers, 15′ x 20′3″ and 14′ x 14′6″, and a delightful dining room, 16′x 23′9″.

In addition to the spacious master's section there are adequate service arrangements, including kitchen, pantry and rooms for four maids. Other rooms for men servants or maids may be had in the building if they are desired.

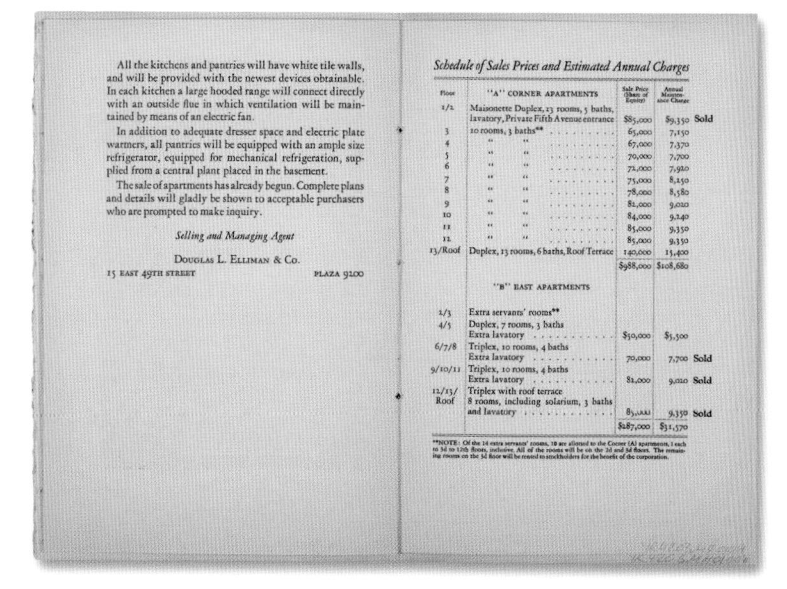

All the kitchens and pantries will have white tile walls, and will be provided with the newest devices obtainable. In each kitchen a large hooded range will connect directly with an outside flue in which ventilation will be maintained by means of an electric fan.

In addition to adequate dresser space and electric plate warmers, all pantries will be equipped with an ample size refrigerator, equipped for mechanical refrigeration, supplied from a central plant placed in the basement.

The sale of apartments has already begun. Complete plans and details will gladly be shown to acceptable purchasers who are prompted to make inquiry.

Selling and Managing Agent

DOUGLAS L. ELLIMAN & CO.

15 EAST 49TH STREET PLAZA 9200

Schedule of Sales Prices and Estimated Annual Charges

Floor	"A" CORNER APARTMENTS	Sale Price (Share of Equity)	Annual Maintenance Charge	
1/2	Maisonette Duplex, 13 rooms, 5 baths, lavatory, Private Fifth Avenue entrance	$85,000	$9,350	Sold
3	10 rooms, 3 baths**	65,000	7,150	
4	" "	67,000	7,370	
5	" "	70,000	7,700	
6	" "	72,000	7,920	
7	" "	75,000	8,250	
8	" "	78,000	8,580	
9	" "	82,000	9,020	
10	" "	84,000	9,240	
11	" "	85,000	9,350	
12	" "	85,000	9,350	
13/Roof	Duplex, 13 rooms, 6 baths, Roof Terrace	140,000	15,400	
		$988,000	$108,680	
	"B" EAST APARTMENTS			
2/3	Extra servants' rooms**			
4/5	Duplex, 7 rooms, 3 baths Extra lavatory	$50,000	$5,500	
6/7/8	Triplex, 10 rooms, 4 baths Extra lavatory	70,000	7,700	Sold
9/10/11	Triplex, 10 rooms, 4 baths Extra lavatory	82,000	9,020	Sold
12/13/ Roof	Triplex with roof terrace 8 rooms, including solarium, 3 baths and lavatory	85,000	9,350	Sold
		$287,000	$31,570	

**NOTE: Of the 14 extra servants' rooms, 10 are allotted to the Corner (A) apartments, 1 each to 3d to 12th floors, inclusive. All of the rooms will be on the 2d and 3d floors. The remaining rooms on the 3d floor will be rented to stockholders for the benefit of the corporation.

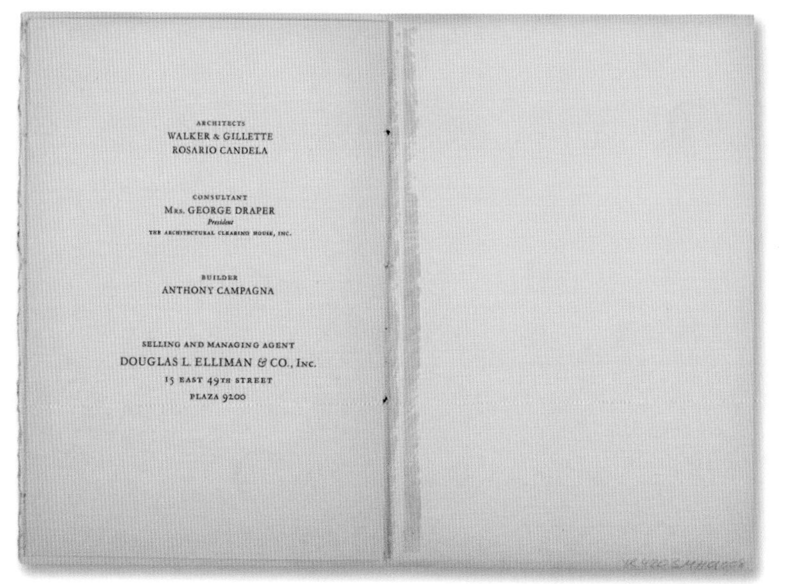

ARCHITECTS
WALKER & GILLETTE
ROSARIO CANDELA

CONSULTANT
MRS. GEORGE DRAPER
President
THE ARCHITECTURAL CLEARING HOUSE, INC.

BUILDER
ANTHONY CAMPAGNA

SELLING AND MANAGING AGENT
DOUGLAS L. ELLIMAN & CO., INC.
15 EAST 49TH STREET
PLAZA 9200

2 East 70th Street (Sales Brochure), Manhattan, Douglas L. Elliman and Co., Inc.

Above: The B-line penthouse triplex once occupied by Jules Stein, renovated by Thierry Despont and decorated by Stephen Sills.

Page 104: In the stair hall hangs Picasso's *Instruments de musique sur un guéridon* (1914), formerly in the collection of Yves Saint Laurent and Pierre Bergé.

Page 105: A view northwest to the Beresford, a building opposite in scale in every way, by Emery Roth.

Opposite: A butler waits to serve lunch in an apartment maintained by an eminent Italian couturier as a pied-à-terre, with decoration by Jacques Grange.

Above: An eclectic collection of nineteenth- and twentieth-century furniture and contemporary art in the living room. Principal rooms at Number 2 have low casement windows with wrought iron French railings.

Above: In the entrance hall a late de Kooning faces the fireplace, out of view on the south wall.

Opposite: A Léger of similar vintage to the building dominates the living room.

WURTS
BROS
N.Y.
816847.
25 SUTTON PLACE. NEW YORK.
DEC. 4th 1945.

25 SUTTON PLACE, 1927

A handsome if stolid Georgian building, 25 Sutton Place has fourteen units, each a full floor except for a duplex maisonette and triplex penthouse.

One of the enigmas of this Candela design, for which Cross & Cross served as supervising architects, is in the orientation and layout of its typical plan, with the main rooms facing west across Sutton Place and addressing city—rather than river—views. Why is this, when all 25's neighbors on the east side of Sutton Place are designed and sited to exploit their blockbuster exposure to the river? It's tempting to speculate that the answer may lie in the row of four-story townhouses lining what is now known as Riverview Terrace, a private cobbled street extending to the north of Sutton Square. Within the exuberant context of the late 1920s economy, and with all of Sutton Place in play, Candela and developer Anthony Paterno could reasonably have expected those townhouses to give way to another apartment building as tall as this one—they may even have been planning to build it themselves—in which case any river views from 25 Sutton Place would have been short-lived. The year 1929 came instead, granting the six townhouses a reprieve (and two of 25's bedrooms on each floor panoramic river views and an unwanted expanse of brick wall) in perpetuity. Or so it seems reasonable to speculate.

Number 25 was originally distinguished by a liberal use of wood shutters on the exterior, now long gone, giving a particularly English flavor to this red brick facade on a two-story limestone base and relating it to the scale and charm of Mott Schmidt's townhouses to the south. Tenants over the years have included Otto Kahn's daughter Nin Ryan, Stavros Niarchos with three of his five wives, and Michel David-Weill.

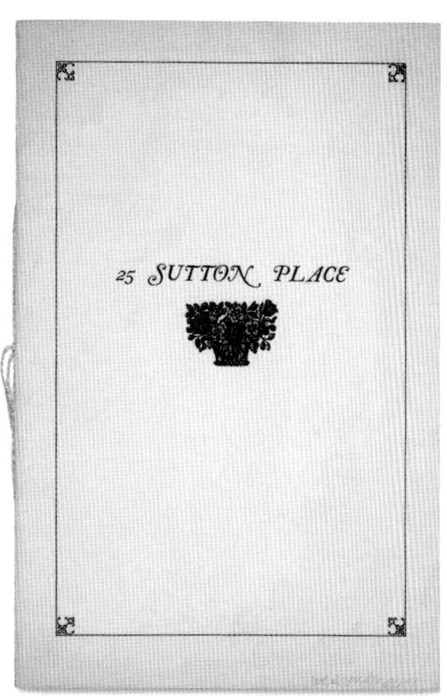

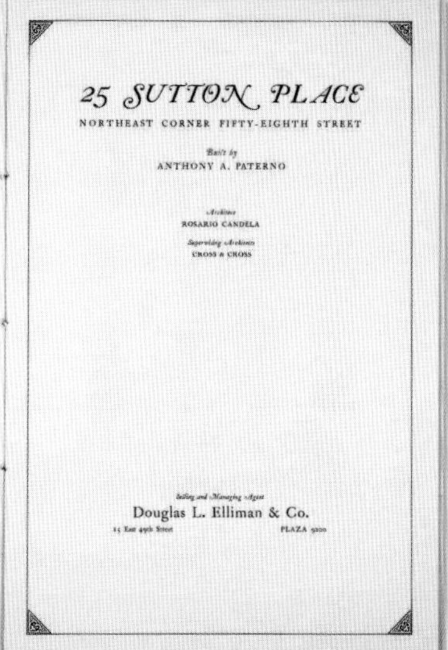

25 SUTTON PLACE

NORTHEAST CORNER FIFTY-EIGHTH STREET

Built by
ANTHONY A. PATERNO

Architect
ROSARIO CANDELA

Supervising Architects
CROSS & CROSS

Selling and Managing Agent
Douglas L. Elliman & Co.
15 East 49th Street PLAZA 9200

25 SUTTON PLACE

IN KEEPING with its heritage from the time when the banks of the East River were lined with the great mansions of Colonial dignitaries, the new co-operative apartment building at 25 Sutton Place has been designed after the best Colonial tradition.

The building is brick, of the deep red color which characterized the English brick used in early American houses, except the first two stories, which are of limestone, so employed as to emphasize the colonial nature of the architecture.

Arches, pilasters and fanlights, which are the most distinctive features of colonial architecture, have been employed in decorating the facades of the building. The broad double doors of the front entrance flanked by tall fluted columns; the trim front steps with their gracefully curving iron railings; and the green of the wooden window-shutters all bring to mind those mansions of another day that once bordered this same river bank.

Here, amid the charming colony of private homes which have recaptured so much of the dignity and beauty that formerly distinguished the banks of the East River, number 25 Sutton Place will be thoroughly in keeping with the spirit of the neighborhood and will continue the traditions of those great houses that once overlooked long green lawns leading to the beautifully varied and picturesque shores.

The rediscovery and reclamation of this garden spot has been enthusiastically welcomed by New Yorkers and no less welcome will be the knowledge of this latest step in the recovery of its former glory. A glory that, even now, has been so far restored, it might be said again, as it once was—"Thither came all of the eminent personages of the day. Men distinguished in important fields—statesmen, financiers, travelers and poets—were frequent visitors in these hospitable homes. The locality was then the finest in all New York and was eagerly seized upon for the establishment of great houses by the opulent merchants and socially important."

OCCUPYING the sunny corner, number 25 Sutton Place will have something over 67 feet on Sutton Place and a long southern frontage of 75 feet on Sutton Square (58th Street). The building will be 14 stories high with roof house and terraces. It will contain 11 complete residences, each occupying a single floor, a Duplex Maisonette with a separate entrance at 1 Sutton Square, and a duplex apartment consisting of the 14th and roof stories with roof terrace.

From more than half the apartments, the sweeping view to the south, over the private houses of the Sutton Place colony, presents a magnificent panorama of the East River; protected for more than forty years from obstruction.

TYPICAL FLOOR

THE TYPICAL PLAN of apartment, which prevails throughout 11 stories, provides for one apartment of 11 rooms and five baths to each floor. A private elevator entry on each of these floors leads to a spacious gallery which opens conveniently into the living room, dining room, and library and is connected by an ample corridor with the masters' chambers, which are well removed from the living section.

Characterized by a splendid spaciousness in the masters'

Previous page: A view of East River Drive during construction (c. 1939) shows the largely blank lot line facade facing east, sacrificing views of the river in anticipation of a building that was never to come.

Above and opposite: An offering brochure compares life at 25 Sutton Place to that in the townhouses of Sutton Square.

Gardens of the Sutton Place Colony

sections which is nicely balanced with adequate service and servants' quarters, these are indeed fine residences. They will immediately appeal to those who are interested in maintaining a city home which is easily accessible and yet removed from the dust and congestion of city traffic.

Located on the corner so that two sides are open to sun and breeze, the living room—27′ 2″ x 19′ 2″—has five large windows and the cheer of a generous wood-burning fireplace. From this room great double doors lead to the dining room, which is 17′ x 19′ 2″ and has two outside windows. Adjoining the living room on the other side is the library which also has two broad windows, opening to the southern sun, and here again there is a cheerful log-burning fireplace.

The masters' section is completed with three comfortable bedrooms, each with its own bath and two commodious closets. Two of these chambers—one 15′ x 23′, the other 14′ 3″ x 19′ 4″—have three windows facing south. The third chamber has two windows and is 12′ 6″ x 19′ 8″.

The service and servants' quarters are more generous than is usual in these days of cramped space. The kitchen —17′ 8″ x 11′ 6″—is large and equipped with every modern convenience. And the serving pantry has been splendidly arranged with an eye to practical usage. The butler's room adjoins the pantry and has its own bath. On the other side of the kitchen are two maids' rooms with connecting bath. These rooms open directly into the spacious servants' hall.

THE DUPLEX MAISONETTE

ENJOYING that complete quiet and seclusion that are assured by freedom from passing traffic, the Duplex Maisonette has its own separate number and entrance at One Sutton Square. This is graced with a neat iron railing giving it an appearance harmonious with the private houses across the Square to the south.

The generous entrance gallery with two coat closets gives easy access to the rooms on both floors of this residence. To the left it opens into the great living room. To the right is the library, and a broad hall leading to the dining room. From this hall a wide stairway curves gracefully to the chambers on the floor above.

The living room in this Maisonette affords a magnificent setting for period furniture and works of art. It is 31′ 10″ x 18′9″; has six splendid windows opening to the South and West, and a cheerful log-burning fireplace.

The comfortable library, 13′ x 11′ 3″, has the convenience of its own lavatory, which also makes it available as a chamber should such use seem desirable.

At the end of the hall is the dining room, 15′ x 20′ 2″. This room has three windows and connects conveniently with the pantry and kitchen, 12′ x 15′. The servants' hall and butler's room are also on this floor.

On the second floor are four comfortable chambers—19′ 2″ x 17′ 8″, 19′ 8″ x 13′ 6″, 23′ x 15′, 18′ 5″ x 12′ 6″—each with its own bath and an abundance of closet space. This floor is completed with rooms for two maids and their bath.

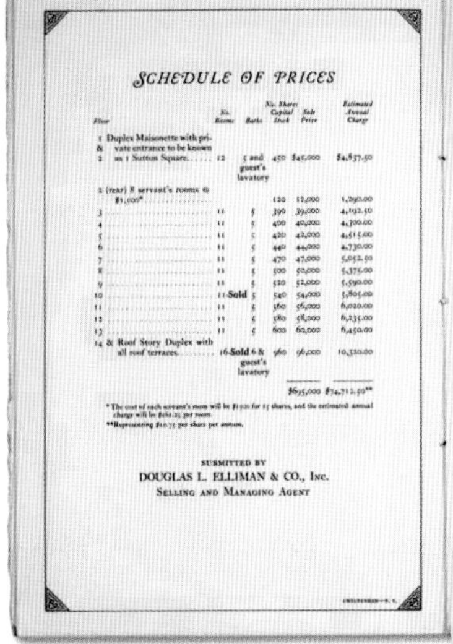

SCHEDULE OF PRICES

Floor		No. Rooms	Baths	No. Shares Capital Stock	Sale Price	Estimated Annual Charge
1 & 2	Duplex Maisonette with private entrance to be known as 1 Sutton Square	12	5 and guest's lavatory	450	$45,000	$4,837.50
2 (rear)	8 servant's rooms @ $1,500*			120	12,000	1,290.00
3		11	5	390	39,000	4,192.50
4		11	5	400	40,000	4,300.00
5		11	5	420	42,000	4,515.00
6		11	5	440	44,000	4,730.00
7		11	5	470	47,000	5,052.50
8		11	5	500	50,000	5,375.00
9		11	5	520	52,000	5,590.00
10		11 Sold	5	540	54,000	5,805.00
11		11	5	560	56,000	6,020.00
12		11	5	580	58,000	6,235.00
13		11	5	600	60,000	6,450.00
14 &	Roof Story Duplex with all roof terraces	16 Sold	6 & guest's lavatory	960	96,000	10,320.00
					$695,000	$74,712.50**

* The cost of each servant's room will be $1500 for 15 shares, and the estimated annual charge will be $161.25 per room.

**Representing $10.75 per share per annum.

SUBMITTED BY

DOUGLAS L. ELLIMAN & CO., Inc.

Selling and Managing Agent

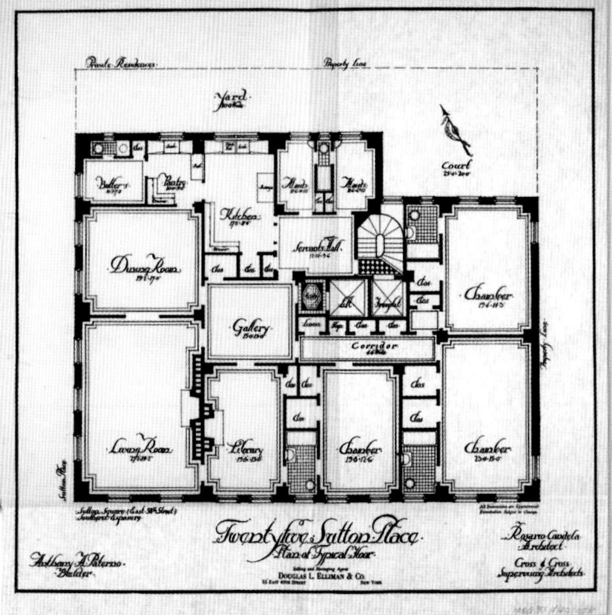

960 FIFTH AVENUE, 1927

If there is a single Candela building that represents everything his architecture is about—a project that exemplifies his skill and ingenuity for spatial planning and external massing alike—it is 960 Fifth Avenue. It was and is his most lavish commission; 834 Fifth and 740 Park come within a nose, but 960 pulls ahead because of the sectional diversity found here and nowhere else. As Peter Pennoyer showed when he essentially provided an MRI of the building in his digital model for the 2018 Museum of the City of New York exhibition *Elegance in the Sky*, 960 is the best project to examine if we seek a case study to understand Candela's talents as they relate to cryptography. It is also a building of firsts.

In 1925, developer Anthony Campagna purchased the William A. Clark house on this site, so solid and massive it had dissuaded several other developers (and did in fact cost $1 million to demolish). Another Fifth Avenue mansion built to settle scores and last one thousand years had stood for barely twenty. Campagna's new building at 77th Street and Fifth Avenue has so far lasted nearly a hundred and was unusual from the start because it was marketed as a cooperative and square footage could be acquired in both horizontal or vertical specifications, with taller ceiling heights ranging from fully two stories to simply "enhanced." This offering plan was most certainly based on the recent success of Warren & Wetmore's 1020 Fifth Avenue of 1925, also built as a cooperative and featuring double-height and step-down living rooms (though unlike 960, these are laid out in a typical repeated plan with three ceiling heights). The patrician firm of Warren & Wetmore are Candela's associate architects here, though no one but Candela could have devised such a puzzle box of units, only two of which are the same (duplexes

Clark House undergoing demolition (1927), with a billboard announcing the soon-to-begin construction of 960

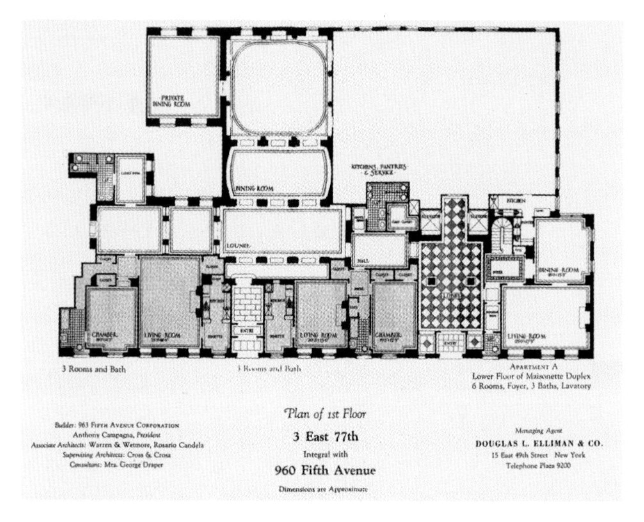

Plan of eastern portion of ground floor showing the reception rooms known as the Georgian Suite, restaurant, and lobby of 3 East 77th Street

5/6 and 7/8B), ultimately delivering two buildings of great internal complexity disguised externally as three.

The resulting nineteen apartments at 960—the adjoining building contains what were originally smaller rental units bearing the side street address of 3 East 77th Street—are part of what amounts to an urban complex, with connecting lobbies and a ground floor dining room for residents' use embedded in what is known as the Georgian Suite. This series of reception rooms for entertaining offers residents essentially the facilities of in-house club and has its own entrance on 77th Street labeled discreetly and somewhat mysteriously as number 1A.

Such a diversity of window arrangements resulting from multiple ceiling heights is managed in two ways: on the Fifth Avenue facade by the anchor device of the massive two-story "loggia" embedded at the tenth and eleventh floors, representing a trianon suspended above Central Park; and on 77th Street by disguising the two buildings as three. The middle "building" in this fiction is defined by vertical quoins and a projecting cornice, implying that an earlier Italian Renaissance–style apartment house has possibly been sandwiched between two Georgian Moderne limestone buildings, more abstract in style and built later. Grander on the corner, more intimately scaled to the east; while 960 has the drama of scale, the stateliness conveyed by its enormous windows and caryatids, 3 East 77th Street has the charm and energy of setback terraces. Here is the first time Candela uses the ziggurat device derived from commercial buildings that was to be scaled up and play such a defining role in buildings to come such as 720, 740, 770, and 778 Park Avenue. Candela's 3 East 77th Street is the dress rehearsal for his other great skill besides the planning of layouts, which was to carve away at the upper stories of a building, in so doing replacing form with light and transforming the restrictions of 1916 into the opportunities of a decade later.

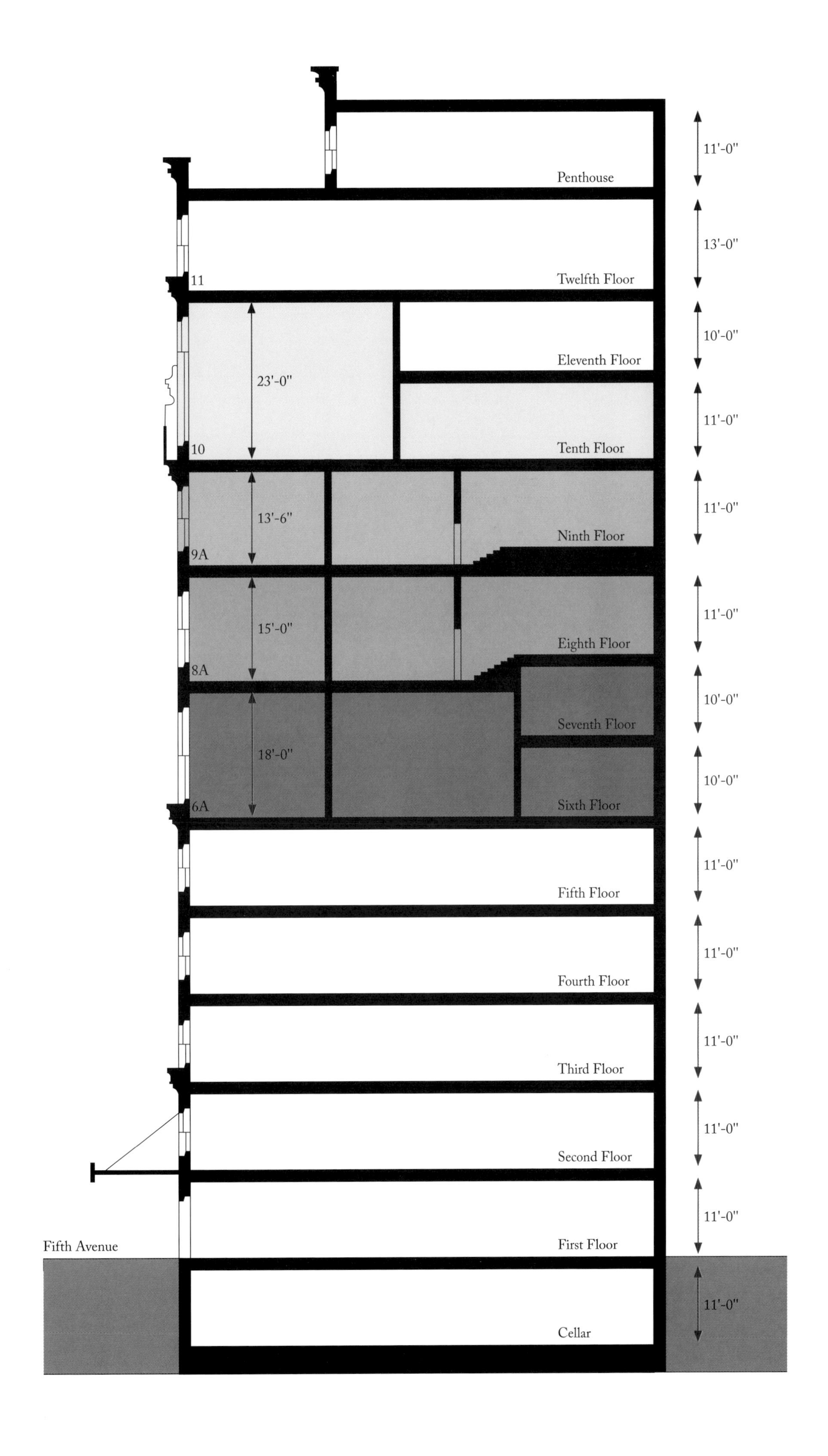
11'-0"
Penthouse
13'-0"
11
Twelfth Floor
10'-0"
23'-0"
Eleventh Floor
11'-0"
10
Tenth Floor
13'-6"
11'-0"
9A
Ninth Floor
15'-0"
11'-0"
8A
Eighth Floor
18'-0"
10'-0"
Seventh Floor
10'-0"
6A
Sixth Floor
11'-0"
Fifth Floor
11'-0"
Fourth Floor
11'-0"
Third Floor
11'-0"
Second Floor
11'-0"
Fifth Avenue
First Floor
11'-0"
Cellar

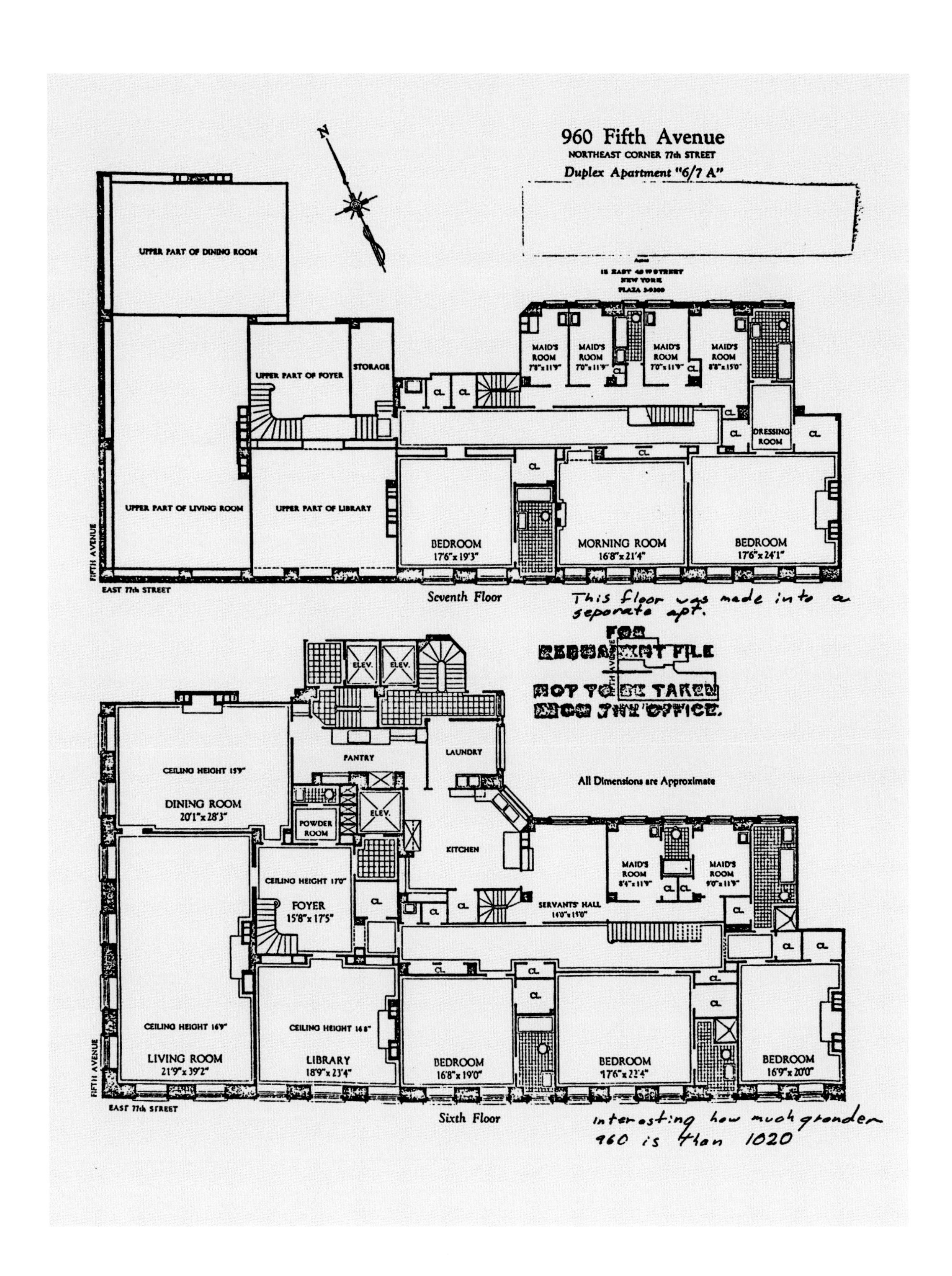

Apartment 6/7A, with six bedrooms (counting the morning room) and ceilings as high as any in the building. Much of the eighteenth-century English furniture in the Metropolitan Museum of Art was once in this apartment, the collection of Judge Irwin Untermyer.

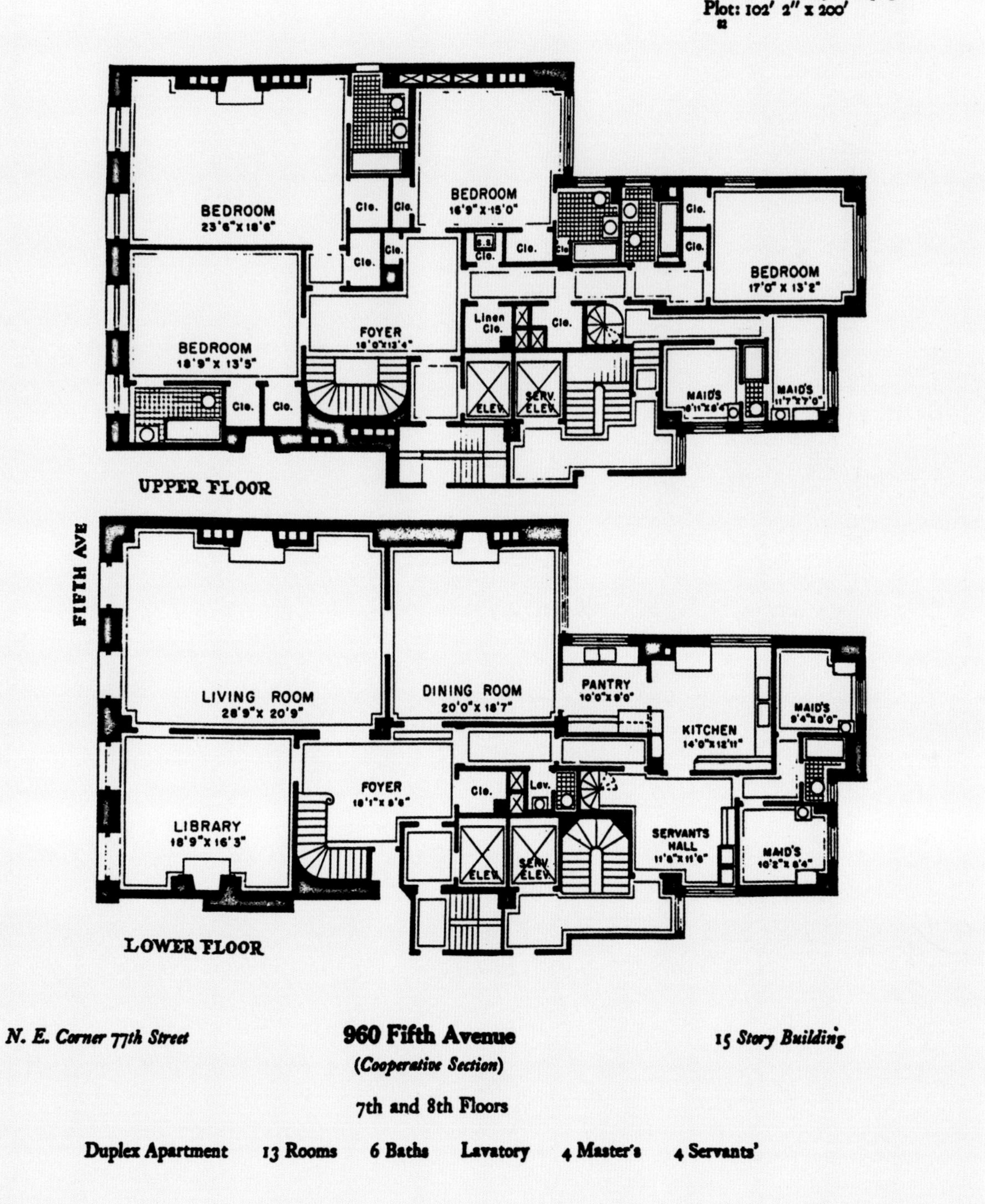
SELECT REGISTER OF APARTMENT HOUSE PLANS

Part Cooperative
Architects: { Warren and Wetmore / Rosario Candela
Builder: Anthony Campagna
Plot: 102′ 2″ x 200′

N. E. Corner 77th Street — **960 Fifth Avenue** (*Cooperative Section*) — *15 Story Building*

7th and 8th Floors

Duplex Apartment 13 Rooms 6 Baths Lavatory 4 Master's 4 Servants'

The two B-line duplexes are the only repeat plans at 960.

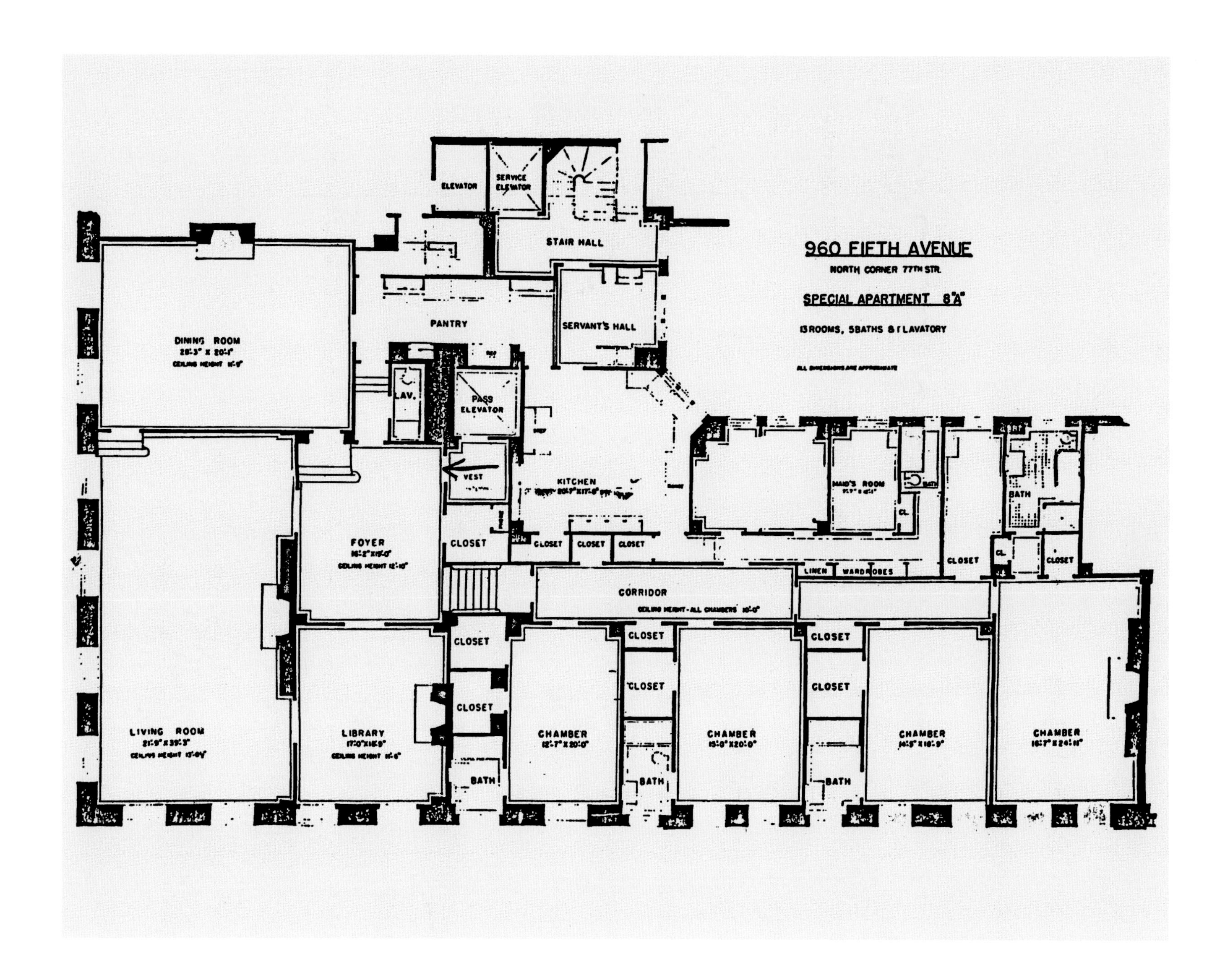

Apartment 8A, once the home of Mr. and Mrs. Claus von Bulow

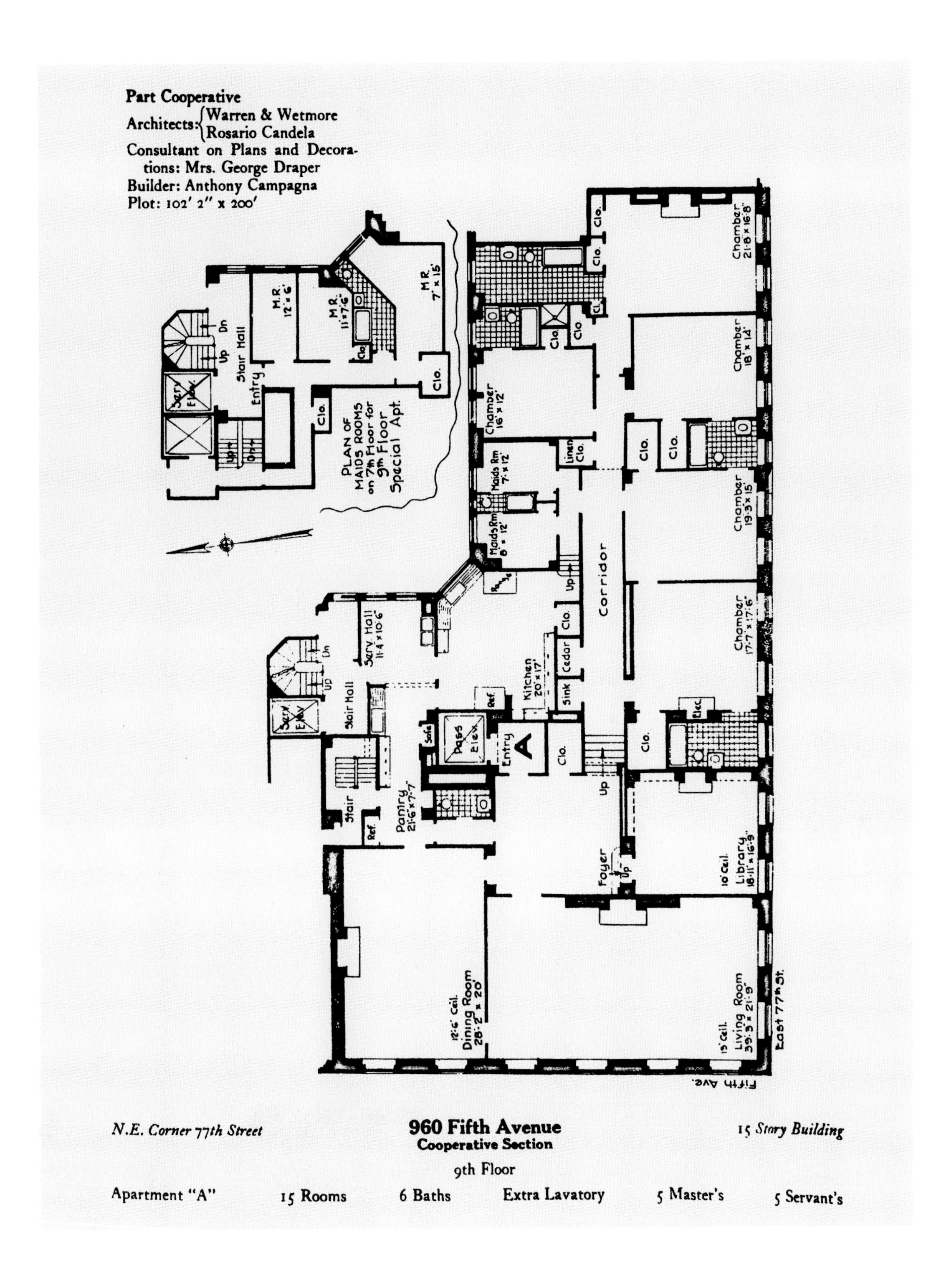

The ninth-floor A-line apartment is a near twin of the floor beneath, with slightly lower ceilings in the front rooms.

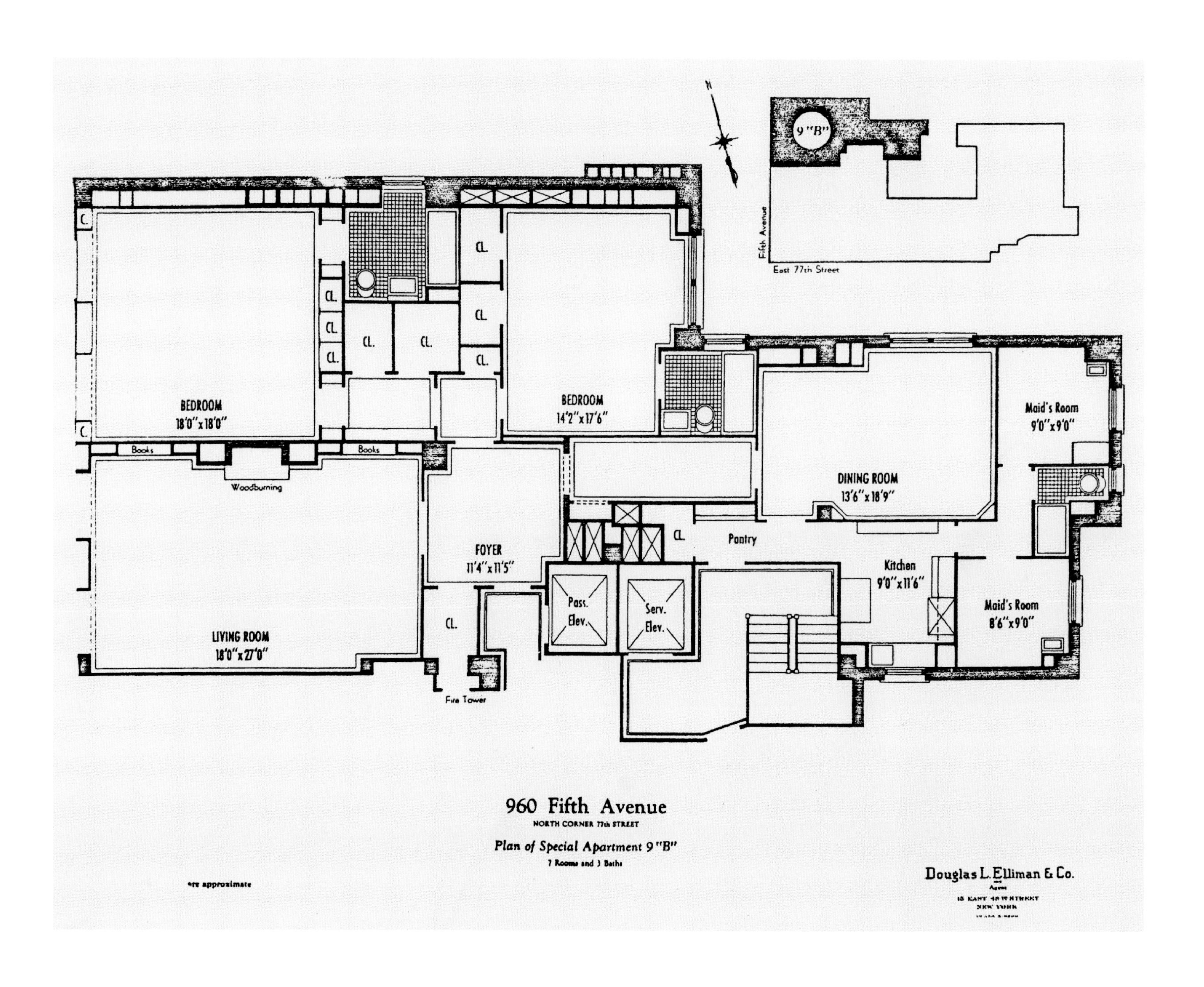

Apartment 9B is uncharacteristically small, with only two bedrooms and no library, but very majestic ceiling heights.

SELECT REGISTER OF APARTMENT HOUSE PLANS

Part Cooperative
Architects: { Warren and Wetmore
Rosario Candela
Builder: Anthony Campagna
Plot: 102′ 2″ x 200′

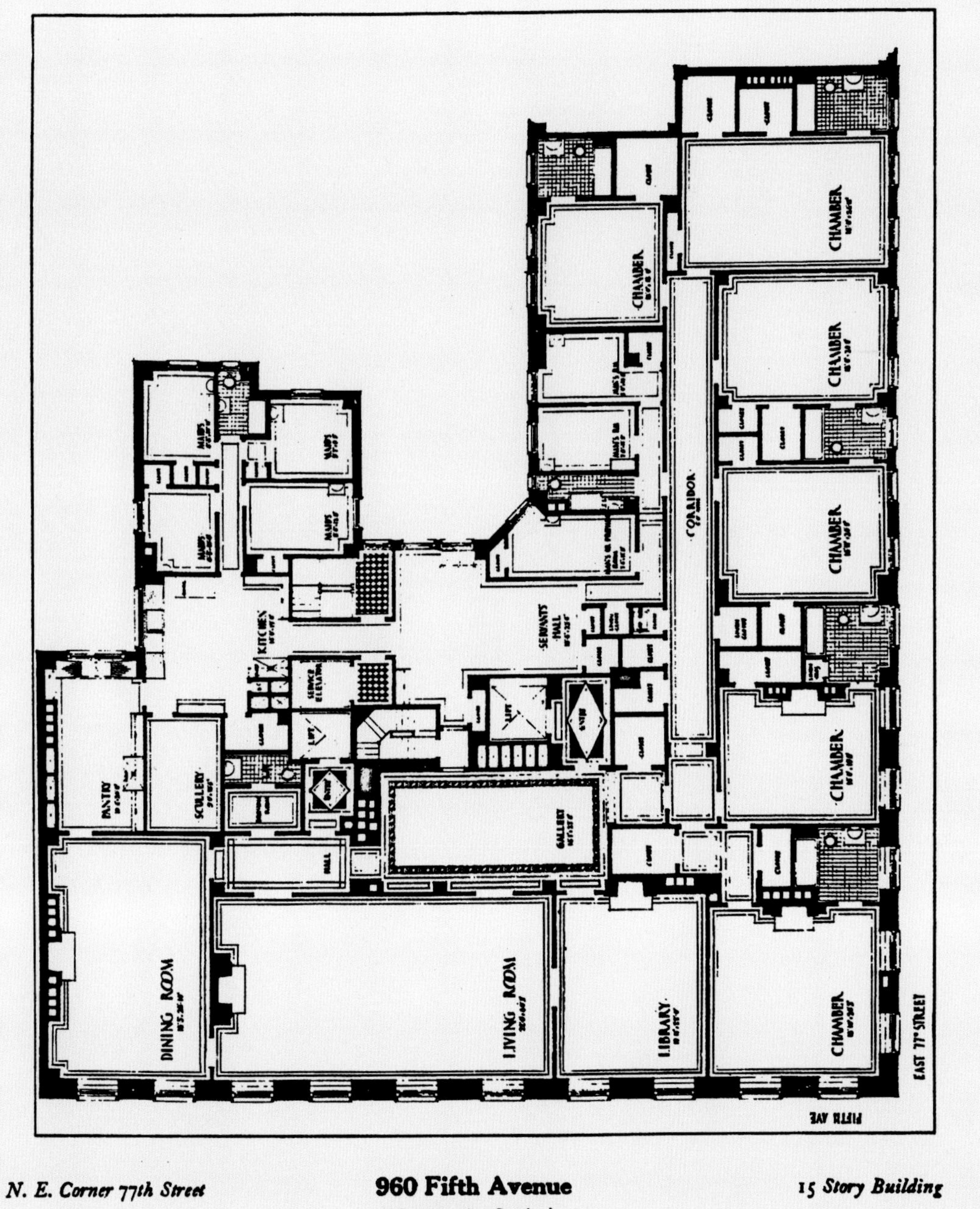

N. E. Corner 77th Street **960 Fifth Avenue** *15 Story Building*

(Cooperative Section)

9th Floor

18 Rooms **7 Baths** **Lavatory** **6 Master's** **7 Servants'**

The mythical Candela apartment that never was. This plan was first reproduced in Andrew Alpern's *Apartments for the Affluent* in 1975. In fact, two full-floor simplexes exist at 960, on the third and twelfth floors—however, neither one has this room arrangement (the ninth floor is divided into two apartments, the ones shown at left and on the previous page; the twelfth floor plan is shown on page 133). The ninth floor as depicted here was never built.

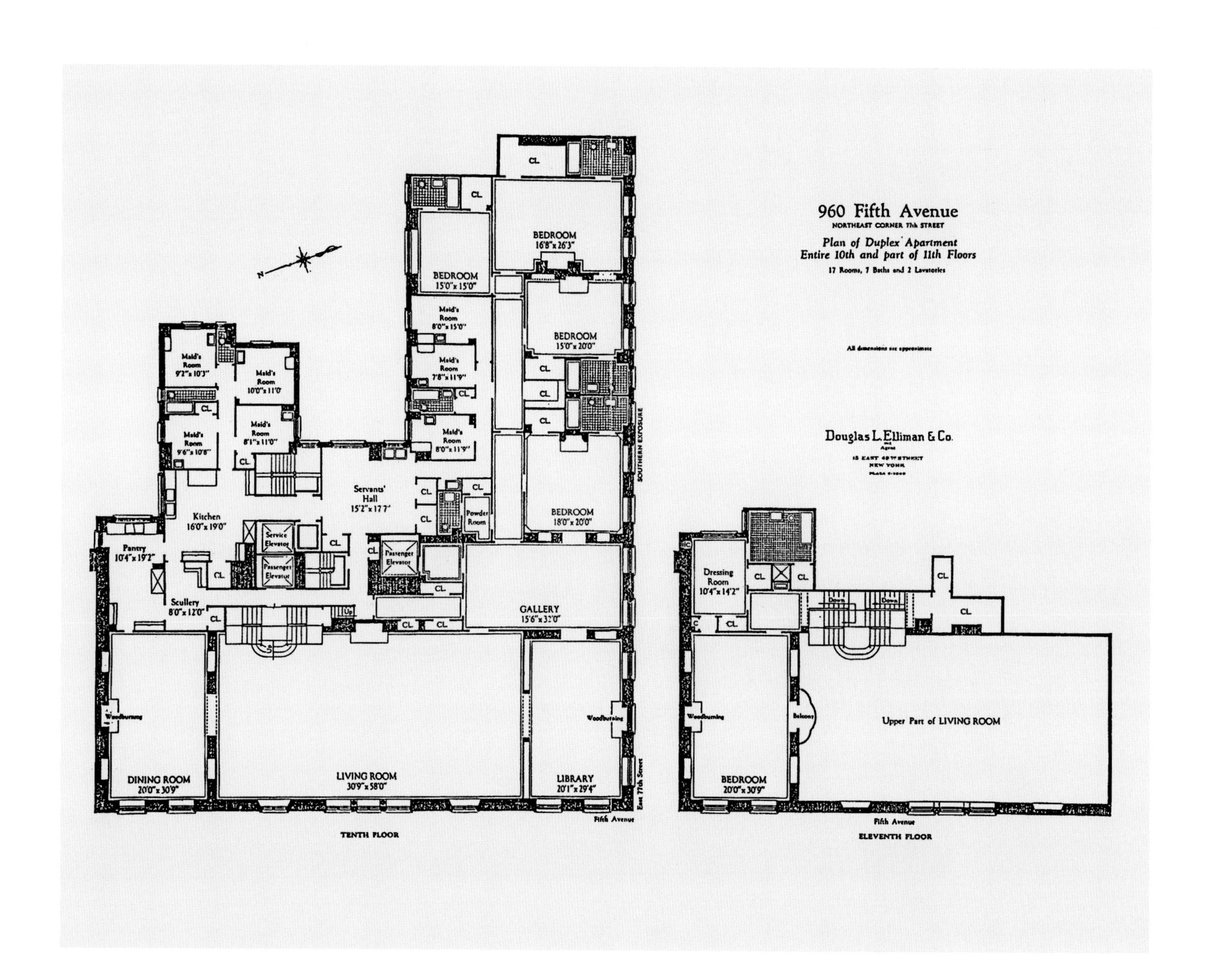

The Satterwhite apartment (tenth and part of the eleventh floors) as originally planned existed until broken up by Candela himself in 1947. The large space of the living room was basically divided in thirds; arched windows at the center became the windows of the dining room of newly formed 10A, for decades the home of Douglas Dillon (secretary of the treasury from 1961 to 1965 and chairman of the board of the Met).

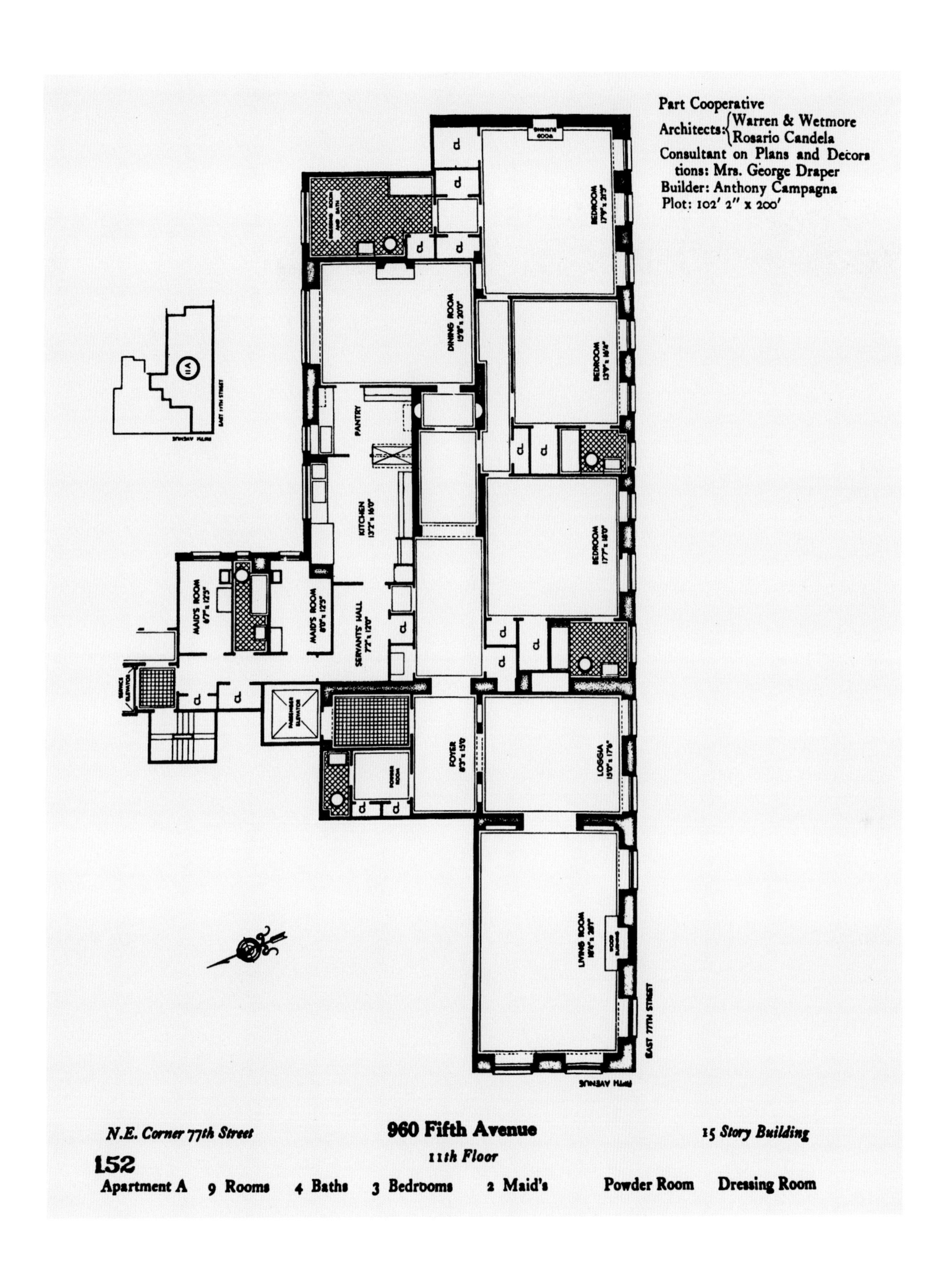

Skirting the upper volume of the Satterwhite living room to the south is 11A, a quirky but successful layout that deploys Candela's illusionistic device of exaggerating the distance between living and dining room to make a compact apartment feel more spacious.

The largest living room of the most expensive apartment in New York as decorated in 1927; the tapestries, around which the space appears to have been designed, may be seen today at the Speed Art Museum in Louisville, Kentucky. The elaborate triple-run staircase leads to the principal bedroom on one side, but two closets on the other. During a recent renovation of 10A by Annabelle Selldorf, it was discovered that the coffered ceiling, covered over in 1947, still exists.

The full one-hundred-foot north-south axis from fireplace to fireplace of the three entertaining rooms was meant to be experienced as a surprise reveal. Guests, having walked through the regular-height entrance gallery and library, were given no hint as to the scale of the space beyond.

Penthouse terrace looking east toward the newly completed Carlyle Hotel, apartment of Mrs. James B. Clemens (1934)

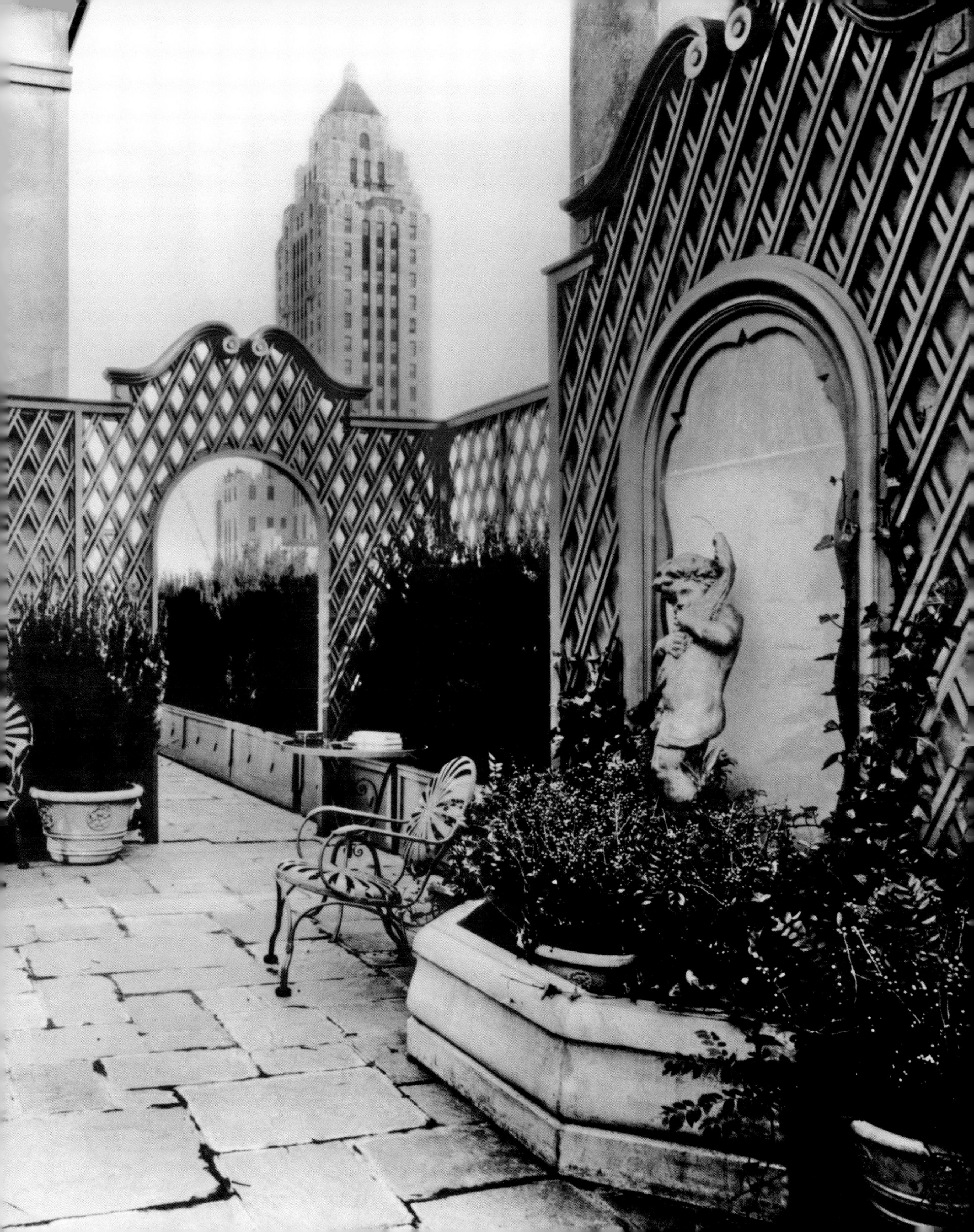

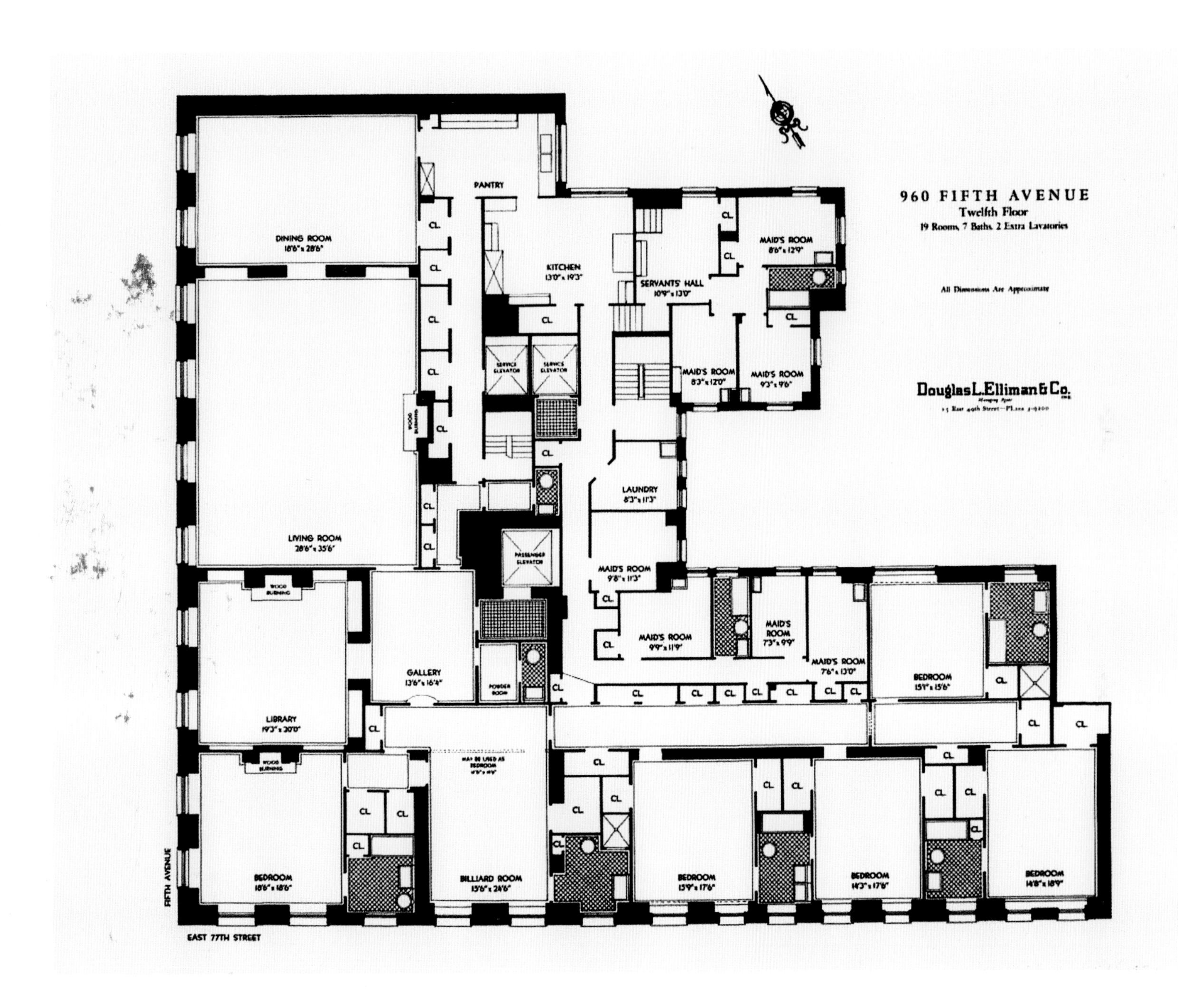

The twelfth floor was originally occupied by Horace Havemeyer and afterward by Ailsa Mellon Bruce, Joan Whitney Payson, and—as seen at left and in the following pages—the late Anne Bass.

The Bass living room. Seating consisted entirely of a suite of Georgian furniture amidst paintings by Mark Rothko, Balthus, Agnes Martin, and Morris Louis. Windows were naked.

"I want my bed to look like a seventeenth-century dress," Mrs. Bass told Mark Hampton, who delivered this sumptuous result within a striking minimalist envelope the color of Gregory Peck's suit.

720 PARK AVENUE, 1928

The couple who owned Macy's and famously decided to perish together on the *Titanic* had seven children, one of whom was a son, Jesse Isidor Straus. Sixteen years after losing his parents at sea, Straus was the builder of this neo-Elizabethan nineteen-story major work by Candela in association with Cross & Cross, and simultaneously of the architecturally slightly less distinguished 730 Park Avenue to the north.

One of Candela's most elaborate buildings by any measure, 720 is also his most picturesque setback composition in both massing and detail. The south facade is disguised as two buildings—a device Candela deploys to obscure disparate window arrangements, especially when working in the Tudor or Lombardic styles. A vertical seam of quoins here divides the A-line simplex apartments from those in the west section of the building (mainly duplexes); above the twelfth floor the setbacks are organized in two sections to continue this illusion. The scale of the duplex Straus created for himself on floors twelve and thirteen is legible in the stone-mullioned windows of the 36 x 27-foot library on the corner.

After the death of Straus's widow Irma in 1970 the apartment sat on the market year after year, unloved and unclaimed, at least by anyone qualified to pay the maintenance (Saul Steinberg, perhaps the only likely taker, was already ensconced at 740). Candela's 720 has always been one of New York's very finest cooperative buildings, but the timing could not have been worse; morale in the city was in free fall at this precise moment, taking the market right along with it. The Straus's unit lingered for a time as the ultimate white elephant, a Norma Desmond–era curiosity in the age of *Rowan & Martin's Laugh-In*, before being broken up into two separate single-floor apartments in 1972.

A steel terrace door at the newly completed 720 with a view south to midtown skyscrapers

A trefoil mullioned window of Jesse Straus's baronial library now belongs to a smaller library, the apartment having been subdivided in 1972.

One story clings to 720, seemingly apocryphal but not, and provides a window into the upper-class social culture surrounding these buildings in the New York of the 1920s (an attitude of "us" and "them," incidentally, which persisted on the part of many co-op boards into the 1990s). It is that Jesse Straus built two buildings at the same time for a reason: 720 was for his own and his family's use and marketed to posh society people (read WASPs); 730 next door was for his Jewish friends.

Opposite: Construction of 720, January 31, 1929. The moment provides an interesting snapshot of life on Park Avenue as it was, and was about to change. At left is the George Blumenthal house, which contained as its courtyard the Vélez Blanco patio now at the Met and represents a scale of life rapidly vanishing from the city. (Billy Baldwin had a disastrous interview in this house, which he speaks of in thinly veiled terms in his 1974 book *Billy Baldwin Remembers.*) To the north, the structural steel is up for Straus's other apartment house project at 730 with architect Lafayette Goldstone. Across 71st Street the Brewster house still stands, not yet demolished to make way for 740 Park Avenue. George S. Brewster is the client for whom the thirty-six-room duplex 15/16B—later widely known as the Rockefeller apartment—was constructed, as an inducement to sell his townhouse and make construction of 740 possible. Mr. and Mrs. John D. Rockefeller Jr. moved in following Brewster's death in 1936.

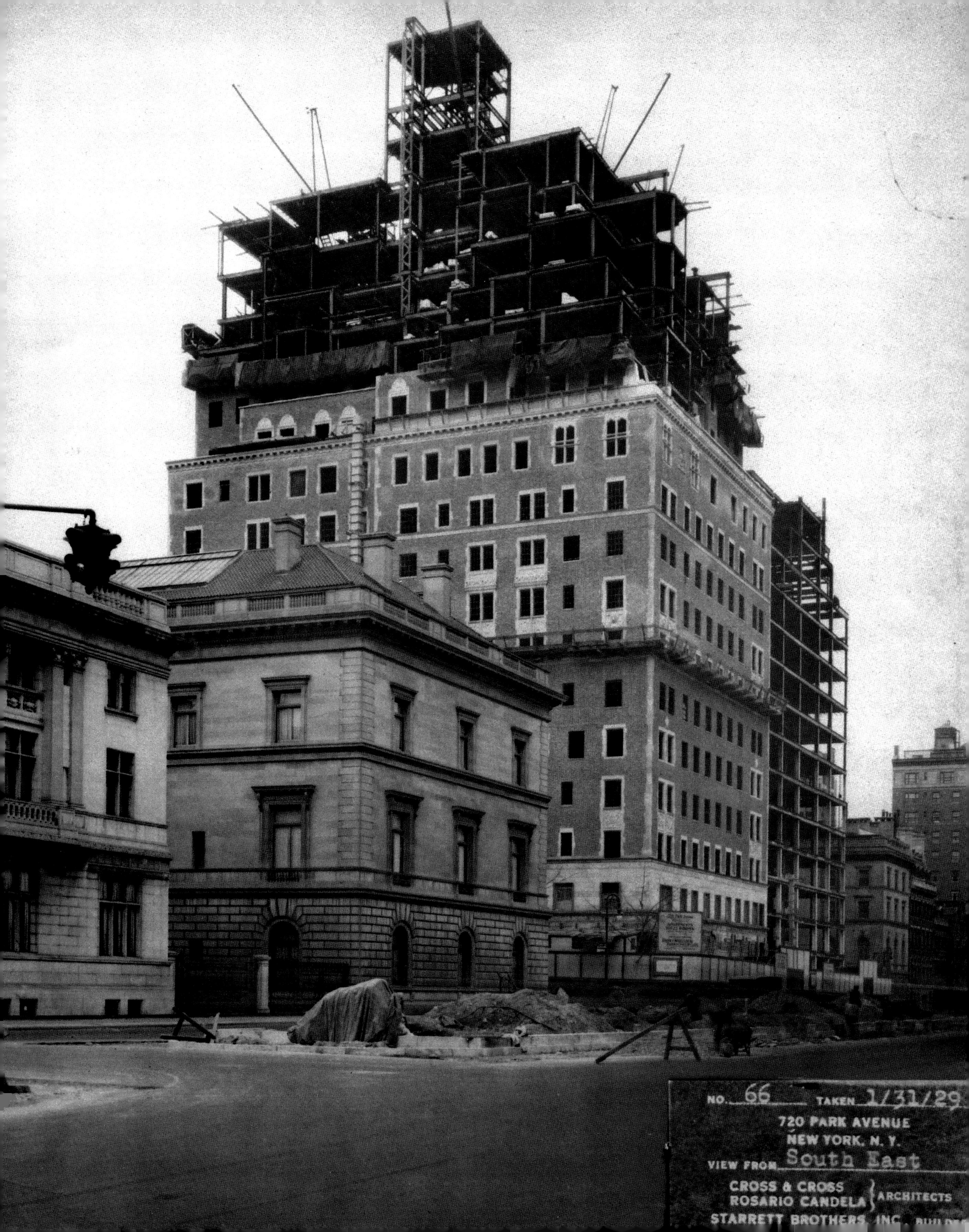
NO. 66 TAKEN 1/31/29
720 PARK AVENUE
NEW YORK, N. Y.
VIEW FROM South East
CROSS & CROSS
ROSARIO CANDELA
ARCHITECTS
STARRETT BROTHERS, INC.

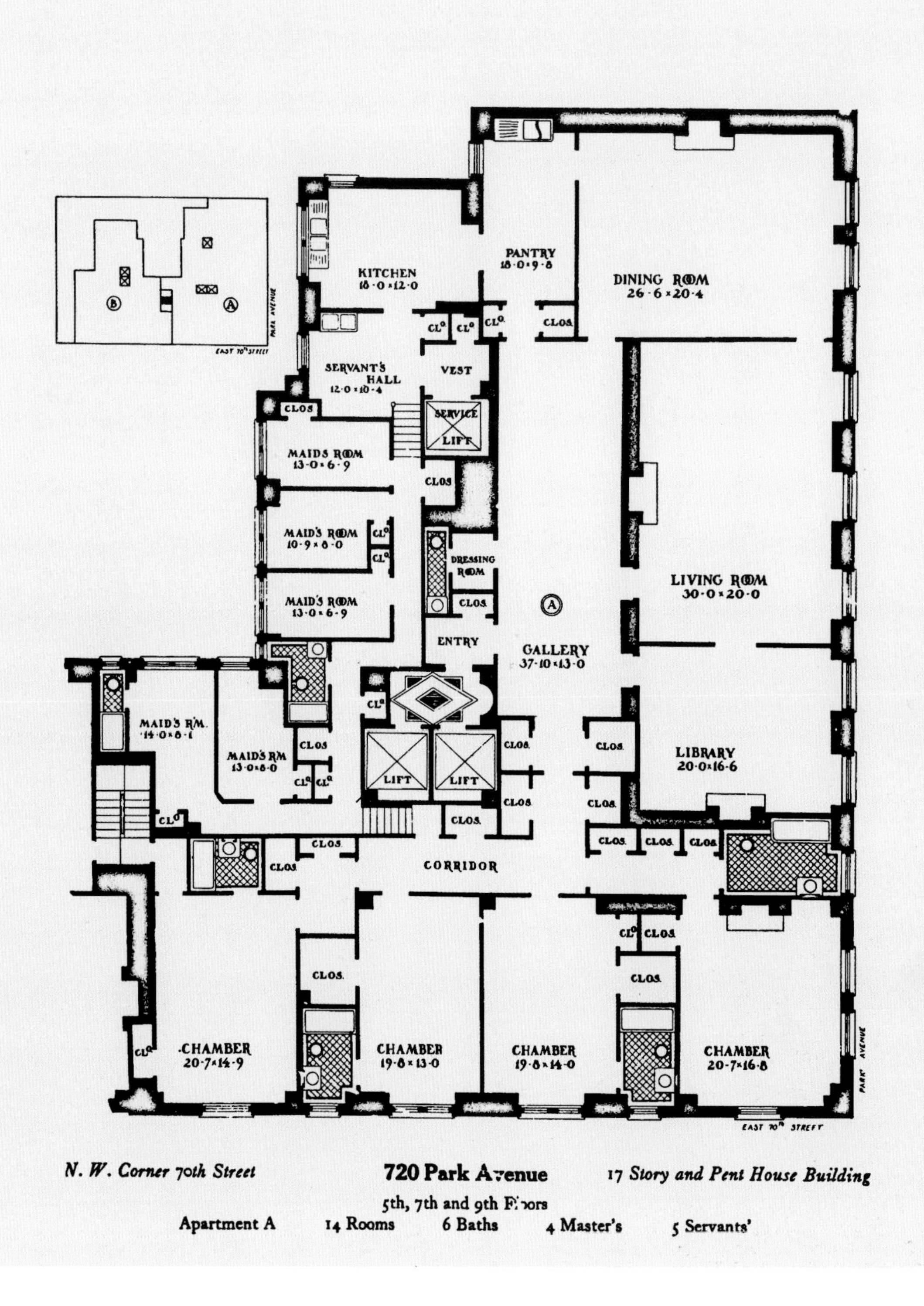

Typical simplex A-line apartment facing Park Avenue, which occurs with minor variations from the fourth to the eleventh floors

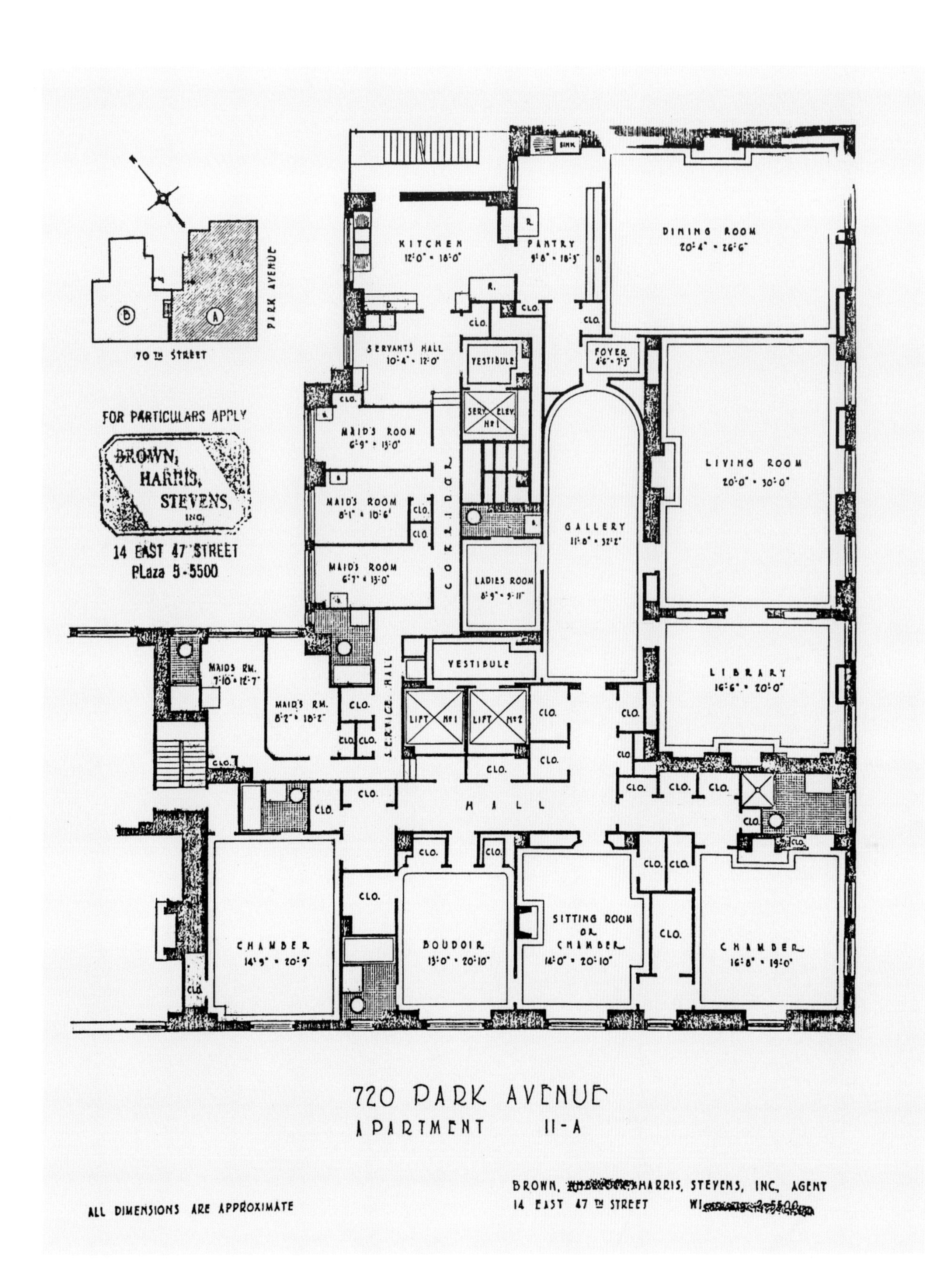

Candela provided extensive customization services to buyers at 720 with features such as the cove-ended gallery of 11A.

Low in the setbacks means lots of space plus the charm of terraces. Apartment 14A and the apartment pictured on pages 156 and 157 (14/14B) have this most desirable combination of romance and scale.

Apartment 15A, pictured in color on pages 158 to 163, has an unusually high number of fireplaces (one in each bedroom). Gianni and Marella Agnelli owned the apartment before they moved to 770 Park.

Apartment 16A contains one of Candela's only asymmetrically shaped living rooms, something he assiduously avoided.

The bottom floor of Apartment 17A, offered as a triplex but not built.

A glass summerhouse has been added to the penthouse duplex, enclosing the terrace off the "Smoking Room."

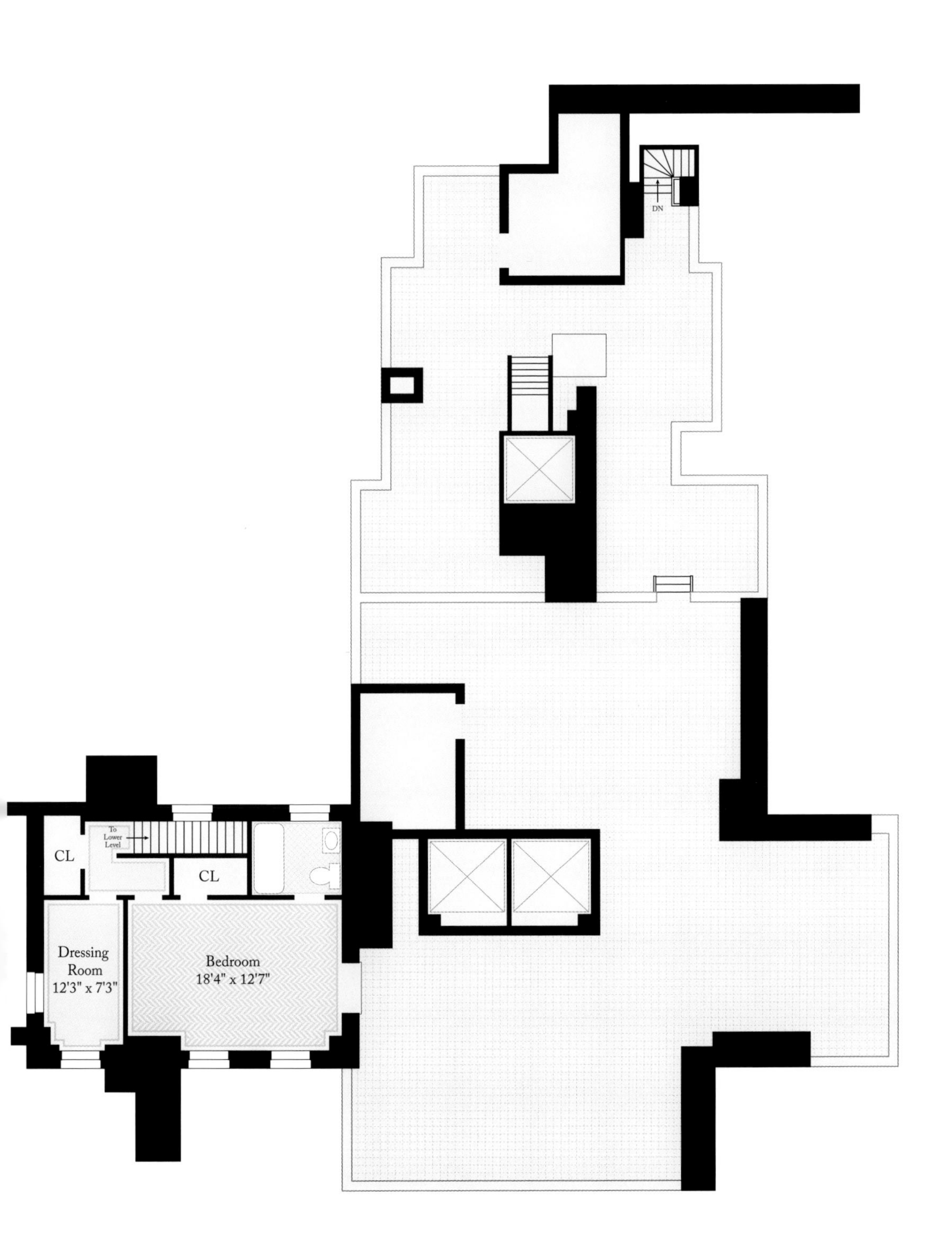

DN
To Lower Level
CL
CL
Dressing Room 12'3" x 7'3"
Bedroom 18'4" x 12'7"

Art Deco library in apartment 8A belonging to Jesse Straus's daughter and son-in-law, one of three family apartments in the building

The original Straus library with its extra-high beamed ceilings, a fragment of which can be seen on page 140. At right, the gallery on the lower level contained a stone staircase in Gothic/French Renaissance style.

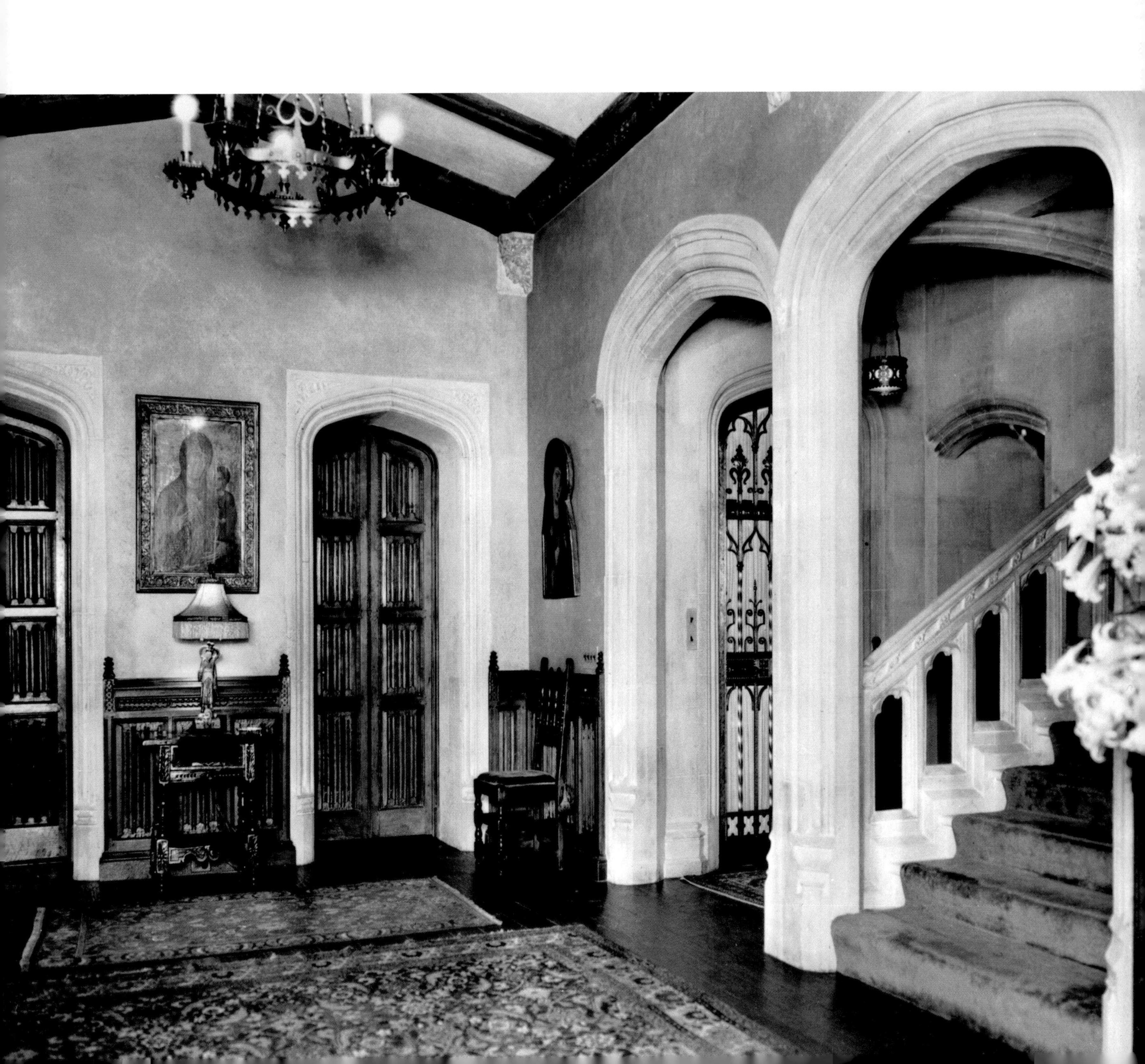

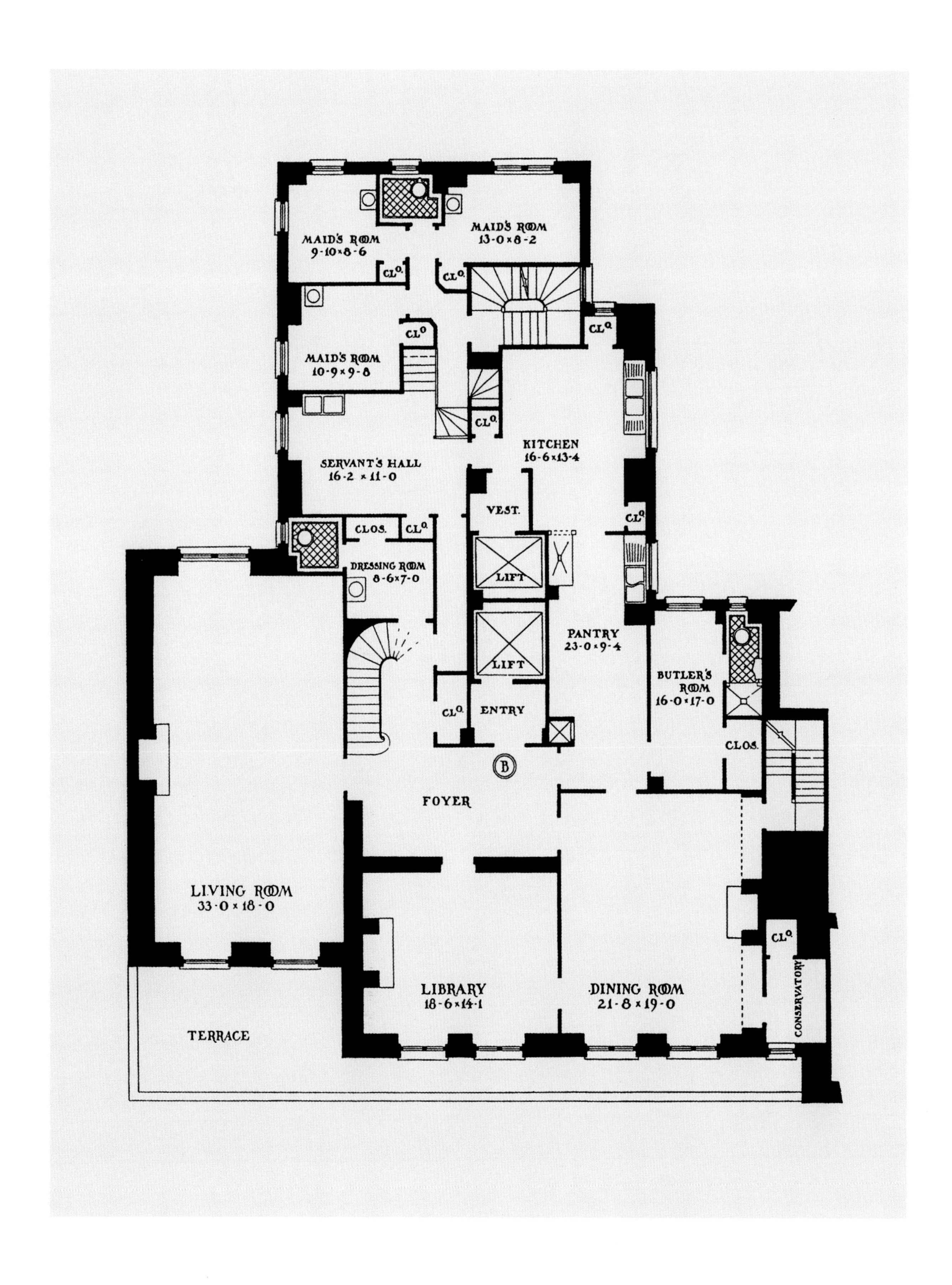

Apartment 14/14B was a seven-bedroom duplex originally occupied by Lucia Chase, founder of American Ballet Theatre

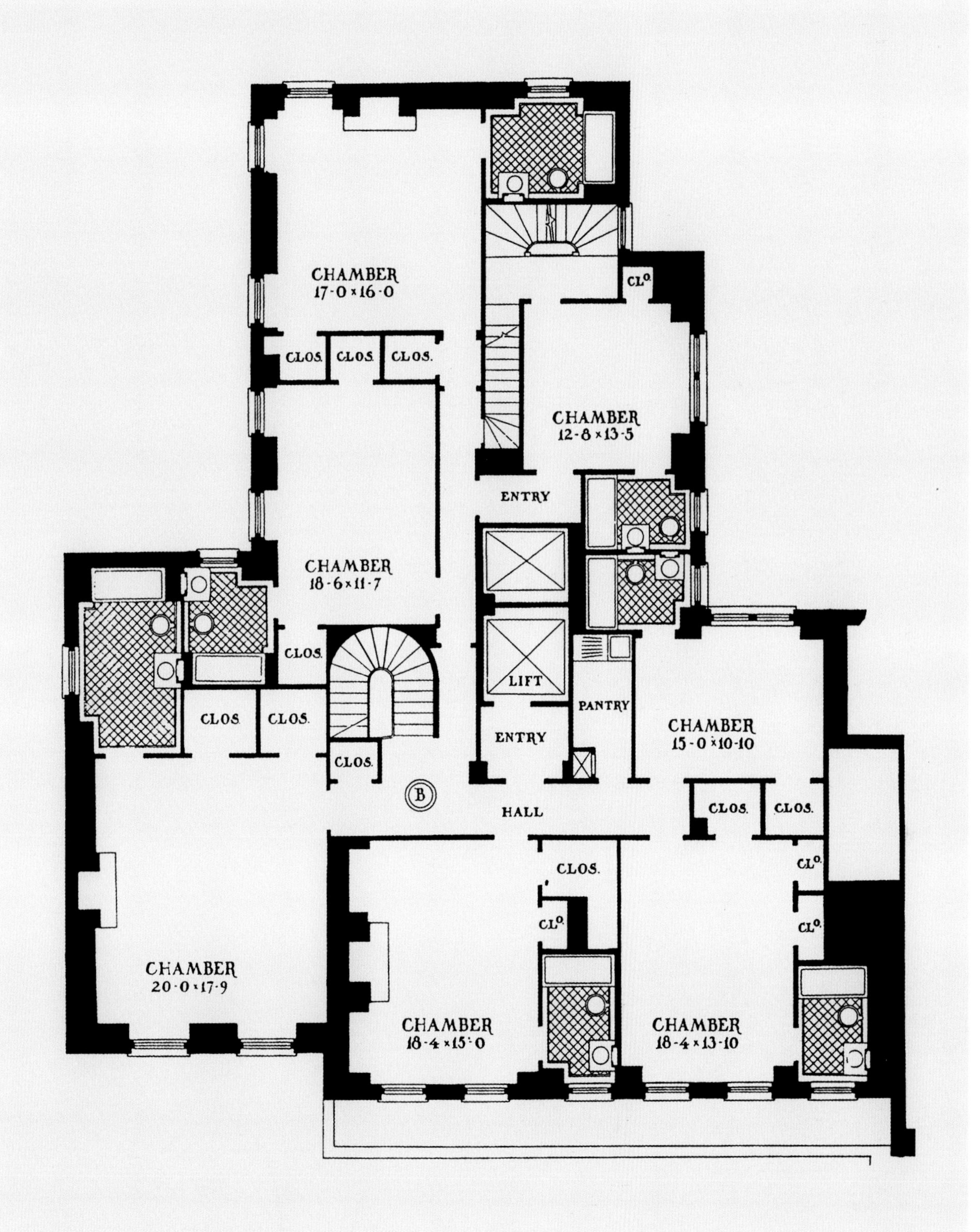
CHAMBER
17·0 × 16·0
CLO.
CLOS.
CLOS.
CLOS.
CHAMBER
12·8 × 13·5
ENTRY
CHAMBER
18·6 × 11·7
CLOS.
LIFT
PANTRY
CLOS.
CLOS.
CHAMBER
15·0 × 10·10
ENTRY
CLOS.
B
HALL
CLOS.
CLOS.
CLOS.
CLO.
CLO.
CLO.
CHAMBER
20·0 × 17·9
CHAMBER
18·4 × 15·0
CHAMBER
18·4 × 13·10

McMillen's treatment of the apartment shown in plan on the preceding pages (late 1980s)

THE HOUSE OF
ISABEL ALLENDE
A DEATH IN THE FAMILY
WATT
Samuel Beckett
THE FLOATING OPERA

Albert Hadley decorated 15A in a beige style that was, if not minimalist, against the mood of prevailing opulence of the 1980s. The stylish individual who still lives here moved upstairs from one of the big A-line simplexes lower in the building.

What was a conservatory in the original plan has been opened up to become an intimate step-up extension the living room.

One of the most admired rooms in New York is the dining room with its aubergine lacquer walls: often imitated, never surpassed.

1 GRACIE SQUARE, 1928

If the south facade of 960 Fifth Avenue is two buildings disguised as three, here we have one disguised as two. When confronted by a disparity of window arrangements, as at 960 and 720 Park Avenue, Candela resorts to camouflage, and the facade becomes as intricately constructed as the plans.

At 1 Gracie Square, the brick and limestone Lombardic-style exterior is split into two vertical halves via a seam of limestone quoins, creating the illusion of two buildings having arisen at two different times. This is most emphatic at street level, where the rustication wrapping the western corner is deliberately more expressive and haphazard than that of the eastern half. The picturesque composition, heavily embellished with Juliet balconies and implied loggias, was crowned by a special fourteen-room penthouse duplex built for Elizabeth F. Howard, whose house formerly stood on the site, and one of Candela's most exuberant water tower enclosures. The penthouse was subdivided in 1938.

The story behind 1 Gracie Square and the design of its unusual facade lies, as is typical when Candela uses this device, in the diversity of its plans. Simplexes, duplexes, and the penthouse dovetail in a fairly compact site on the corner of 84th Street and East End Avenue. This building was the first of the three that would form the southern "wall" of Carl Schurz Park. Its panoramic northwest views over the park toward the Hell Gate Bridge were likely considered more desirable than those of the direct river frontage developed later for 10 Gracie Square. The associate architect for this project was William Lawrence Bottomley.

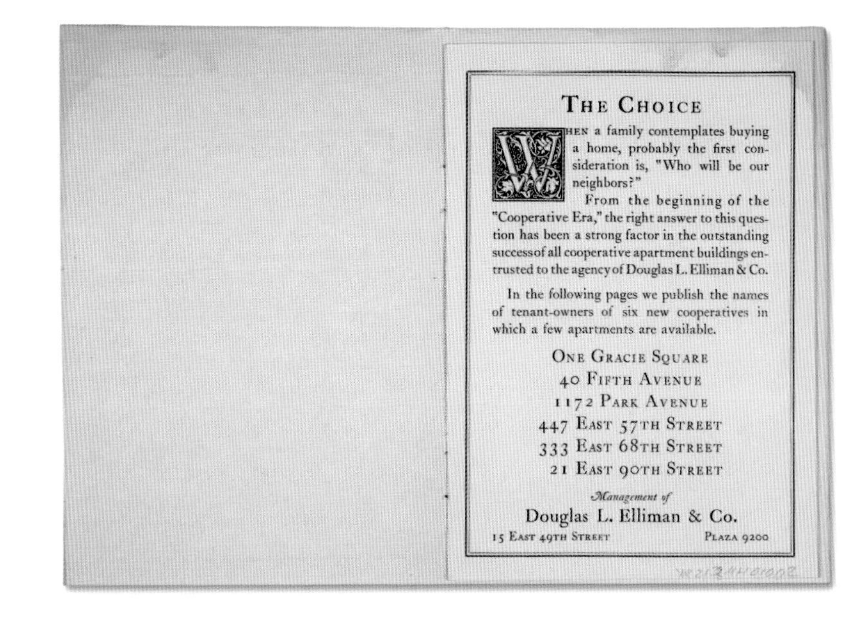

The Choice

When a family contemplates buying a home, probably the first consideration is, "Who will be our neighbors?"

From the beginning of the "Cooperative Era," the right answer to this question has been a strong factor in the outstanding success of all cooperative apartment buildings entrusted to the agency of Douglas L. Elliman & Co.

In the following pages we publish the names of tenant-owners of six new cooperatives in which a few apartments are available.

One Gracie Square
40 Fifth Avenue
1172 Park Avenue
447 East 57th Street
333 East 68th Street
21 East 90th Street

Management of
Douglas L. Elliman & Co.
15 East 49th Street — Plaza 9200

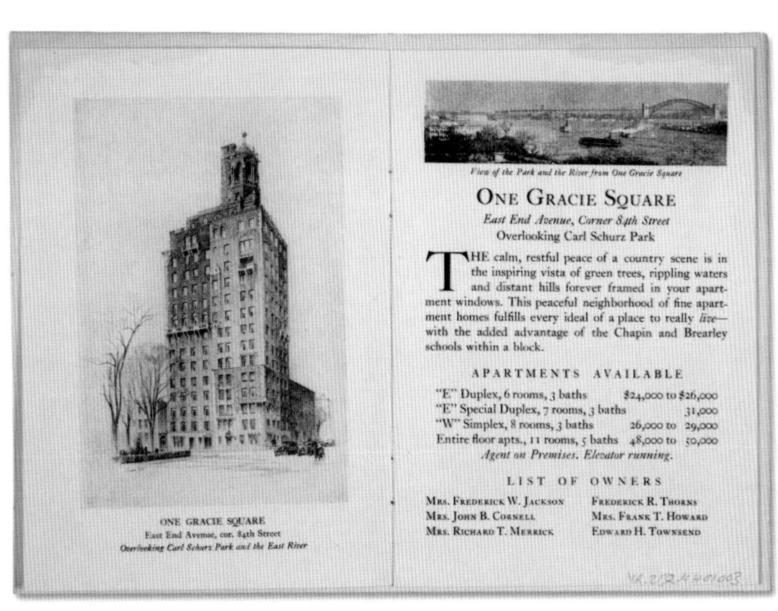

ONE GRACIE SQUARE
East End Avenue, cor. 84th Street
Overlooking Carl Schurz Park and the East River

View of the Park and the River from One Gracie Square

One Gracie Square

East End Avenue, Corner 84th Street
Overlooking Carl Schurz Park

The calm, restful peace of a country scene is in the inspiring vista of green trees, rippling waters and distant hills forever framed in your apartment windows. This peaceful neighborhood of fine apartment homes fulfills every ideal of a place to really *live*—with the added advantage of the Chapin and Brearley schools within a block.

Apartments Available

"E" Duplex, 6 rooms, 3 baths $24,000 to $26,000
"E" Special Duplex, 7 rooms, 3 baths 31,000
"W" Simplex, 8 rooms, 3 baths 26,000 to 29,000
Entire floor apts., 11 rooms, 5 baths 48,000 to 50,000

Agent on Premises. Elevator running.

List of Owners

Mrs. Frederick W. Jackson
Mrs. John B. Cornell
Mrs. Richard T. Merrick
Frederick R. Thorns
Mrs. Frank T. Howard
Edward H. Townsend

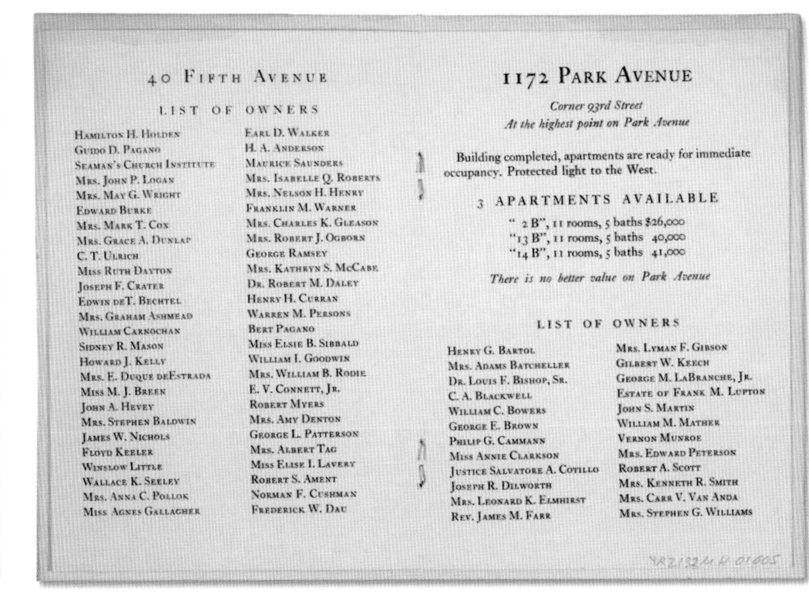

40 Fifth Avenue

List of Owners

Hamilton H. Holden
Guido D. Pagano
Seaman's Church Institute
Mrs. John P. Logan
Mrs. May G. Wright
Edward Burke
Mrs. Mark T. Cox
Mrs. Grace A. Dunlap
C. T. Ulrich
Miss Ruth Dayton
Joseph F. Crater
Edwin deT. Bechtel
Mrs. Graham Ashmead
William Carnochan
Sidney R. Mason
Howard J. Kelly
Mrs. E. Duque deEstrada
Miss M. J. Breen
John A. Hevey
Mrs. Stephen Baldwin
James W. Nichols
Floyd Keeler
Winslow Little
Wallace K. Seeley
Mrs. Anna C. Pollok
Miss Agnes Gallagher
Earl D. Walker
H. A. Anderson
Maurice Saunders
Mrs. Isabelle Q. Roberts
Mrs. Nelson H. Henry
Franklin M. Warner
Mrs. Charles K. Gleason
Mrs. Robert J. Ogborn
George Ramsey
Mrs. Kathryn S. McCabe
Dr. Robert M. Daley
Henry H. Curran
Warren M. Persons
Bert Pagano
Miss Elsie B. Sibbald
William I. Goodwin
Mrs. William B. Rodie
E. V. Connett, Jr.
Robert Myers
Mrs. Amy Denton
George L. Patterson
Mrs. Albert Tag
Miss Elise I. Lavery
Robert S. Ament
Norman F. Cushman
Frederick W. Dau

1172 Park Avenue

Corner 93rd Street
At the highest point on Park Avenue

Building completed, apartments are ready for immediate occupancy. Protected light to the West.

3 Apartments Available

" 2 B", 11 rooms, 5 baths $26,000
"13 B", 11 rooms, 5 baths 40,000
"14 B", 11 rooms, 5 baths 41,000

There is no better value on Park Avenue

List of Owners

Henry G. Bartol
Mrs. Adams Batcheller
Dr. Louis F. Bishop, Sr.
C. A. Blackwell
William C. Bowers
George E. Brown
Philip G. Cammann
Miss Annie Clarkson
Justice Salvatore A. Cotillo
Joseph R. Dilworth
Mrs. Leonard K. Elmhirst
Rev. James M. Farr
Mrs. Lyman F. Gibson
Gilbert W. Keech
George M. LaBranche, Jr.
Estate of Frank M. Lupton
John S. Martin
William M. Mather
Vernon Munroe
Mrs. Edward Peterson
Robert A. Scott
Mrs. Kenneth R. Smith
Mrs. Carr V. Van Anda
Mrs. Stephen G. Williams

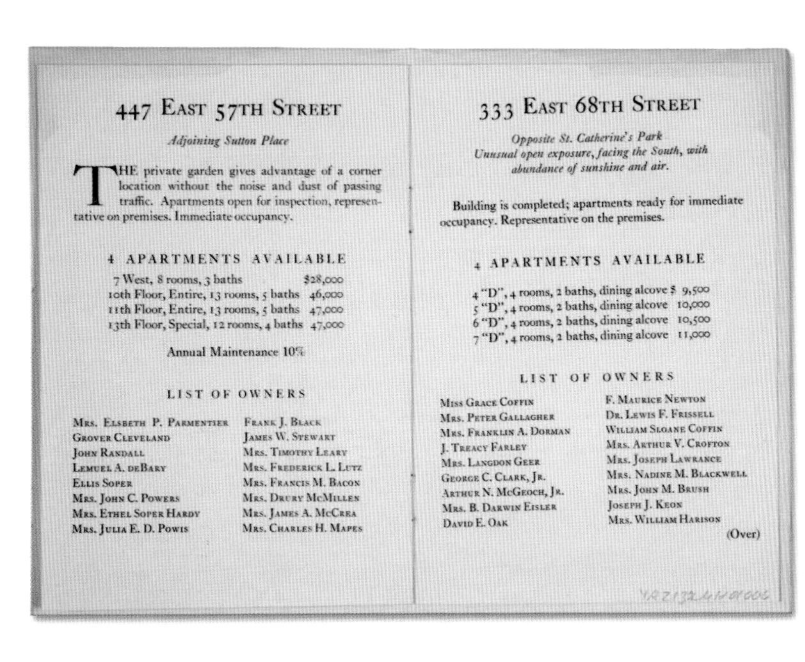

447 East 57th Street

Adjoining Sutton Place

The private garden gives advantage of a corner location without the noise and dust of passing traffic. Apartments open for inspection, representative on premises. Immediate occupancy.

4 Apartments Available

7 West, 8 rooms, 3 baths $28,000
10th Floor, Entire, 13 rooms, 5 baths 46,000
11th Floor, Entire, 13 rooms, 5 baths 47,000
13th Floor, Special, 12 rooms, 4 baths 47,000

Annual Maintenance 10%

List of Owners

Mrs. Elsbeth P. Parmentier
Grover Cleveland
John Randall
Lemuel A. deBary
Ellis Soper
Mrs. John C. Powers
Mrs. Ethel Soper Hardy
Mrs. Julia E. D. Powis
Frank J. Black
James W. Stewart
Mrs. Timothy Leary
Mrs. Frederick L. Lutz
Mrs. Francis M. Bacon
Mrs. Drury McMillen
Mrs. James A. McCrea
Mrs. Charles H. Mapes

333 East 68th Street

Opposite St. Catherine's Park
Unusual open exposure, facing the South, with abundance of sunshine and air.

Building is completed; apartments ready for immediate occupancy. Representative on the premises.

4 Apartments Available

4 "D", 4 rooms, 2 baths, dining alcove $ 9,500
5 "D", 4 rooms, 2 baths, dining alcove 10,000
6 "D", 4 rooms, 2 baths, dining alcove 10,500
7 "D", 4 rooms, 2 baths, dining alcove 11,000

List of Owners

Miss Grace Coffin
Mrs. Peter Gallagher
Mrs. Franklin A. Dorman
J. Treacy Farley
Mrs. Langdon Geer
George C. Clark, Jr.
Arthur N. McGeoch, Jr.
Mrs. B. Darwin Eisler
David E. Oak
F. Maurice Newton
Dr. Lewis F. Frissell
William Sloane Coffin
Mrs. Arthur V. Crofton
Mrs. Joseph Lawrance
Mrs. Nadine M. Blackwell
Mrs. John M. Brush
Joseph J. Keon
Mrs. William Harison

(Over)

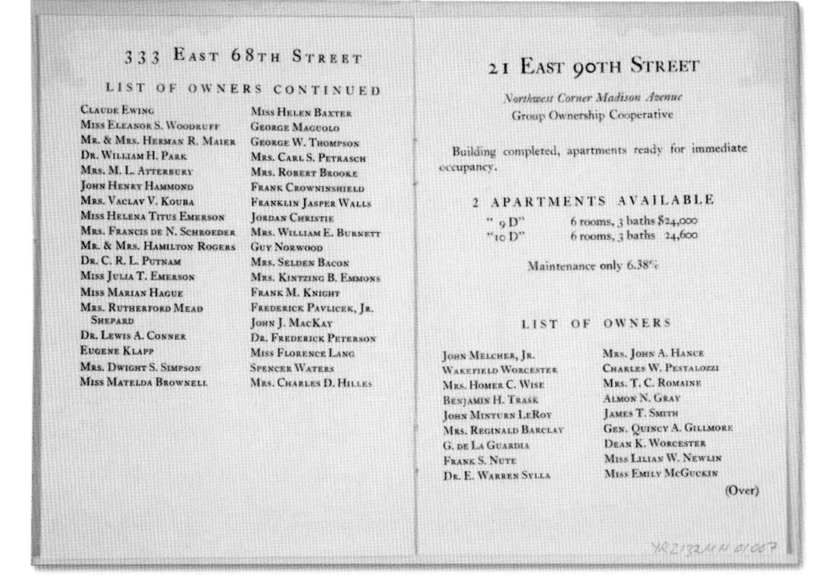

333 East 68th Street

List of Owners Continued

Claude Ewing
Miss Eleanor S. Woodruff
Mr. & Mrs. Herman R. Maier
Dr. William H. Park
Mrs. M. L. Atterbury
John Henry Hammond
Mrs. Vaclav V. Kouba
Miss Helena Titus Emerson
Mrs. Francis de N. Schroeder
Mr. & Mrs. Hamilton Rogers
Dr. C. R. L. Putnam
Miss Julia T. Emerson
Miss Marian Hague
Mrs. Rutherford Mead Shepard
Dr. Lewis A. Conner
Eugene Klapp
Mrs. Dwight S. Simpson
Miss Matelda Brownell
Miss Helen Baxter
George Maguolo
George W. Thompson
Mrs. Carl S. Petrasch
Mrs. Robert Brooke
Frank Crowninshield
Franklin Jasper Walls
Jordan Christie
Mrs. William E. Burnett
Guy Norwood
Mrs. Selden Bacon
Mrs. Kintzing B. Emmons
Frank M. Knight
Frederick Pavlicek, Jr.
John J. MacKay
Dr. Frederick Peterson
Miss Florence Lang
Spencer Waters
Mrs. Charles D. Hilles

21 East 90th Street

Northwest Corner Madison Avenue
Group Ownership Cooperative

Building completed, apartments ready for immediate occupancy.

2 Apartments Available

" 9 D" 6 rooms, 3 baths $24,000
"10 D" 6 rooms, 3 baths 24,600

Maintenance only 6.38%

List of Owners

John Melcher, Jr.
Wakefield Worcester
Mrs. Homer C. Wise
Benjamin H. Trask
John Minturn LeRoy
Mrs. Reginald Barclay
G. de La Guardia
Frank S. Nute
Dr. E. Warren Sylla
Mrs. John A. Hance
Charles W. Pestalozzi
Mrs. T. C. Romaine
Almon N. Gray
James T. Smith
Gen. Quincy A. Gillmore
Dean K. Worcester
Miss Lilian W. Newlin
Miss Emily McGuckin

(Over)

The Choice (Pamphlets), Manhattan, New York.
Douglas L. Elliman and Co., Inc.

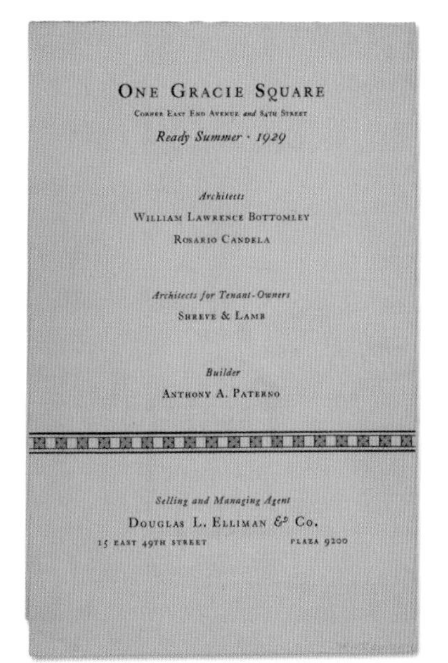

ONE GRACIE SQUARE
CORNER EAST END AVENUE *and* 84TH STREET
Ready Summer · 1929

Architects
WILLIAM LAWRENCE BOTTOMLEY
ROSARIO CANDELA

Architects for Tenant-Owners
SHREVE & LAMB

Builder
ANTHONY A. PATERNO

Selling and Managing Agent
DOUGLAS L. ELLIMAN & CO.
15 EAST 49TH STREET PLAZA 9200

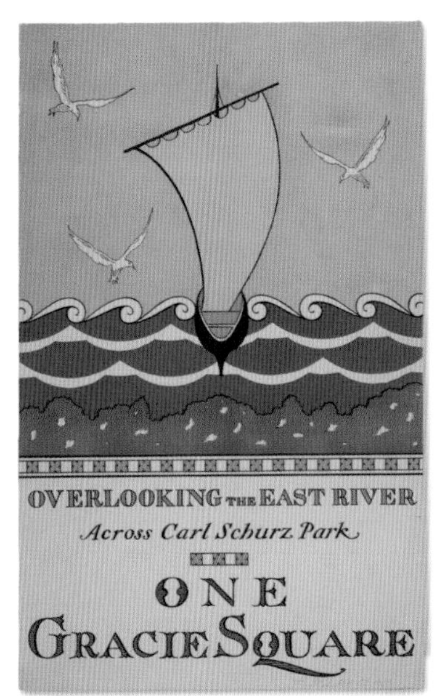

ONE GRACIE SQUARE

SOUTHEAST CORNER OF EAST END AVENUE AND 84TH STREET

Overlooking the East River across Carl Schurz Park

THE wooded effect of the Park, the everchanging charm and fascination of the river viewed from a distinguished residence—these are the elements of a rare combination possible for the permanent enjoyment of a few families through the construction of ONE Gracie Square, just as it was a hundred years ago when this very same bend in the river was chosen as New York's most desirable suburban residential district. ONE Gracie Square has today caught the spirit of the location that lured the fashionables of a former century. Overlooking the Archibald Gracie Mansion, which still stands as an example of the best architecture of that day, it harmonizes with the country manor atmosphere which rightfully clings to this socially restored district.

Directly opposite ONE Gracie Square are the low charming buildings and pleasant grounds of The Chapin School, while but two short blocks away is the Brearly School for Girls.

In planning the apartments in this distinctive cooperative, every effort has been made to give each tenant full enjoyment of the charming views and sweeping vistas its location makes possible. There is a choice of 6 and 7-room Duplex Apartments, 8-room Simplex and 11-room Complete Floor Apartments. All have wood-burning fireplaces, electrical refrigeration, tiled baths and kitchens, and the service facilities which the modern apartment owner requires as a matter of course.

We invite an early inspection of the building and discussion of terms.

Selling and Managing Agents
DOUGLAS L. ELLIMAN & CO.
15 EAST 49TH STREET PLAZA 9200

The Plan

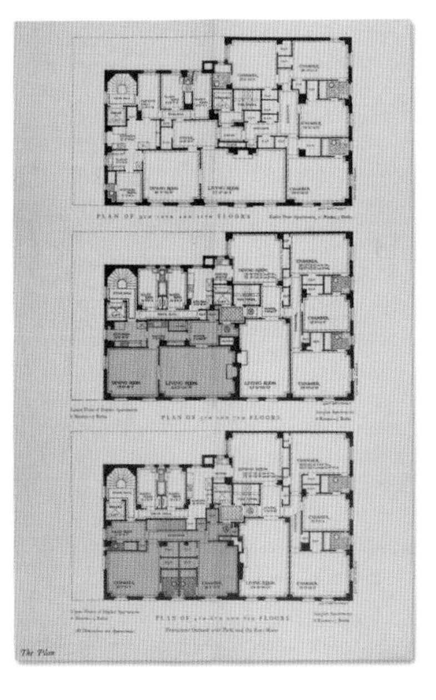

VER SHOP
VER SHOP

133 EAST 80TH STREET, 1929

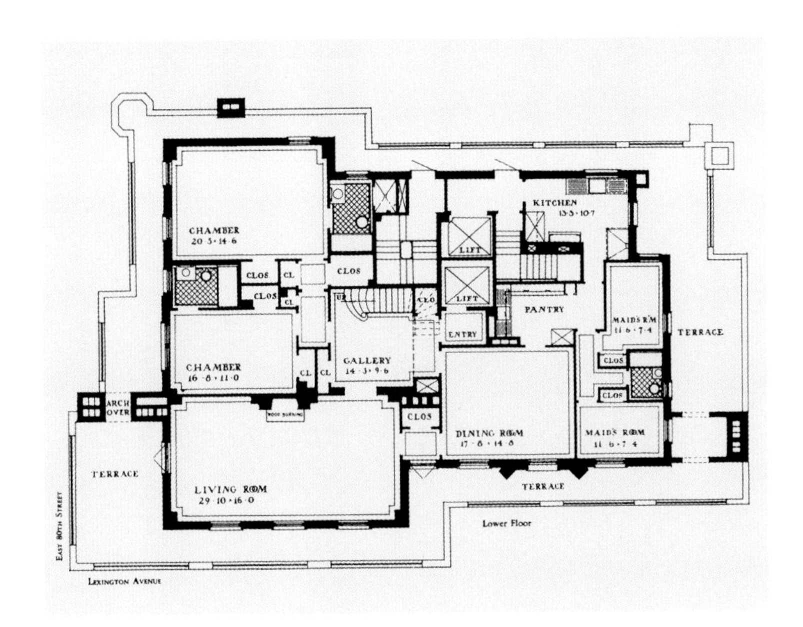

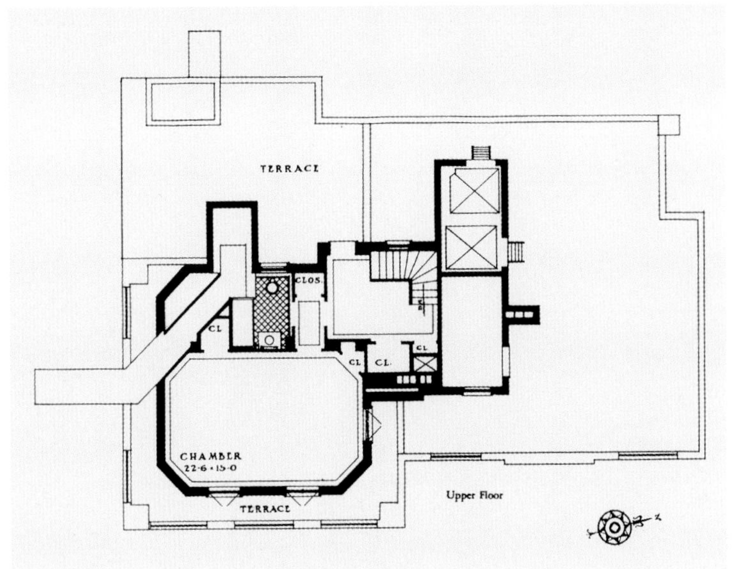

A "quietly important" little building, 133 East 80th Street anchors the corner at Lexington Avenue and springs into greatness above the twelfth floor, where gargoyles sprout—heralding an especially successful setback and water tower composition in the French Gothic style.

As Andrew Alpern notes in his book, the length of construction here was unusually fast, and probably a record (begun January 4 and completed August 19, 1930). Even for the era that saw the Empire State Building completed in fourteen months, this is extraordinary. The building is not extravagant economically (structural beams are visible in the rooms, instead of concealed in the floor sandwich; if not compact, layouts are sensible rather than extravagant), but it is designed with all the care and character of Candela's major Park Avenue buildings, a defining ornament to the neighborhood from its elevated position on Lenox Hill. The likely catalysts in choosing this site were the "anchor tenants" nearby of Vincent Astor's house at Number 130 (Mott Schmidt, 1927), and adjacent neighbors 116, 120, and 124 East 80th Street, a group of double-width Colonial Revival and Georgian facades which form one of the grandest rows in Manhattan.

Moses Ginsberg, who developed the Carlyle Hotel, was the builder here. The Carlyle went into receivership in 1931; thanks to its "in between" scale, 133 East 80th Street weathered the Depression intact, and its six- to eleven-room suites have never been subdivided.

WURTS

740 PARK AVENUE, 1929

Any discussion of this building should begin by referring to the definitive long-form account of its history that already exists, *740 Park: The Story of the World's Richest Apartment Building* written by Michael Gross in 2005. This book delivers the goods on 740 in a social/architectural/investigative journalism project, which amounts to a form of literature that may never have happened before: a biography of an apartment building. Several Candela addresses could have merited this treatment, but 740 is the one that got its own book.

Developer James T. Lee based the concept for his building, with typical floors consisting of multiple duplexes, on J. E. R. Carpenter's AIA Award–winning 812 Park Avenue of 1927. In its plans 740 is quite literally a super-luxury, scaled-up version of 812; externally, however, things could not be more different. Candela's 740 sprouts his most ambitious setback program and is clad completely in severely detailed limestone, its abstraction foreshadowing the fascist classicism of Albert Speer as well as the WPA. Any resemblance to the Empire State Building here is not a coincidence: Arthur Loomis Harmon was the associate architect, and as much as Candela alone could have devised the plans and setbacks, it's difficult to read the facade treatments as anything but pure Shreve, Lamb & Harmon (the Empire State Building and 740 were under construction at the same time).

Because of the wealth of its occupants, and in particular the association with the Rockefeller name, 740 has acquired a mythic stature in New York City folklore; that Lee's granddaughter Jacqueline Bouvier spent her early years at 740 does not diminish this. Some of the greatest art in the city has passed through the service entrance on its way upstairs, and plenty still resides here today. But one thing that explains the enduring desirability and glamour

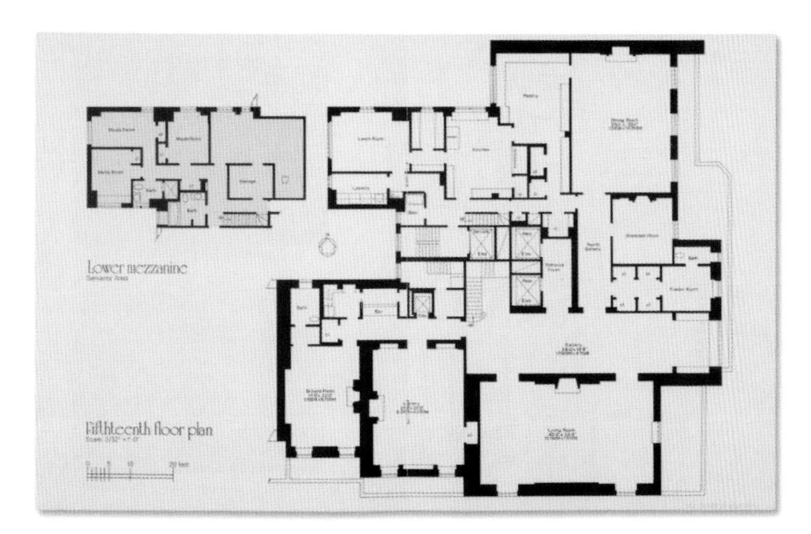

Lower floor of special duplex 15/16B

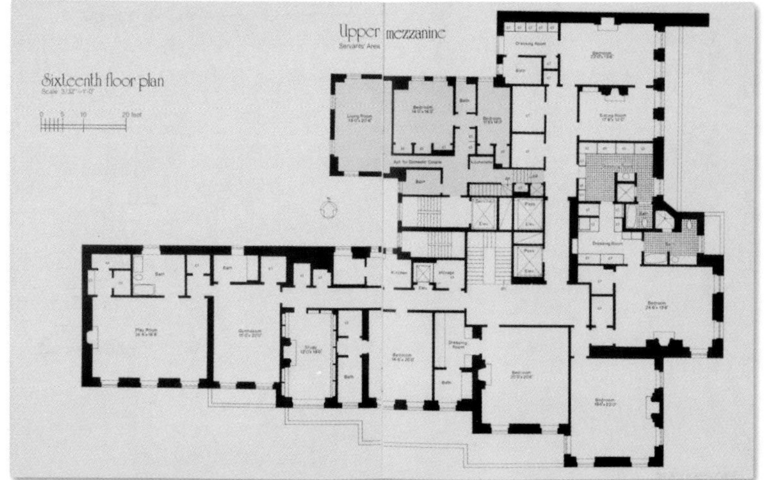

Upper floor of special duplex 15/16B

of 740 is not often pointed out, and that is the power of its architectural style to signify a future across multiple eras: its modernism. Despite its opulence, stylistically it is the least stuffy building on Park Avenue. This explains why the Brewster/Rockefeller/Steinberg apartment is still the most valuable in the city, while the Straus duplex at 720 has long since ceased to exist.

Opposite: Candela Row by Slim Aarons (1953). Shades are down, indicating that Mr. and Mrs. John D. Rockefeller Jr. (and many of their neighbors) are away for the summer. Windows for the penthouse have not yet been altered by the Bronfmans, as they would be in 1962; 17A looks empty because it is owned by the Rockefellers and kept empty to store furniture and air conditioning equipment for the duplex below; an early window unit makes an appearance here, in the corner bedroom of 12/13B.

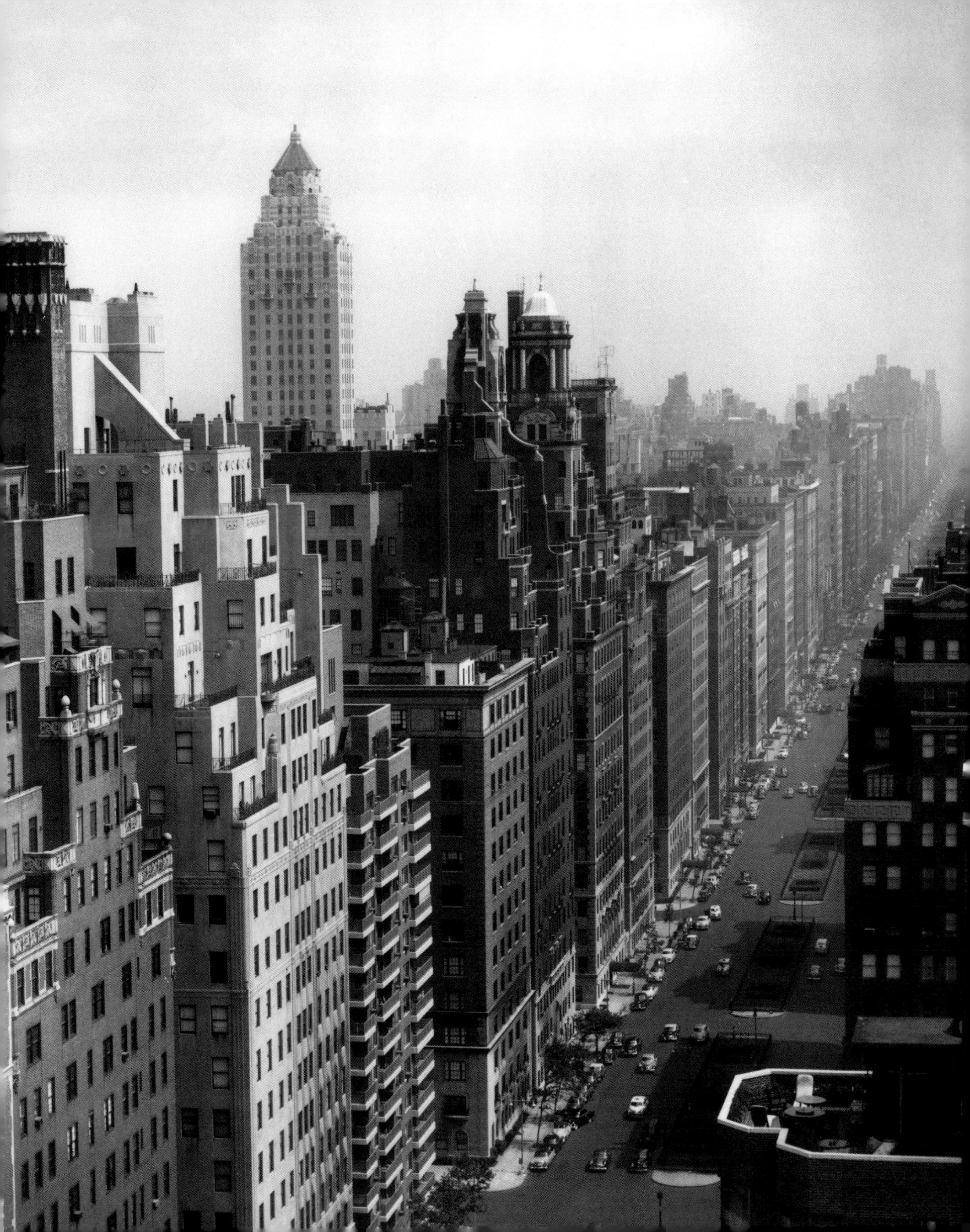

SELECT REGISTER OF APARTMENT HOUSE PLANS

100% Cooperative
Architects: { Rosario Candela / ArthurLoomisHarmon
Builder: James T. Lee
Plot: 220′ x 102′ 2″

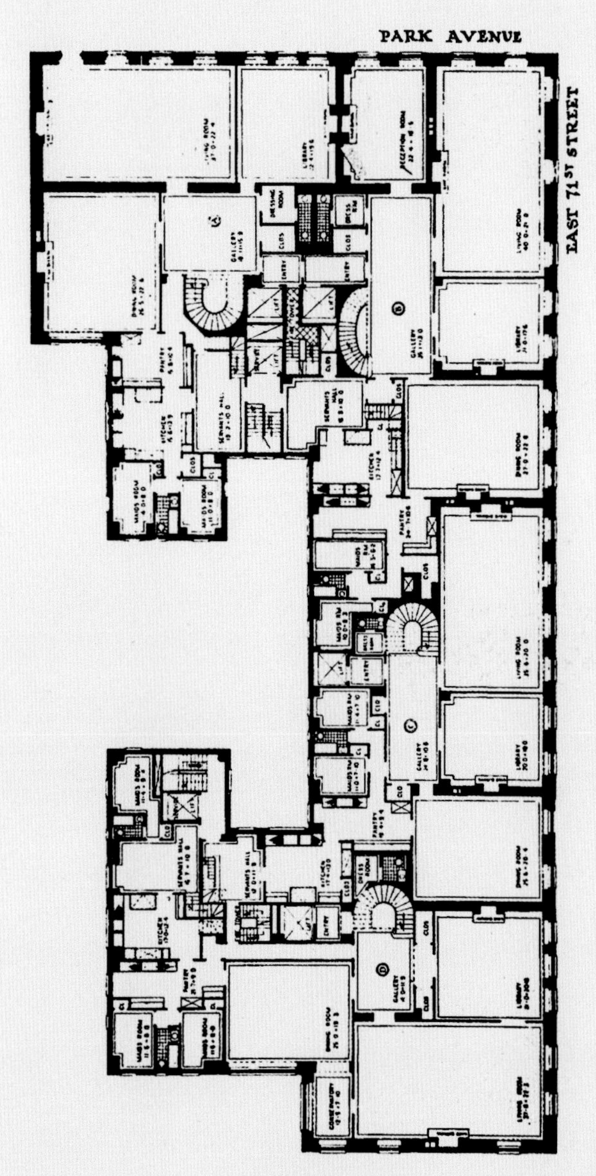

N. W. Corner 71st Street **740 Park Avenue** 11 *Story and Penthouse Building*

Typical Lower Floor Plan

Duplex Apartment A	14 Rooms	6 Baths	Lavatory	4 Master's	5 Servants'
Duplex Apartment B	18 Rooms	8 Baths	Lavatory	6 Master's	6 Servants'
Duplex Apartment C	14 Rooms	6 Baths	Lavatory	4 Master's	5 Servants'
Duplex Apartment D	16 Rooms	8 Baths	Lavatory	5 Master's	6 Servants'

Typical floors at 740

100% Cooperative
Architects: { Rosario Candela
{ Arthur Loomis Harmon
Builder: James T. Lee
Plot: 220' x 102' 2"

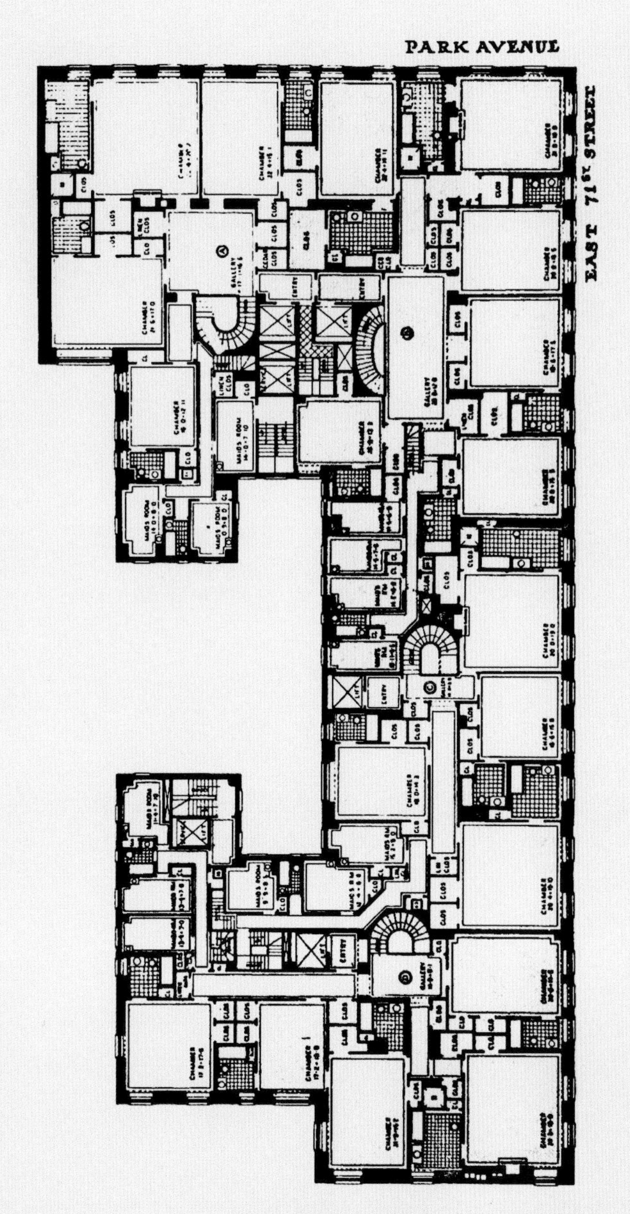

W. Corner 71st Street

740 Park Avenue

Typical Upper Floor Plan

18 *Story and Penthouse Building*

Duplex Apartment A	14 Rooms	6 Baths	Lavatory	4 Master's	5 Servants'
Duplex Apartment B	18 Rooms	8 Baths	Lavatory	6 Master's	6 Servants'
Duplex Apartment C	14 Rooms	6 Baths	Lavatory	4 Master's	5 Servants'
Duplex Apartment D	16 Rooms	8 Baths	Lavatory	5 Master's	6 Servants'

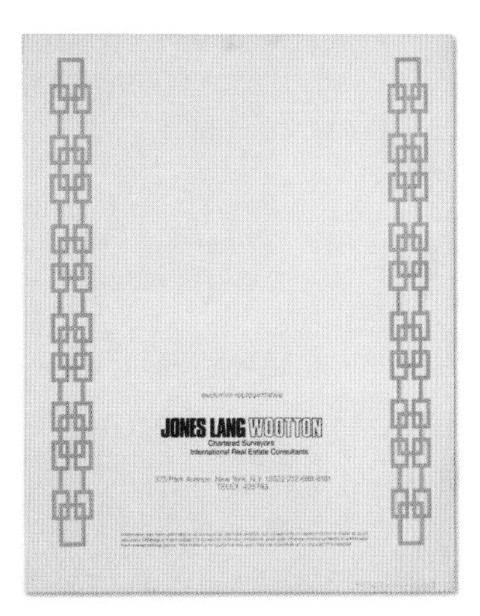

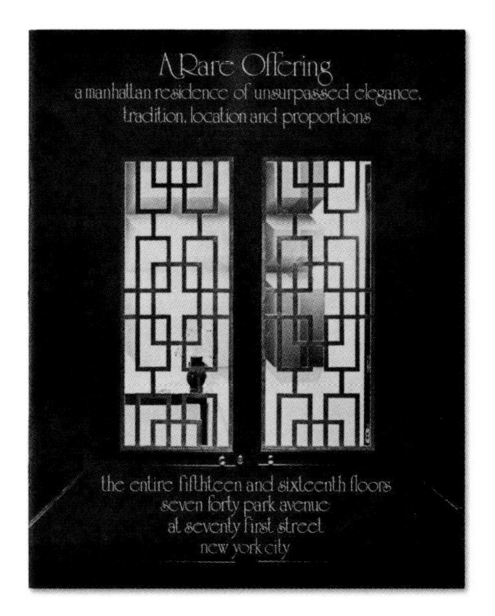

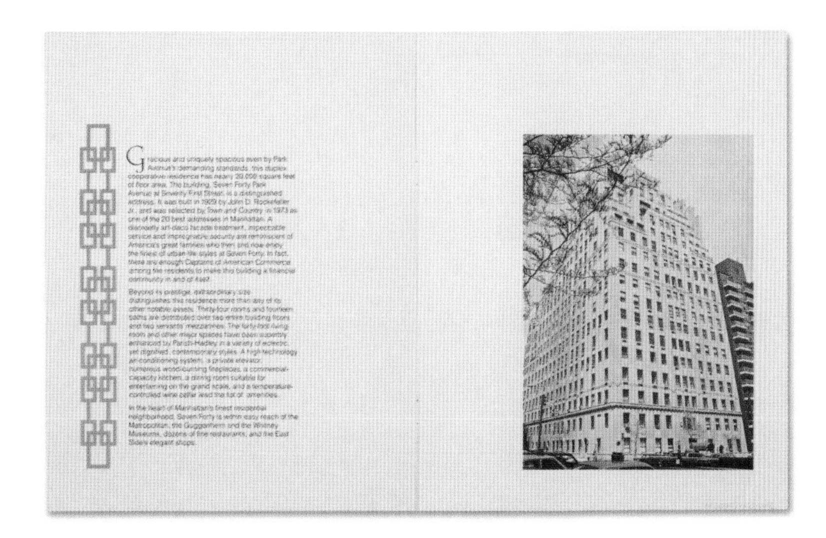

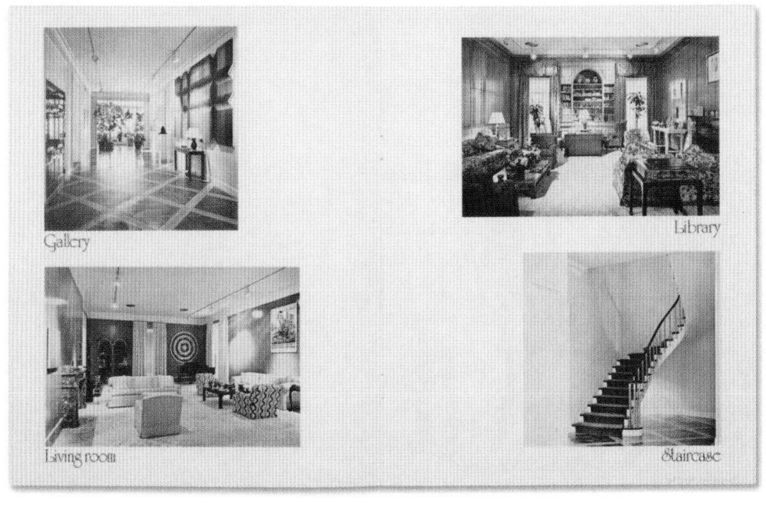

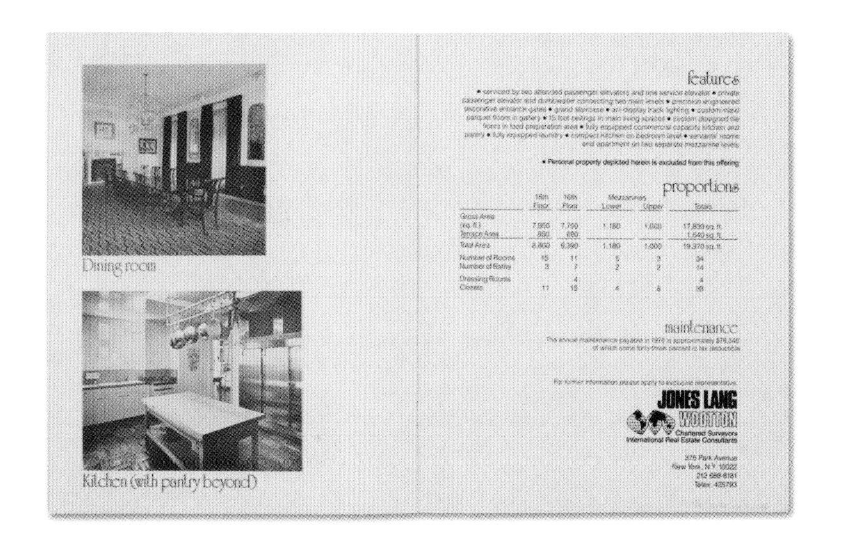

Brochure offering the Steinberg apartment for sale in 1981—priced not to sell at a then unheard-of $10 million

Rockefeller entrance gallery, looking east toward the terrace on Park Avenue. Much of the furniture and carpets can be seen in photos of the Rockefeller townhouse at East 54th Street—torn down to make room for MoMA—from which they moved to live here.

Transfer of Power. At left, the dining room during the Rockefellers' time, 1950. At right, in 1985, Jacob Jordaens's *The King Drinks* provides an appropriate backdrop as Mrs. Saul Steinberg (Gayfryd) checks place settings (from a *Town & Country* story titled "Barony on Park Avenue" with photographs by Arnold Newman).

That was then, that was then. Goya has been replaced by Titian and Rubens, but Old Masters dominate the living room of 15/16B in both 1950 and 1985. Gayfryd's dress is by Arnold Scaasi.

Above: The Library of John D. Rockefeller Jr., a chef d'oeuvre of restraint and English needlepoint.

Opposite: Philippe de Montebello pays a house call under track lighting amidst decoration by Tom Collum (1985).

The entrance hall of 17/18D as decorated by Albert Hadley for Enid Haupt

Mrs. Haupt had a phobia of ash and dirt, so incredibly all the fireplaces were sealed during her renovation. The library was a comparatively masculine room for a woman who lived alone.

770 PARK AVENUE, 1929

Because of its fenestration, 770 is one of the Candela buildings easiest to read from the exterior. The window arrangement reveals duplexes up to the sixteenth floor, with window heights and spacing—full height with balconies in the living and dining rooms, closer together on the upper bedroom floors—spelling out the A- and B-line layouts.

Above that is the roofscape of setbacks culminating in a water tower that, among all his buildings, most resembles an Italian hill town. Special larger apartments take advantage of the now properly recognized opportunity of the setbacks; this is 1929, with the tentative experiment to comply with code at 3 East 77th Street only two years past—yet here the setbacks *are* the point. Indeed, 770 is defined by the ziggurat of its upper stories, visually and internally. A penthouse triplex sadly did not include the great arched window of the water tower, as Emery Roth would find a way to do across town at the Beresford, and in 1944 this apartment was broken up into two smaller but still very desirable units. There are thirty-five apartments in the building.

Of all the distinguished treatments of Candela's architecture and enhancements to his intended plans, the Agnelli apartment stands among the best. Marella and Gianni Agnelli were already fans of his work, having owned 15A at 720 Park; in the mid-1980s they purchased two adjacent upper-level duplexes at 770, and with the help of Peter Marino and Renzo Mongiardino combined them to create one of the fabled interiors in the history of decorative arts in New York. The romance of 770's terraced special apartments has always attracted whales: a previous big combination was effected by Winthrop Rockefeller, who altered 16A significantly after his marriage in 1948, changing room arrangements, adding a bay window and a loggia to

Daniel Craig's apartment in Netflix's *Glass Onion* is set at 770 in a CGI rendering so accurate you have to look to buildings to the north to understand it isn't real (spoiler alert: limestone rustication is random on the real building, but orderly here).

the Park Avenue frontage, and incorporating three bedrooms from 16D. This apartment still exists today.

Candela's 770 made an appearance as the home of Benoit Blanc (played by Daniel Craig) in the 2022 Netflix film *Glass Onion*. The distinctive buttress, which carries the A-line chimney flues over the eighteenth-floor terrace attaching them to the water tower above, was faithfully reproduced by CGI, and it takes a sharp eye to realize this is not the actual building. Eighty-six years after his rooftop lantern makes its appearance in *Follow the Fleet*—a skyline amalgam of 770 and 778—the architecture of Rosario Candela and this building in particular is still inspiring Hollywood's depiction of romantic imagery of New York.

Opposite: The buttress (containing chimney flues) and lantern (water tower enclosure) use architectural necessities to form the composition of Candela's most picturesque roofscape.

Following pages: The real Benoit Blanc's terrace, belonging to apartment 19A

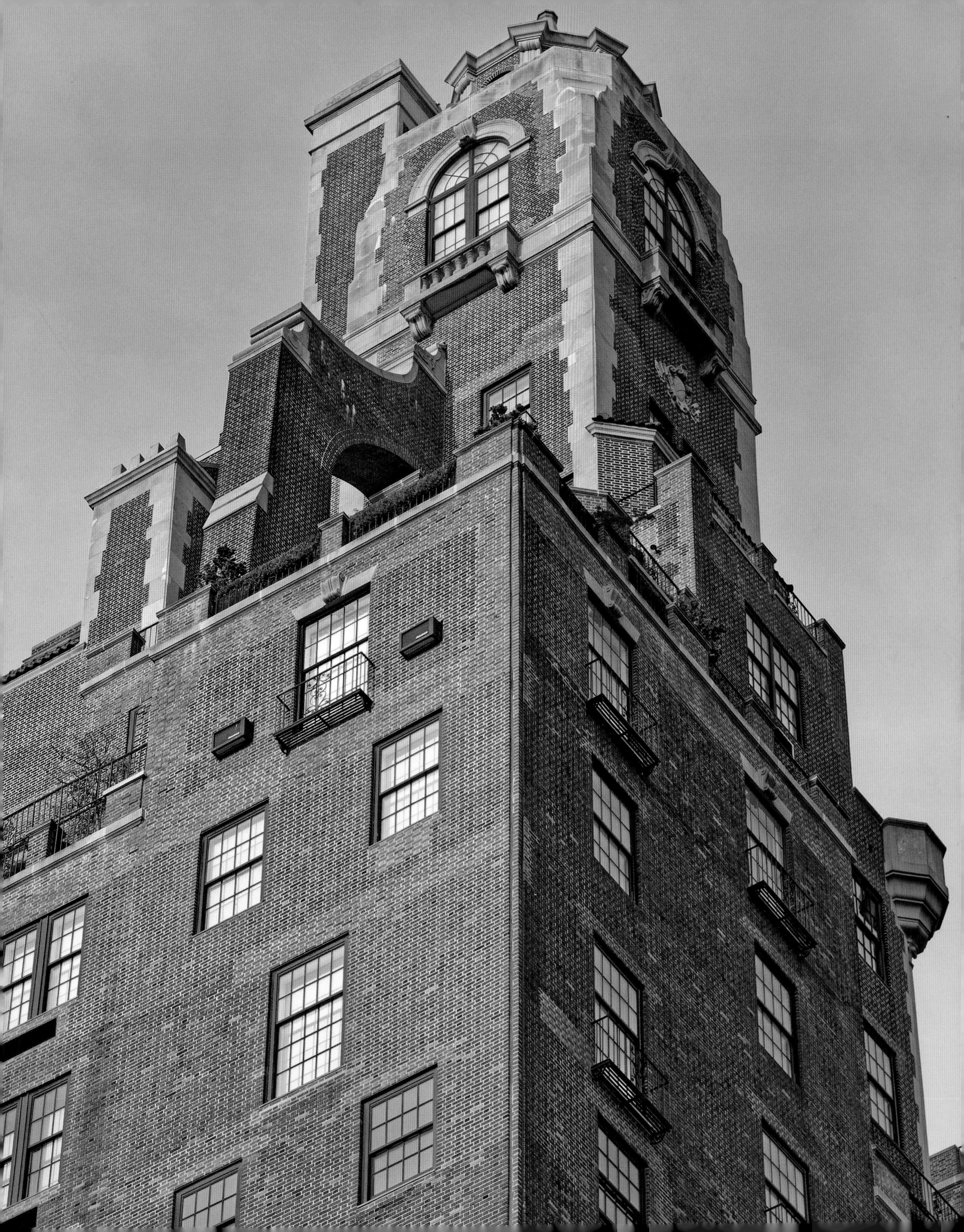

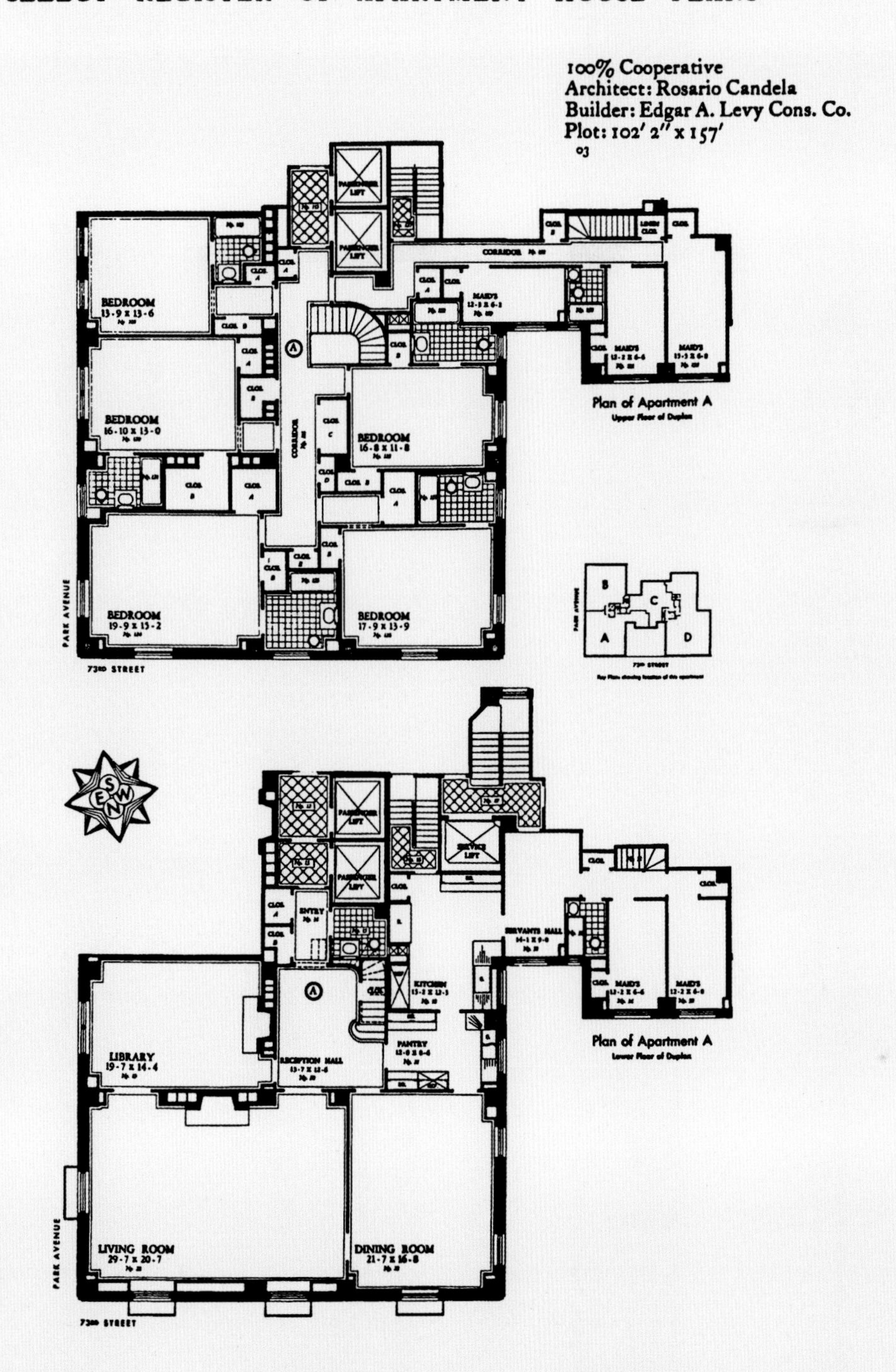

Opposite: B-line stair and veneered entrance hall in a swashbuckling art deco style

Above: Typical A-line corner duplex with five bedrooms, front and back stairs, and low windows with balconies to the living and dining rooms

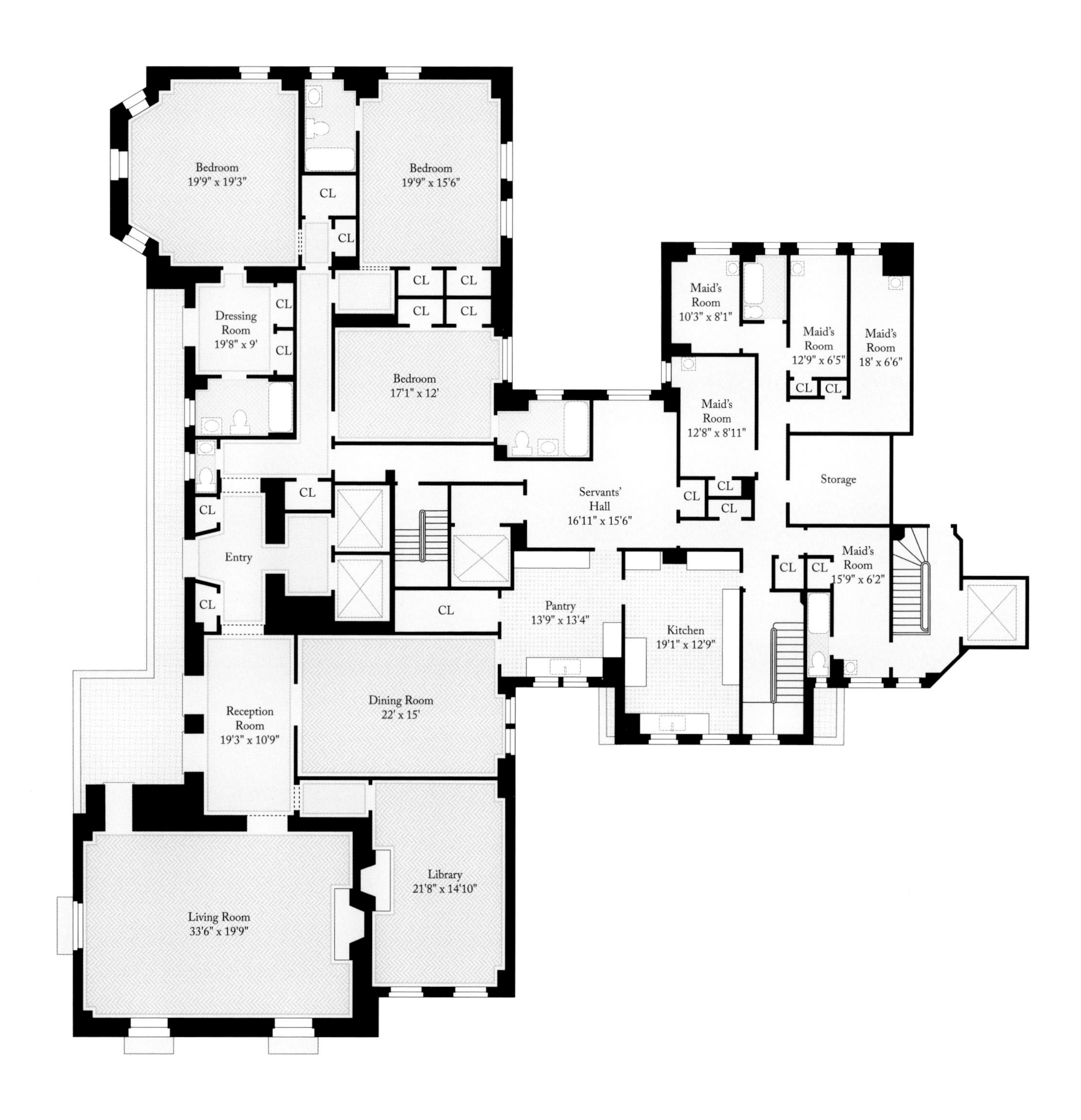

Apartment 16A as originally planned, before enlargements by Winthrop Rockefeller in 1948

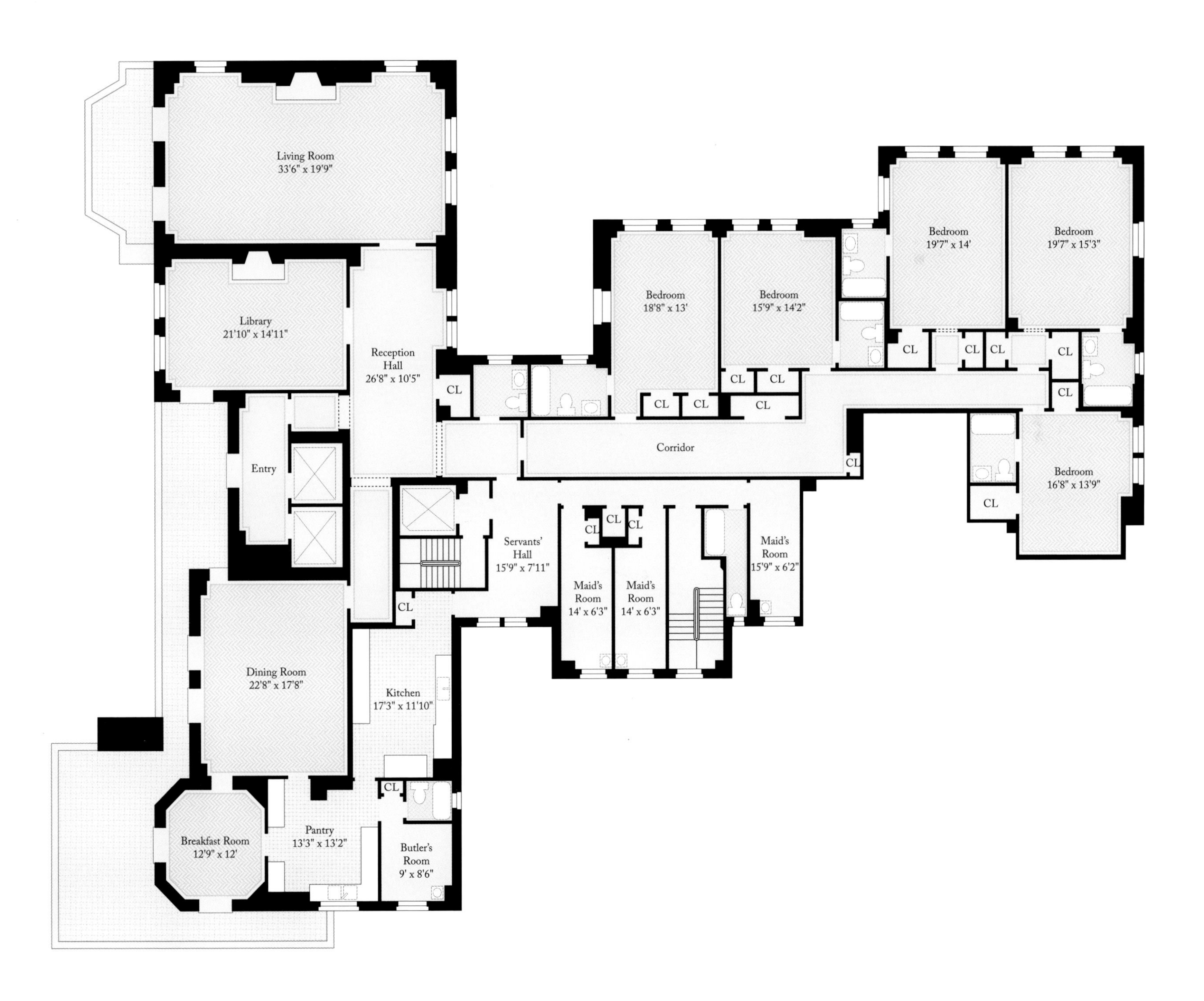

Apartment 17A contains the octagonal breakfast room shown on page 205.

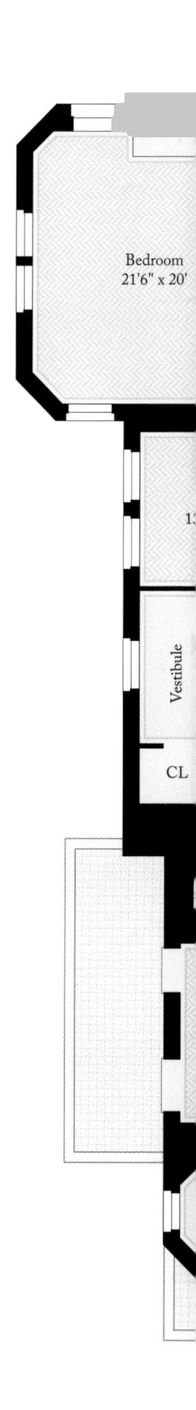

Original penthouse triplex plan

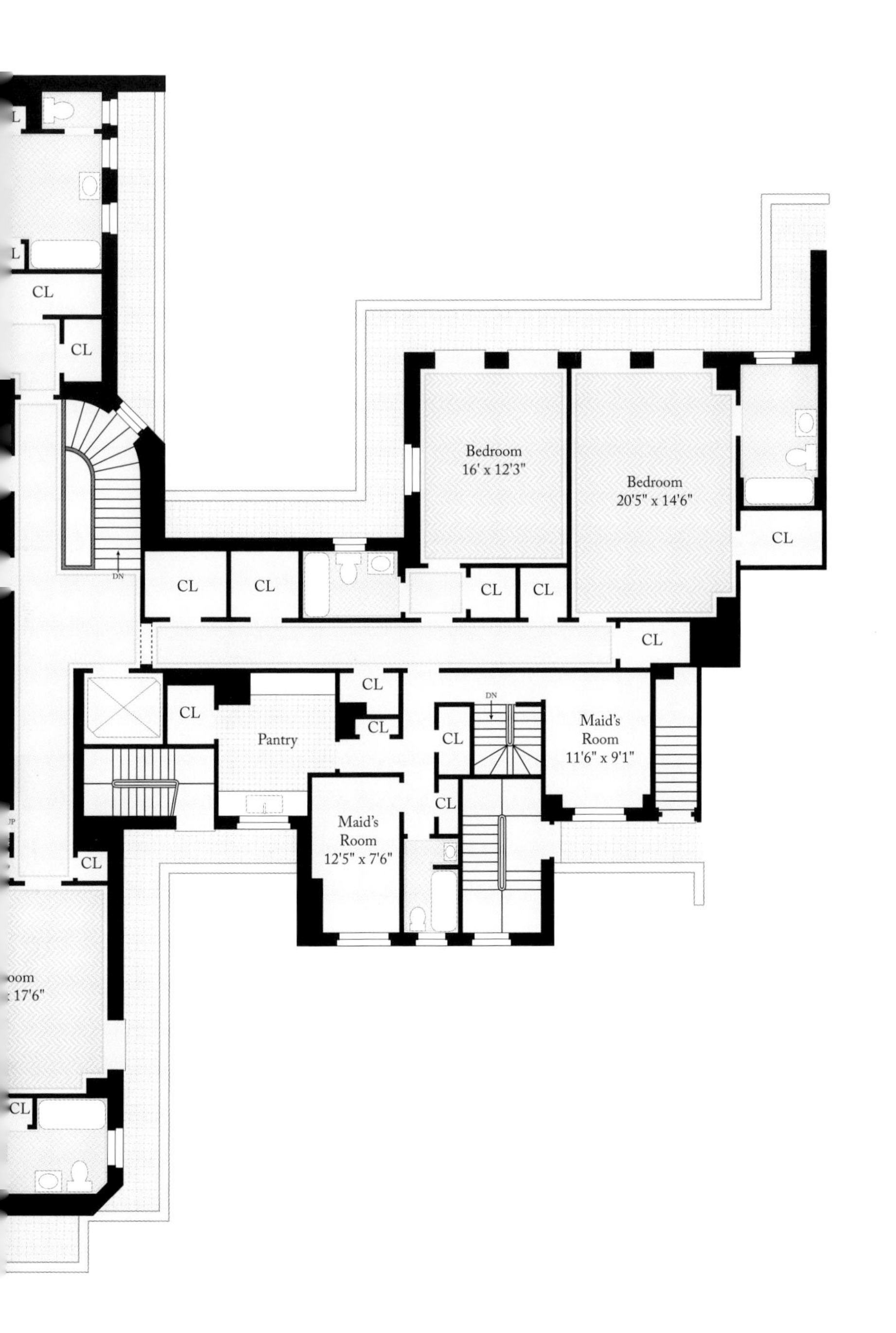

L
L
CL
CL
DN
CL
CL
CL
CL
Bedroom
16' x 12'3"
Bedroom
20'5" x 14'6"
CL
CL
CL
CL
CL
Pantry
CL
DN
Maid's
Room
11'6" x 9'1"
CL
CL
Maid's
Room
12'5" x 7'6"
CL
oom
17'6"
CL

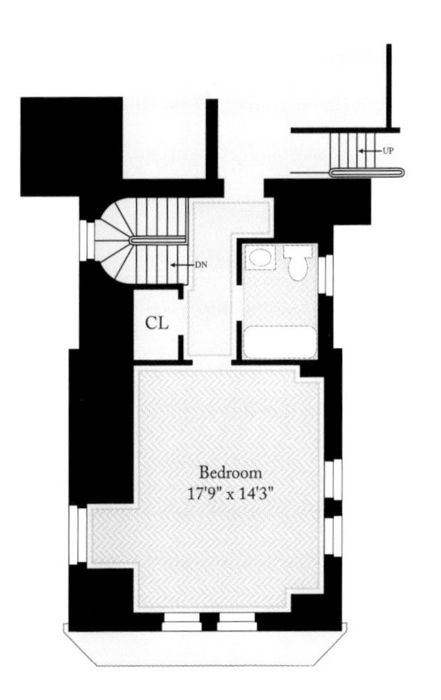

UP
DN
CL
Bedroom
17'9" x 14'3"

Opposite: A rare photo from the 1940s showing clearly the upper stories of 770. Winthrop Rockefeller's renovation of 16A has not yet transformed the Park Avenue frontage into a loggia, as can be seen in the photo on pages 218 to 219.

This page: An axonometric drawing shows the triplex's ascent from floors eighteen to twenty. The unsettling thought may or may not have ever crossed the mind of those nestled into bed at the base of the tower that ten thousand gallons of water are directly overhead.

Opposite: Entry hall of special simplex 17A

Above: Floating above Park Avenue is 17A's octagonal breakfast room, its wraparound terrace facing east and north.

Left and following pages: The Agnelli apartment, the apotheosis of European style in New York. Gianni Agnelli's cork-lined study contained a suite of Hoffmann seat furniture and a magnificent Louis XVI desk by Leleu known as the Flahaut bureau plat; on it are a Tizio lamp and a 1940s wooden boat model that opens to hold paper clips. The rings were for impromptu gymnastics during boring phone calls.

Living room with windows facing north and west. Renzo Mongiardino has covered the walls in thick corduroy channeled velvet.

The windowed entrance gallery was not original to the plan, but fashioned by Peter Marino out of the combined apartments.

Above: Agnelli guest room.

Opposite: A properly run establishment requires two laundresses, and sheets ironed twice—once in the laundry and once on the bed.

778 PARK AVENUE, 1929

The more northerly of what Paul Goldberger christened "great gates across 73rd Street" was filed in March 1929. Construction began in August of that year and was completed in July 1931—an almost perfect swan dive into the depths of the Depression. By the time 778 hit the market, the demand for lavish seventeen-room full-floor suites and penthouse setbacks, which included Candela's only freestanding tea house, was next to nonexistent. And so, in terms of its financial success, one of Candela's most admired buildings was brought into the world stillborn. The top three floors were originally offered as a triplex, but darkening economic conditions caused these plans to be abandoned in favor of a compact penthouse duplex of essentially one bedroom (replacing what had originally been a library or observation room under the water tower on the twentieth floor). The footprint of the stair that would have connected the bedroom floor of the three stories forms a curved wall in the entrance hall of the eighteenth-floor apartment, built as a three-bedroom simplex.

Mr. and Mrs. William F. Buckley lived here in a maisonette, Gary Cooper married his wife, Veronica, at her mother's apartment in 1933, but the most prominent resident of 778 has undoubtedly been Brooke Astor, who moved to the building after the death of her husband Vincent in 1959. Originally she had both the sixteenth and fifteenth floors; the latter housing her mother. After her mother's death, Mrs. Astor sold off the lower apartment but retained two of its bedrooms and attached them to the sixteenth floor. One of these became the famous "Money Room," decorated by Parish Hadley and so-named because it was the home office from which the Astor philanthropy flowed.

Brooke Astor photographed in her library for the December 6, 1980, edition of the *New York Times*, before her dinner for Pesident-elect Ronald Reagan

Watercolor illustration by Mita Corsini Bland showing Albert Hadley's legendary red lacquer and brass modernistic treatment of this room

In December 1980 president-elect Ronald Reagan came to dinner at Mrs. Astor's apartment, and for a night, all eyes in New York City were on 778. The evening served to put Candela's architecture squarely in the spotlight as a backdrop for the kind of use for which it had always been intended, and prefigured the success of the Reagans as hosts who would go on to dazzle socially in the White House. The sixty guests included Candela residents and residents-to-be Bill Blass, Oscar de la Renta, and Douglas Dillon—but also Jewell Jackson McCabe, of the organization 100 Black Women, who was given the seat of honor next to the incoming president. "Thanks to Brooke Astor's logistics," she told the *Washington Post*, "everybody was able to meet the Reagans, and the president-elect's willingness to mingle with such a cross section seems to me a very good step."

Opposite: Axonometric drawings of the fourteenth and fifteenth floors showing how plans, position of fireplaces, steel columns, etc., remain consistent even as ascending setbacks erode the floor area. The section labeled lower part of duplex shows the two bedrooms added by Brooke Astor from this apartment to the floor above.

Following pages: The freestanding tea house on the nineteenth floor. Originally an open belvedere, this structure is now glazed following a recent renovation.

Upper Part of Duplex
15th Floor
Lower Part of Duplex
14th Floor

Skyline by Rosario Candela (1931). The Italian and Georgian upper stories of 770 and 778 Park Avenue—seven stories that amount to a city unto themselves surmounted by towers—are, in Paul Goldberger's words, "Great gateways to Central Park."

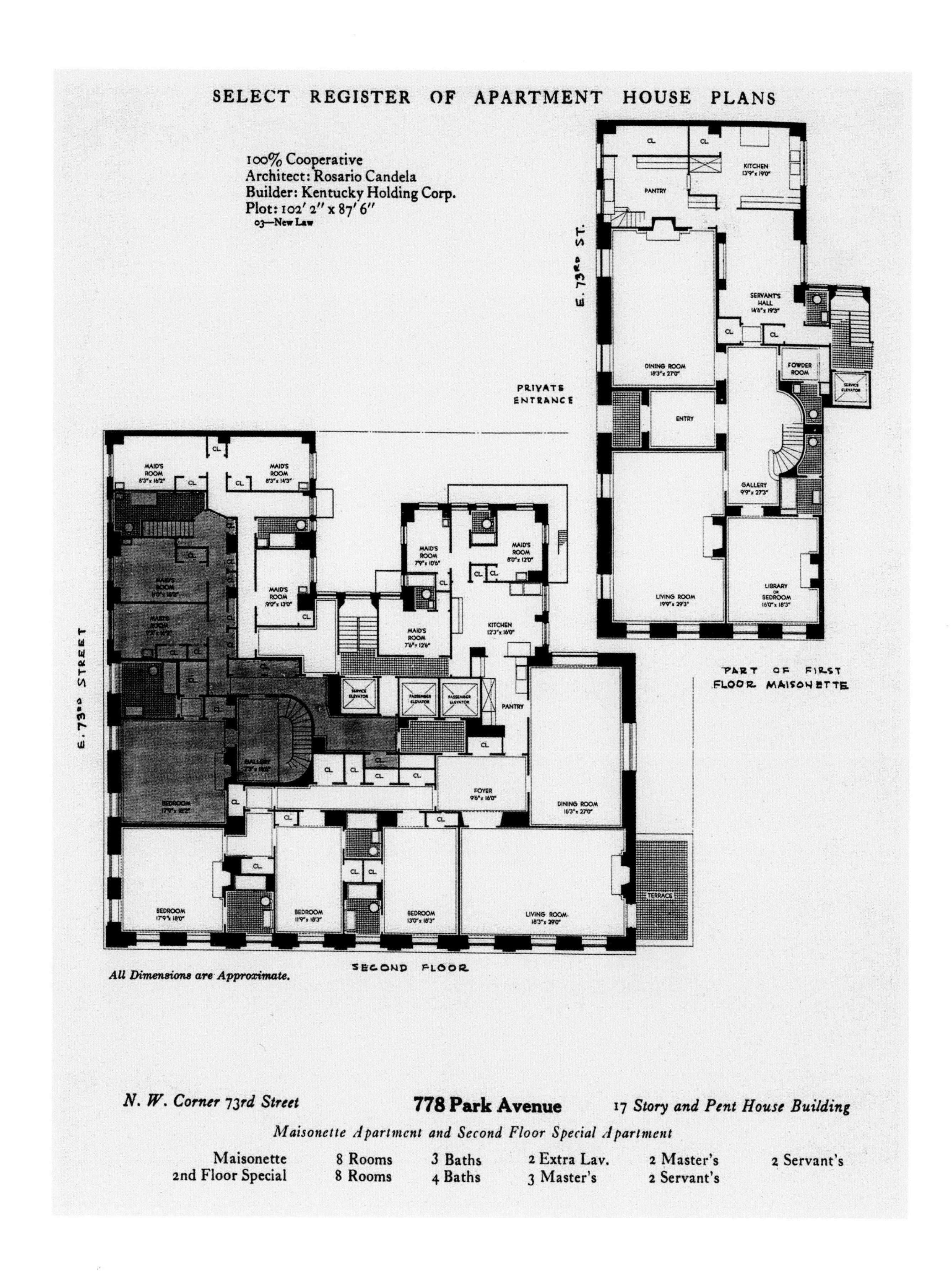

Duplex maisonette once occupied by William F. Buckley and second-floor special apartment (full-floor simplexes begin on the third floor)

SELECT REGISTER OF APARTMENT HOUSE PLANS

100% Cooperative
Architect: Rosario Candela
Builder: Kentucky Holding Corp.
Plot: 102′ 2″ x 87′ 6″
03—New Law

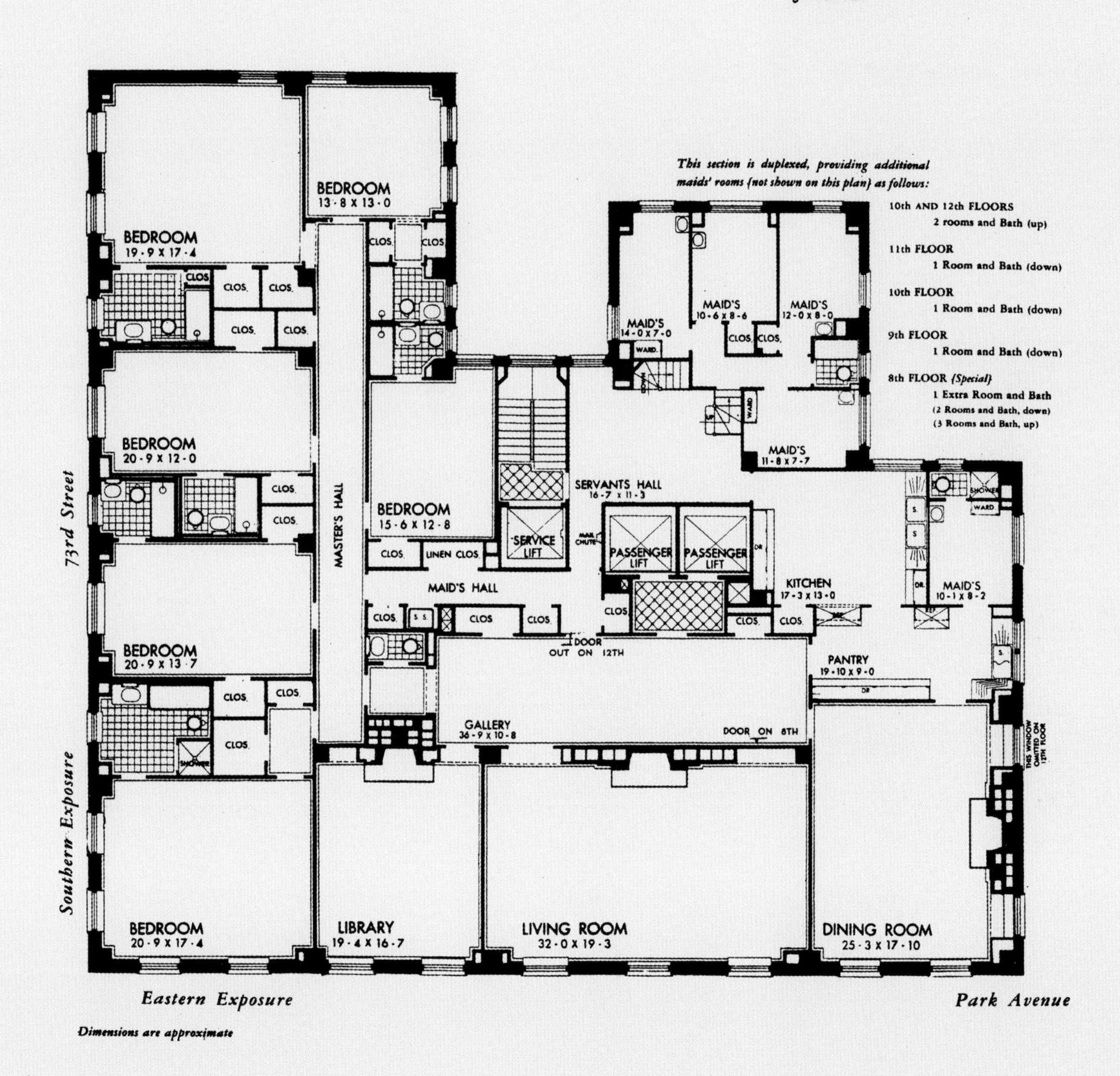

N. W. Corner 73rd Street **778 Park Avenue** *17 Story and Pent House Building*

8th, 9th and 12th Floors

8th and 9th Floors	17 Rooms	9 Baths	Extra Lav.	6 Master's	5 Servant's
12th Floor	18 Rooms	9 Baths	Extra Lav.	6 Master's	7 Servant's

Generous typical plans at 778, with six bedrooms and a regal thirty-six-foot entrance gallery

Apartment 14. The setbacks begin to form a ziggurat with the appearance of corner terraces on the fourteenth floor.

These two bedrooms now duplexed to sixteenth floor above

Apartment 15. In a remarkable feat of cryptographic solution-seeking, as we ascend through the upper levels the room arrangement/layout is maintained. This occurs even as floor area is reduced, and structural steel and fireplace flues—elements that dictated the plan diagram in the first place—change position in relation to rooms.

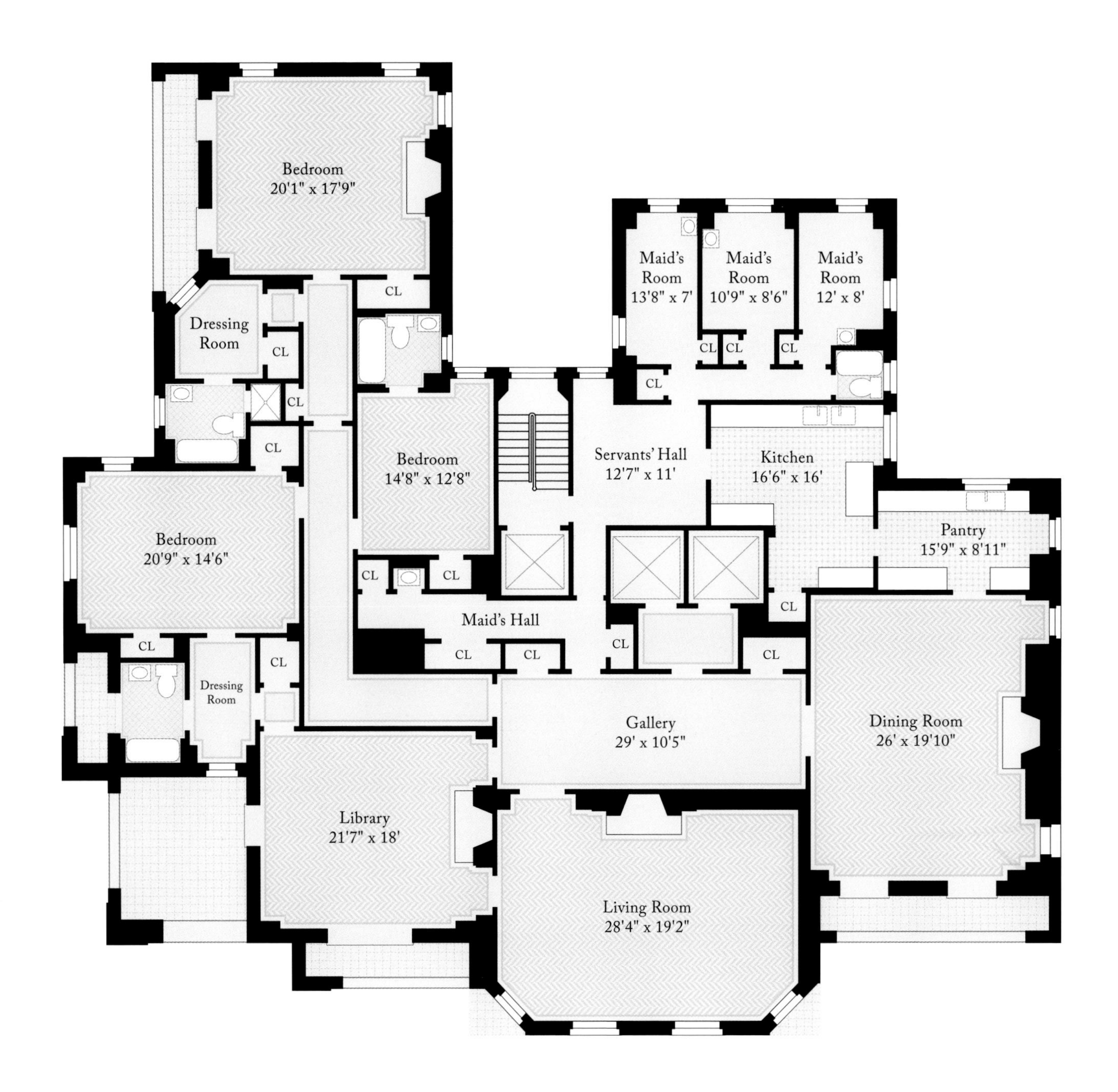

Apartment 16. In the longtime home of Brooke Astor, two bedrooms are now attached to this apartment from the floor below.

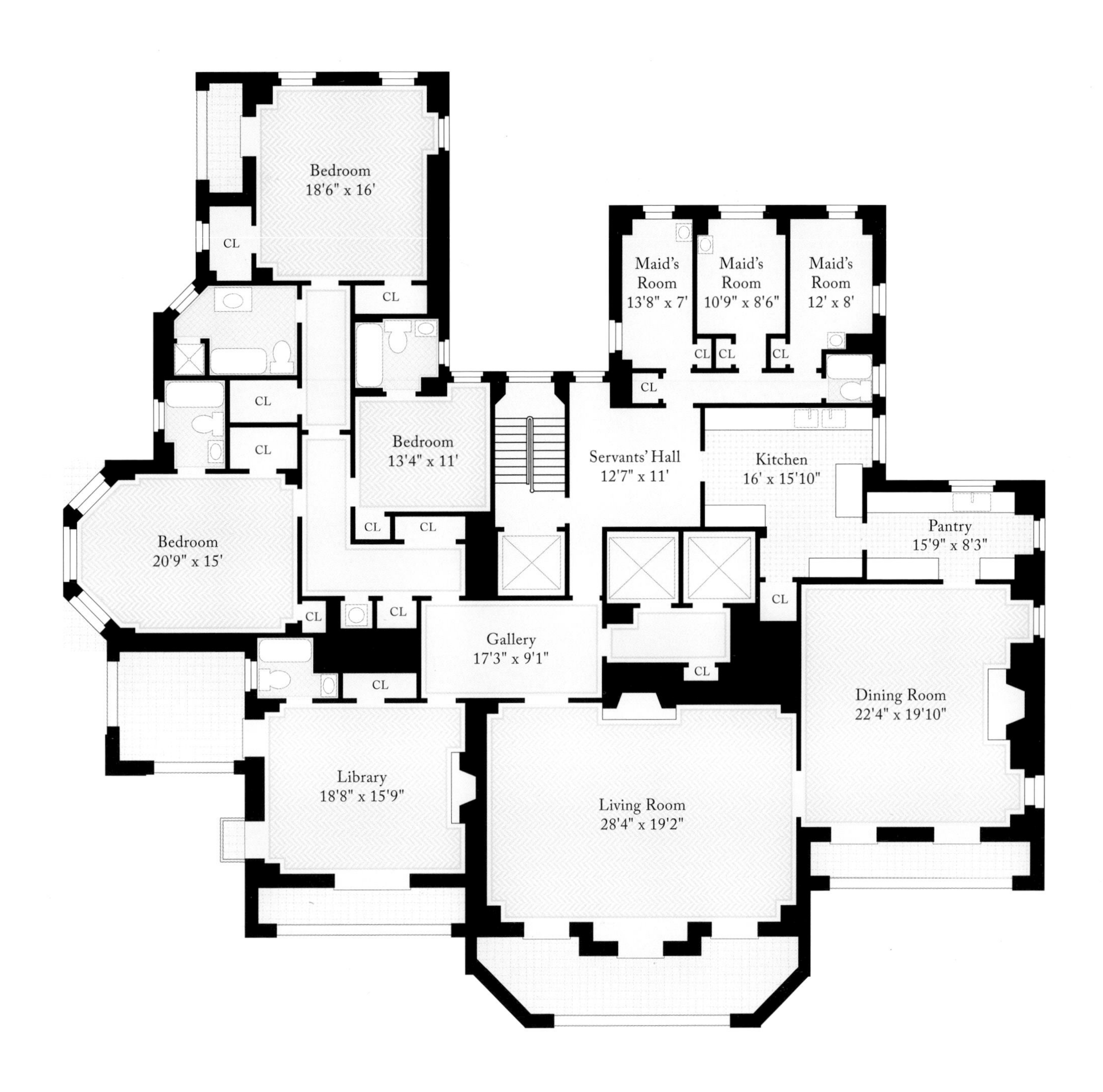

Apartment 17. By this level the gallery has shrunk, but other features have sprouted such as small terraces and a bay-windowed bedroom. Candela still makes sure staff can get to the front of the house without going through the dining room.

Apartment 18. The bedroom floor of the triplex that wasn't to be is today one of the most charming simplex apartments in New York (photos as decorated by Mariette Himes Gomez on pages 232 to 233).

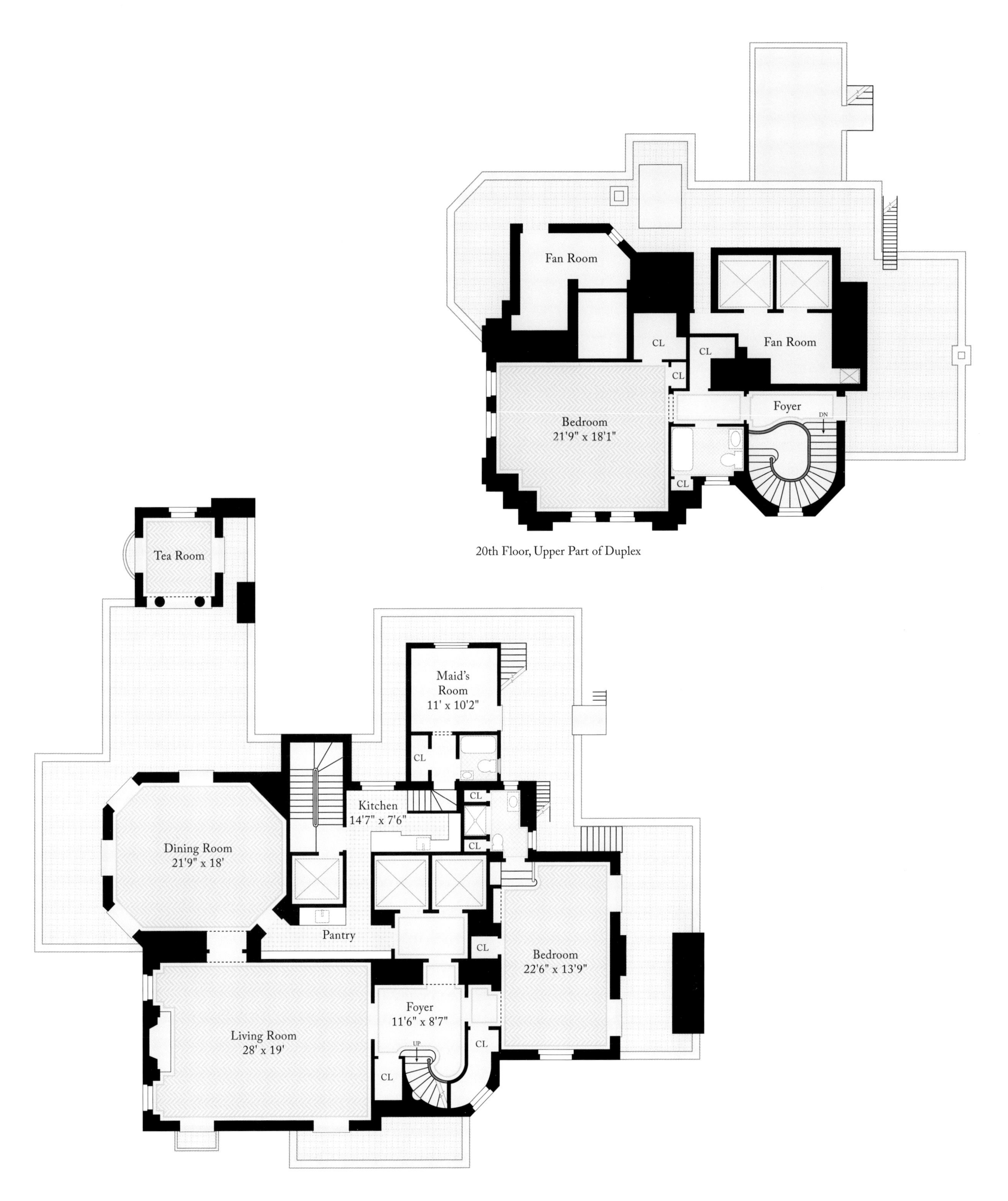

Apartment 19/20. A two-bedroom duplex with the unique feature of a freestanding tea house. In the triplex plan, the octagonal space labeled dining room was a music room.

Eighteenth Floor. Living room and (right) entry hall, with curved wall to accommodate the bottom run of the stair in what was originally planned as a penthouse triplex. This level, lowest and with the most floor space, would have contained the bedrooms.

1021 PARK AVENUE, 1929

Number 1021 Park Avenue is hard to categorize. With its entrance in the center of a wide facade facing East 84th Street and only an understated, much narrower side facing grander Park Avenue, it would seem, at first glance, to be a sibling to 990 Fifth Avenue or 2 East 70th Street, Candela's slim slabs that present slender ends to Central Park and have their main facades on side streets. But there is much more going on at 1021. The side-street facade calls to mind two of Candela's finest, but often overlooked, buildings, 1 Gracie Square and 133 East 80th Street, elements of which Candela has integrated into something new and different here. The hundred-foot long, south-facing facade on 84th Street is broken up into three sections, not unlike the way the facade of 1 Gracie Square is designed to look like two buildings.

It is another one of Candela's fictions, an imaginary composition, this time of three buildings, two matching ones at the ends with three-story limestone bases, and a center section with a base in brick, set in the diamond pattern that Candela used at 133 East 80th Street. The pretense of multiple buildings here is driven not by the need to control disparate window arrangements (as Candela did in the south facade of 960 Fifth Avenue) but in the service of visual pleasure and comfortable scale. Creating the impression of distinct buildings here was a way of breaking apart what could have been a monotonous facade and relating it at least somewhat more closely to the scale of the nearby townhouses.

And in the case of at least two nearby townhouses, Candela was concerned about more than just scale. Number 1021 sits between two important mansions: John Russell Pope's vaguely Elizabethan Reginald De Koven house of 1913 to the north, and Ernest Flagg's Federal-style house for Lewis G. Morris of 1914

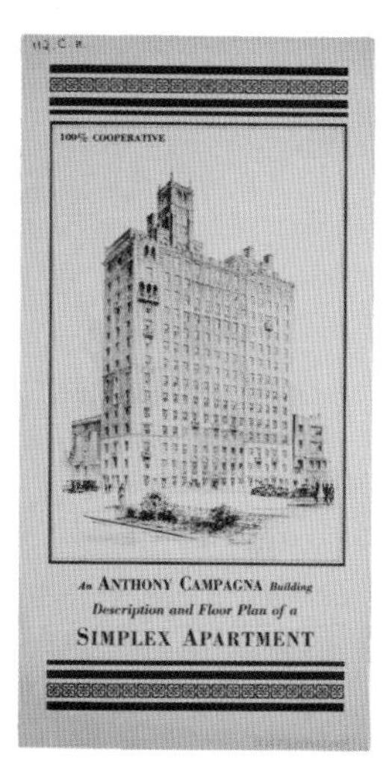

1021 PARK AVENUE

NORTHEAST CORNER OF EIGHTY-FIFTH STREET

100% COOPERATIVE

THE northeast corner of Park Avenue and Eighty-fifth Street has long been a center of social distinction, as the roster of its tenants testifies.

Now, Anthony Campagna, builder of many outstanding cooperatives, has erected on this distinguished site, a 100% cooperative apartment building which will afford many families the advantage of this famous address. But more than that, 1021 Park Avenue is a building of unusually effective design and its apartments are an outstanding value even if considered only as an investment. In plan, 1021 Park Avenue takes the form of an "L" which allows a much greater exposure than customary, and naturally, a greater number of windows. Exposure is greatest to the south, on 85th Street, while the north, east and west are protected by low buildings. The naturalistic garden of Mrs. Reginald de Koven, within the "L" shape, which all the apartments overlook, offers a pleasant vista.

There are only eight apartments now available, the other nineteen apartments all having been sold within four months of the first offering. This record-breaking sale indicates the exceptional approval of the plans and details of the apartments. In every refinement of detail these apartments live up to the reputation for superior value for which Campagna-built cooperatives are known.

An early inspection of the building and discussion of details is urged. The selling agents will be glad to show a list of those who have already bought apartments.

Management of PEASE & ELLIMAN, INC.

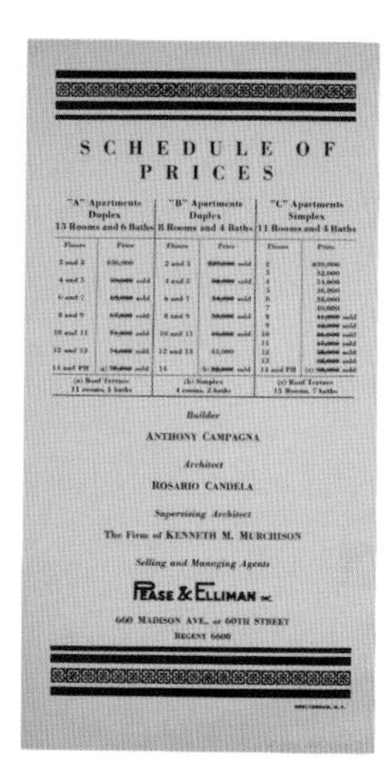

SCHEDULE OF PRICES

"A" Apartments Duplex 13 Rooms and 6 Baths		"B" Apartments Duplex 8 Rooms and 4 Baths	
Floors	Price	Floors	Price
2 and 3	[illegible]	2 and 3	[illegible] sold
4 and 5	[illegible] sold	4 and 5	[illegible] sold
6 and 7	[illegible] sold	6 and 7	[illegible] sold
8 and 9	[illegible] sold	8 and 9	[illegible] sold
10 and 11	[illegible] sold	10 and 11	[illegible] sold
12 and 13	[illegible] sold	12 and 13	42,000
14 and PH	(a) [illegible] sold	14	(b) [illegible] sold
(a) Roof Terrace 11 rooms, 5 baths		(b) Simplex 4 rooms, 2 baths	

"C" Apartments Simplex 11 Rooms and 4 Baths	
Floors	Price
2	[illegible]
3	32,000
4	34,000
5	36,000
6	38,000
7	40,000
8	[illegible] sold
9	[illegible] sold
10	[illegible] sold
11	[illegible] sold
12	[illegible] sold
13	[illegible] sold
14 and PH	(c) [illegible] sold
(c) Roof Terrace 15 Rooms, 7 baths	

Builder
ANTHONY CAMPAGNA

Architect
ROSARIO CANDELA

Supervising Architect
The Firm of KENNETH M. MURCHISON

Selling and Managing Agents
PEASE & ELLIMAN INC.
660 MADISON AVE., at 60TH STREET
REGENT 6600

across 84th Street to the south. Candela had the assignment of slipping a tall apartment building in between two of the Upper East Side's better townhouses; it is no surprise that he thought first of breaking down the scale, but he also had the challenge of not wanting to let his building clash violently with either of these two very different houses. His solution is eclectic, weaving together elements like limestone framing that vertically joins pairs of windows to subtly allude to the large Elizabethan windows of the Pope house, and then using more conventional six-over-six windows set into brick that suggest the Flagg house. Neither house is imitated but both are respected, and Candela never loses sight of the responsibility that the architect of a large building has to the pre-existing small buildings around it—buildings that, happily, remain to this day.

Further separating 1021 from the narrow buildings that it seems to resemble is its footprint, which is shaped like a letter L turned on its side, with the east end of the building extending farther to the north than the section along Park Avenue. Candela placed three units on each floor, two duplexes and one simplex. The A-line apartments are the grandest, with Park Avenue frontage; the B-line duplexes are smaller, but they contain what is surely one of the earliest appearances of "his and hers" primary bathrooms: off a dressing room (itself a rarity, even in the most luxurious apartment designs of the time) there is a small "powder room" for the use of the husband, presumably to shave. The extension of the building to the north at the east end yields a gracious, expansive simplex, with the service spaces and the dining room carefully tucked into the midblock extension, which presumably gets minimal sunlight.

The building, completed in the incredibly short period of 264 days, has long been considered desirable; more than half of the apartments were sold within five weeks of the announcement. It has always been a quiet, discreet building, with a strong preference for residents with a low profile—something the board asserted in 1969 when it rejected Barbra Streisand's $240,000 offer for an apartment.

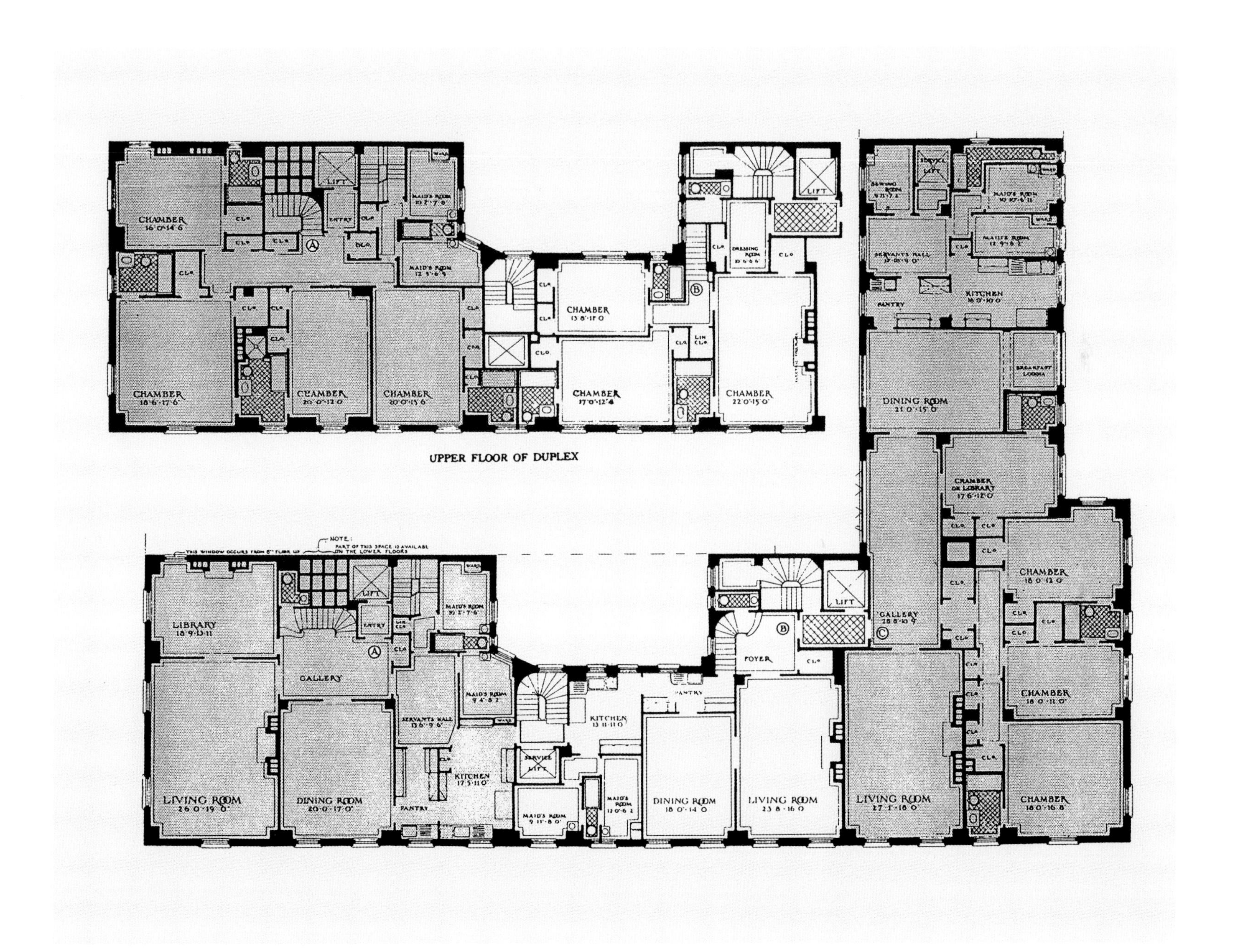

Typical plans, with two duplexes and one simplex per floor

View from the dining room to the entrance hall in the apartment of Frank P. Shepard

1220 PARK AVENUE, 1929

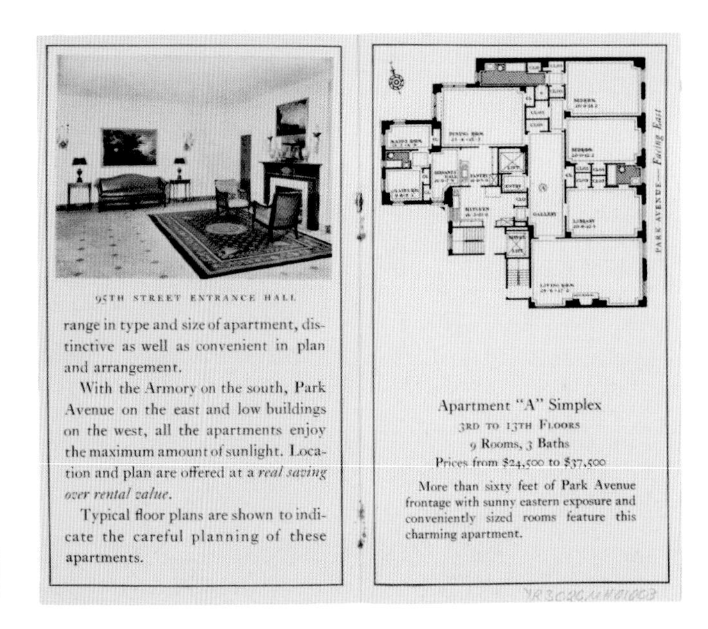

Unlike most Candela buildings, which replaced brownstones or other smaller structures, 1220 Park Avenue at the northwest corner of 95th Street was built on an empty lot. That may have been happenstance, since by the time it went up in 1929 there were plenty of houses and several apartment buildings in that section of Carnegie Hill, including Schwartz & Gross's distinguished full-block courtyard building at 1185 Park Avenue. Still, the fact that it was built on "virgin" land underscores the extent to which 1220, the most northerly of Candela's full flower late "ziggurat" buildings, was a pioneer, constructed to bring a new level of luxury to the upper reaches of the Upper East Side. Its location could be described either as the crown of Carnegie Hill or as close to Harlem than any building of its stature had been. It is just one block south of the point at which the New York Central railroad tracks, buried discreetly under Park Avenue from Grand Central Terminal through the Upper East Side, burst out to become an elevated line through Harlem.

But if the site of Number 1220 represented something of a risk for Joseph Paterno, its developer, the architecture was equivalent to Candela's best designs in 1220's better-known siblings twenty blocks down the avenue—1220 looks as if it had been designed to prove to apartment dwellers that they could live as well at 95th Street as at 65th or 75th. Candela produced a beautifully massed, sumptuous brick and limestone structure, with a three-story limestone base, elegant setbacks that recall 770 and 778 Park Avenue, and a handsome water tower anchoring the corner of 95th Street and Park Avenue, recalling the towers of those buildings but in this case clearly meant to enhance 1220's role as an uptown beacon.

Inside, there are generally four apartments per floor, simplexes and du-

Portrait of Joseph Paterno, 1908

plexes, most of which are classic Candela: with spacious rooms and generous proportions, and expansive views to the rest of the Upper East Side and midtown from the upper floors on the 95th Street side; the western portion of the building, which would seem to be the rear and might normally be expected to have lesser apartments, actually contains many of the building's most desirable units, with open views made better still by the presence of a low building, now a school, that fills the block to the south. The climax of 1220 is a special twelve-room triplex penthouse with a solarium at the top level, tucked under the building's water tower.

Paterno's gamble paid off. Number 1220, along with its non-Candela neighbor at 1185, has long been viewed as the most desirable address on Park Avenue in the 90s.

Even all the way up on 95th Street, the real roots of these buildings—and how their forms came to be—lie downtown in the skyscrapers of the Financial District, as a journalist conveyed with mawkish yet tender insight in this passage from Joseph Paterno's obituary in the June 14, 1939, edition of the *New York Times*:

> On a raw, gusty day in November, 1889, Joseph, then a newsboy, shivering at his post in Park Row, watched construction of a huge office structure across the street.
>
> "Papa," he asked, "why do they make the business buildings so high?"
>
> "Because it pays," the father replied.
>
> "The higher the building, the more rent it brings its owner. I would not do so in Italy, but this is the American way."
>
> The bright-eyed newsboy wrinkled his head and frowned, while making change for a customer. "But papa, if that is so why don't they make the houses and tenements high, too, so they will bring more rent?"
>
> The father smiled and patted his son's curly head. "You have an eye for business, my son. Perhaps someday you may build some high houses."

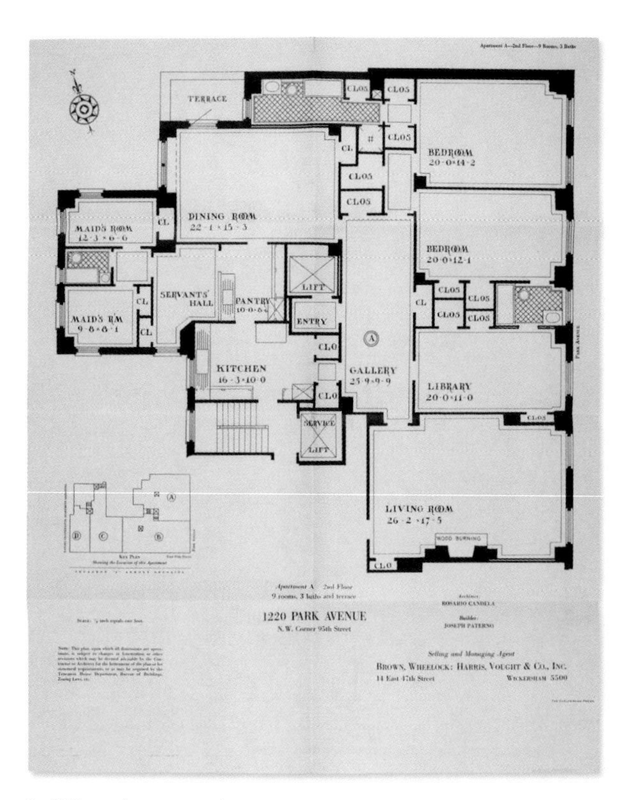

2nd Floor, Apartment A

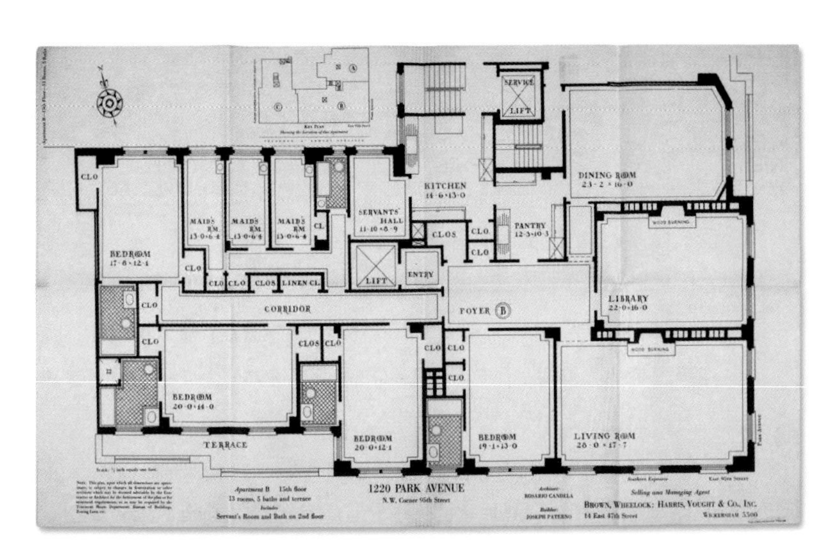

15th Floor, Apartment B

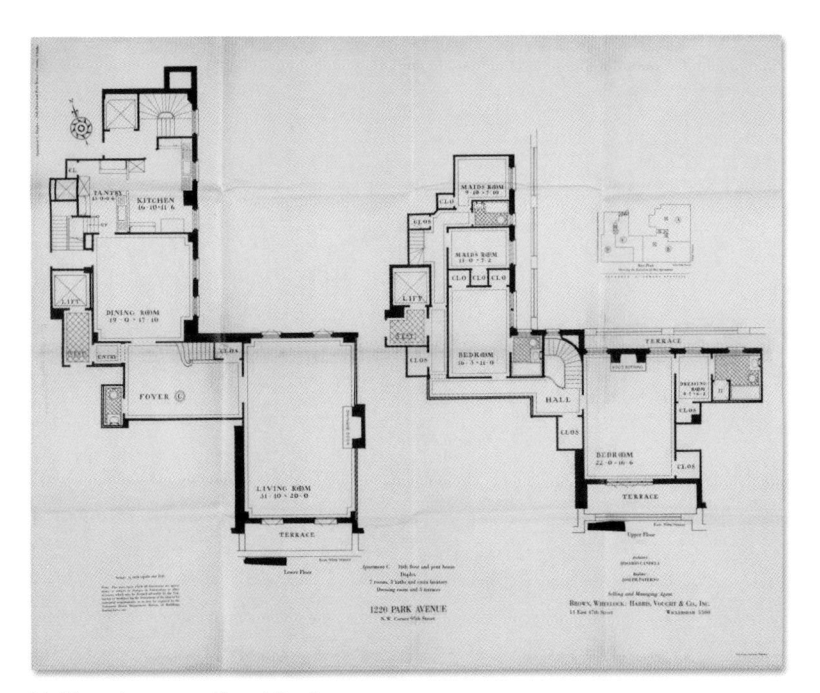

6th Floor, Apartment C, and Penthouse

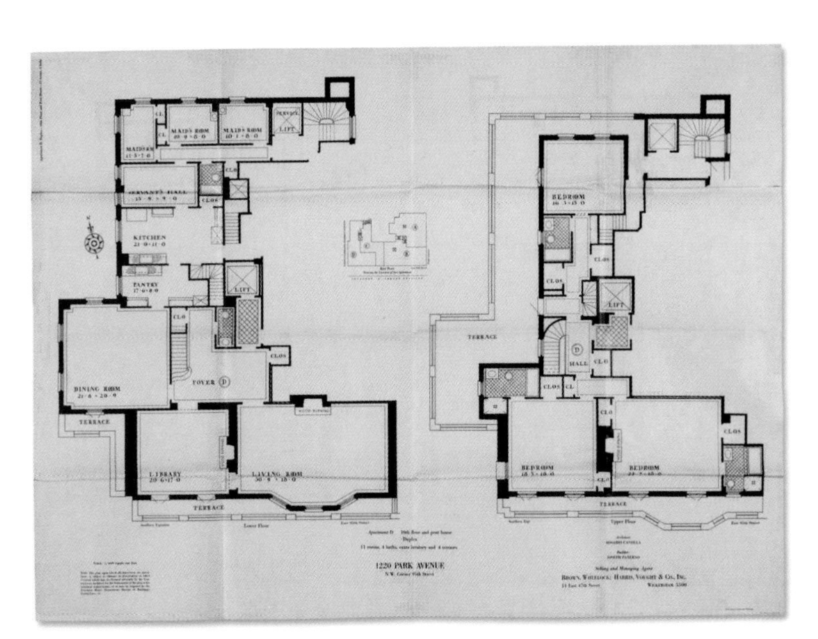

16th Floor, Apartment D, and Penthouse Duplex

A variety of plans at 1120, with duplexes on higher floors no less desirably laid out than those at 770 or 778 Park

834 FIFTH AVENUE, 1929

One of Candela's three most opulent buildings (960 Fifth and 740 Park make up the trio), 834 has perhaps the most interesting story behind the events that led to its final appearance and form. After developer Anthony Campagna's failure to acquire the James Ben Ali Haggin townhouse at the corner of 64th and Fifth, work was begun on a mid-block site on October 21, 1929, with promotional renderings showing a symmetrical composition crowned at the center with a water tower. Then, in April 1930, with structural steel already erected and limestone cladding in place as high as the third floor, the widow of the charismatic California Gold Rush character gave in (she would move into the building and was to live there until her death in 1965); the townhouse lot was incorporated into an expanded, now asymmetrical composition wrapping the corner to graft seven duplexes and a tiny four-room penthouse onto the initial building to the north: enter 834 2.0. By November 14, 1930, the *New York Times* was announcing the sale of the largest of these to Chase Bank's Carl Schmidlapp for $275,000.

Laurance Rockefeller moved to the penthouse in 1944, a triplex to which he added two bedrooms from the apartment below (for a time, he too owned the entire building before overseeing its conversion to a co-op, mirroring his father John D. Rockefeller Jr.'s situation at 740 Park). The modernist renovation of this apartment features enormous single-pane windows that changed the external character of the upper regions of 834 significantly, though not unsuccessfully. The design was overseen by Rockefeller family architect Wallace Harrison, also a resident here.

Besides being a Candela building that has consistently set co-op price records and played host to various defining "leg up" moments of the New York

Fifth Avenue looking north (early 1920s). The only interloper in an unbroken wall of mansions is 4 East 66th Street (J. E. R. Carpenter, 1920). In well under a decade nearly all would be gone.

A holdout, but not forever. Structural steel for 834 is already up; limestone cladding reaches as high as the fourth floor.

real estate market—a building that makes news—834 has made New York design history. Apartments here have been decorated by François Catroux, David Easton, Lee Mindel, Stephen Sills, Peter Marino, Christian Liaigre, John Stefanidis, Thierry Despont, Jacques Grange, Henri Samuel, and Jansen (the cover of the 1971 Jansen book, *Jansen Decoration*, is the dining room of 7/8A during ownership by Mr. and Mrs. Watson Blair). The windowed staircase of 11/12A floating above the park has always been one of the most, if not the most, expressive and singularly elegant features of any Candela apartment—a visual clue to the scale of the spaces inside, almost as if one of his signature water towers has climbed down to become embedded in the wall of the building.

Form 104 LEM/IMcC 39-2093-27-Bt.

22 **Tenement House Department**

OF THE CITY OF NEW YORK

Municipal Building, Centre and Chamber Streets
BOROUGH OF MANHATTAN

MUNICIPAL BUILDING
JORALEMON AND COURT STREETS
BOROUGH OF BROOKLYN

BERGEN BUILDING
TREMONT AND ARTHUR AVENUES
BOROUGH OF THE BRONX

NEW YORK, 6/18/30 192

BUREAU OF BUILDINGS OF THE CITY OF NEW YORK

TO THE SUPERINTENDENT OF BUILDINGS,

Received JUN 19 1930

BOROUGH OF MANHATTAN

FURTHER BOROUGH OF MANHATTAN

DEAR SIR:

Plans and specifications have been submitted to the Tenement House Department for the erection of one multiple dwelling located at 833--836 FIFTH AVE., 1 EAST 64th ST.

Borough of Manhattan by

Architect Rosario Candela; Address 578 Madison Ave.

Owner #833 Fifth Ave. Corp. Address 551 - 5th Ave.
A. Campagna, Pres.

and have been approved by the Tenement House Department on 6/18/30. A copy of the approved plans is herewith forwarded to your department.

Yours respectfully,

Roll. William F. Deegan

COMMISSIONER

Tenement House Commissioner

aw 1153

By F. R. Robertson

Plan No. N.B. 281/29 192

JUN 18 1930

Receipt for the Buildings Department application for the southern addition to 834—the most palatial multiple dwelling in the city, but technically still a Tenement House—dated June 18, 1930. This means Candela drew the working plans for what, in terms of scope, amounts to an entirely separate building in fewer than three months.

New York Times,
April 12, 1929

BUILDERS PURCHASE NEW HOUSING SITES

Lexington Av. Corner at 89th St. Is Bought for a 12-Story Apartment House.

PROJECT ON EAST 108TH ST.

Campagnas Add to Fifth Avenue Plottage on Which They Plan to Erect a Tall Flat—Other Deals.

The southwest corner of Lexington and Eighty-ninth Street has been purchased by Max Rosenfeld and Paul Herring, operators and builders, for improvement with a twelve-story apartment house with stores, representing an investment of $2,000,000, it was announced yesterday.

The site fronts 100 feet on the avenue and 144 feet on the street and is now improved with six three-story houses and three flats. The sale was negotiated by F. V. Calder & Co., brokers.

The corner portion of the plot was sold by the 1,101 Park Avenue Corporation, Michael E. Paterno, president, and 116-118 East Eighty-ninth Street was sold by Mary A. Drury of Washington, D. C. Henry I. Cooper was associate broker in the sale of the Paterno plot.

A large housing operation for the upper east side was announced yesterday when Michael and Armino Campagna purchased the five-story apartment house at 7 East 108th Street, 25 by 100 feet. The Campagnas recently acquired the northeast corner of East 108th Street and Fifth Avenue and now have a plottage of 15,000 square feet at this point.

They plan to improve the site with a fifteen-story apartment house. Construction work is to begin in the Fall for occupancy in October, 1930. The operation will represent an investment of $2,000,000, according to the Wood-Dolson Company, broker in the sale of both parcels.

The William B. May Company, ...Inc., has sold fo[illegible] ...Street Company the ...ent house

New York Times,
April 18, 1929

5TH AV. SITE IS SOLD FOR 36-STORY HOTEL

Anthony Campagna Buys Plot at 65th St. for $10,000,000 Cooperative Apartments.

3 HOUSES, SCHOOL TO GO

Skyscraper Will Replace Homes of Mrs. A. Guggenheim, Frank J. Gould and Frederick Lewisohn.

Three homes of prominent families on Fifth Avenue and a private school were doomed to pass before the northward movement of skyscraper housing projects yesterday, when the four structures were purchased by a builder for a thirty-six-story apartment hotel, representing an investment of $10,000,000. The proposed building is to be operated on a 100 per cent cooperative basis. It is the first housing operation of its kind, with the hotel feature, to invade the Fifth Avenue section.

The houses just sold are at 833, 834, 835 and 836 Fifth Avenue and were owned by Mrs. Aimee S. Guggenheim, Frank J. Gould, Frederick Lewisohn and the Bovee School, respectively. They have been bought by Anthony Campagna, builder, through Brown, Wheelock: Harris, Vought & Co., brokers. This purchase gives Mr. Campagna a plot fronting 120 feet on the east side of Fifth Avenue, between Sixty-fourth and Sixty-fifth Streets, with a depth of 110 feet. The entire plot has a ground area of 13,000 square feet.

The Guggenheim house is a five-story building on a lot 35 by 100 feet and has been held in the seller's ownership since 1914. The residence at 834 Fifth Avenue is a similar house and was sold by the Three States Realty Company, representing Frank J. Gould, who has been living abroad for thirteen years. The home of Frederick Lewisohn, who now lives in Germany, is a five-story structure on a lot 25 by 125 feet. Mr. Lewisohn has held the property since 1916, and negotiations for its sale were carried on with the seller by cable.

The most northerly of the four buildings sold is at 836 Fifth Avenue. It is a four-story structure, occupied by the Bovee School. The 1929 assessment, for taxation purposes, on the four properties is as follows:

	Land.	Land and Building.
833	$265,000	$450,000
834	265,000	450,000
835	195,000	350,000
836	175,000	260,000
Total	$900,000	$1,510,000

The purchase gives Mr. Campagna control of the entire blockfront on Fifth Avenue, in the block just south of the new Temple Emanu-El, which replaced the home of Vincent Astor, with the exception of the two corner houses at 830, title to which is held by Margaret B. Haggin, and 837, title to which is held by Sophia A. Sherman.

Negotiations for the purchase of the plot have been carried on by Mr. Campagna for two years.

The builder is having plans prepared by Rosario Candela, architect, for the new thirty-six-story 100 per cent cooperative apartment hotel, which is to be one of the tallest structures on Fifth Avenue, north of Fifty-ninth Street.

Last Floor in Cooperative On Gary Site Is Purchased

Joseph B. Terbell, president and chairman of the board of the American Brake Shoe and Foundry Company, has bought an apartment of fourteen rooms and six baths, occupying a floor in the 100 per cent cooperative recently completed at 855 Fifth Avenue, corner of Sixty-seventh Street, by the 855 Fifth Avenue Corporation, Michael E. Paterno, president, from plans by Warren & Wetmore and Rosario Candela. All the space in the structure, a twelve-story and penthouse building erected on the site of the former Gary residence, is now sold, according to Brown, Wheelock: Harris, Vought & Co., Inc., the brokers.

Candela's 834 makes the newspaper of record, April 1929.

FIFTH AVENUE

MOST FAMOUS RESIDENTIAL THOROUGHFARE IN THE WORLD

Wealthy and aristocratic old New York families, who formerly occupied their palatial homes on this world-renowned street, have one by one gradually succumbed to changing conditions, and abdicated in favor of enterprising real estate operators who have been so aggressive in erecting towering apartment buildings on Fifth Avenue. The result during the past few years is an almost completely transformed and *NEW* Fifth Avenue.

Massive white marble residential skyscrapers now replace the old brownstone and granite-fronted dwellings. Thirty, forty and even sixty and seventy families now live on a plot of ground that formerly accommodated less than half a dozen individuals and servants.

New York has grown so phenomenally, real estate values have increased so rapidly, and taxes risen so steadily, that even New York's multi-millionaires found housekeeping on Fifth Avenue "a bit expensive" and finally capitulated to the new order of things.

Words convey but a faint idea of the luxury, the regal grandeur and the superb magnificence of many of these palatial apartment buildings which for over two miles face Central Park in almost unbroken continuity. It is estimated that from 59th Street to 110th St. (the length of Central Park) the actual value or amount of money invested in these fifty short blocks is over

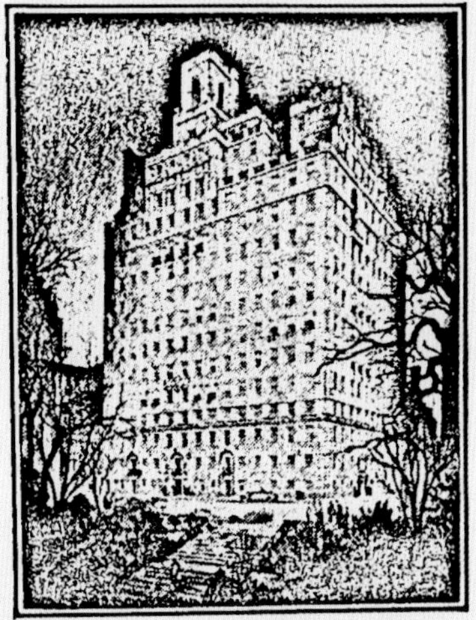

Louis H. Dreyer

834 FIFTH AVE.

N. E. Cor. 64th Street.

Cost.................$7,000,000
230 feet high.........16 Floors
Completed................1931
Arch..........Rosario Candela
Bldr.....Anthony Campagua
Sell. & Man. Agents.
Brown Wheelock Harris & Co.

CO-OPERATIVE OWNED

ONE OF THE MOST REGAL RESIDENTIAL PALACES IN ALL THE WORLD

$250,000,000

The interior decoration and furnishings of many of these homes beggars description. Rare paintings and tapestries costing a ransom, blend with oriental rugs, and costly draperies which cannot be excelled in even the old palaces of Europe.

There are three sections of the city recognized as the outstanding residential districts of New York's aristocracy and greatest wealth:

FIFTH AVENUE and vicinity
PARK AVENUE and vicinity
EAST RIVER DEVELOPMENTS

Pease & Elliman Co., Douglas L. Elliman & Co., and Brown Wheelock Harris & Co. have been most active in this district. New York owes a great deal of its indisputable supremacy in the way of both its commercial and residential palaces, to the promotive genius and aggressiveness of these three enterprising firms.

278

W. Parker Chase in *New York: The Wonder City* describes 834 as "One of the most regal residential palaces in all the world," for once not an exaggeration.

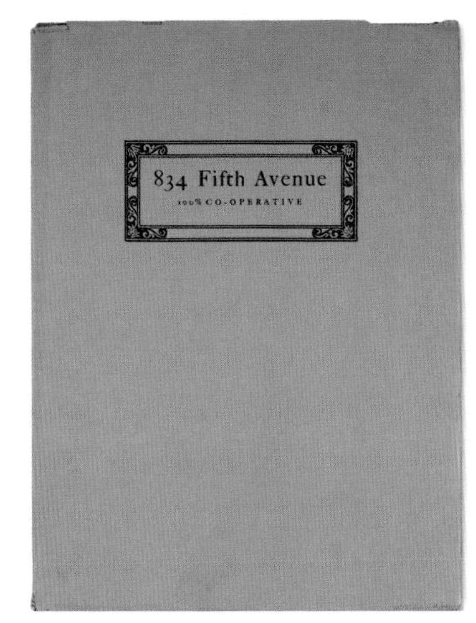

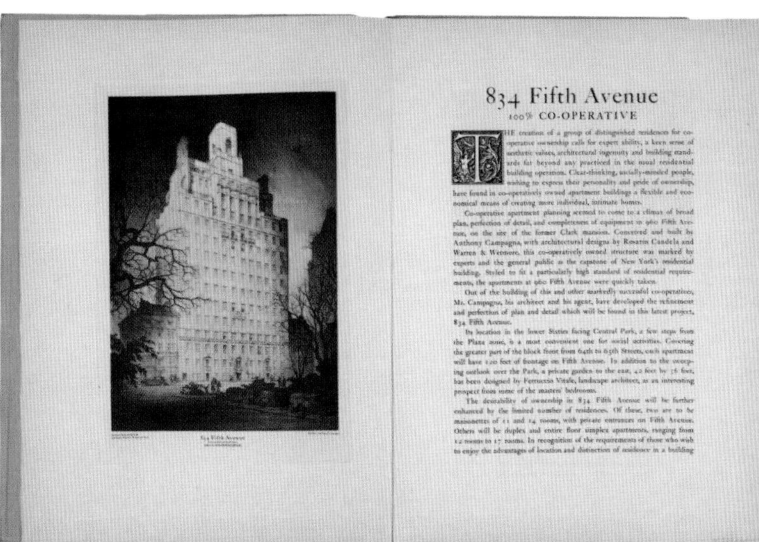

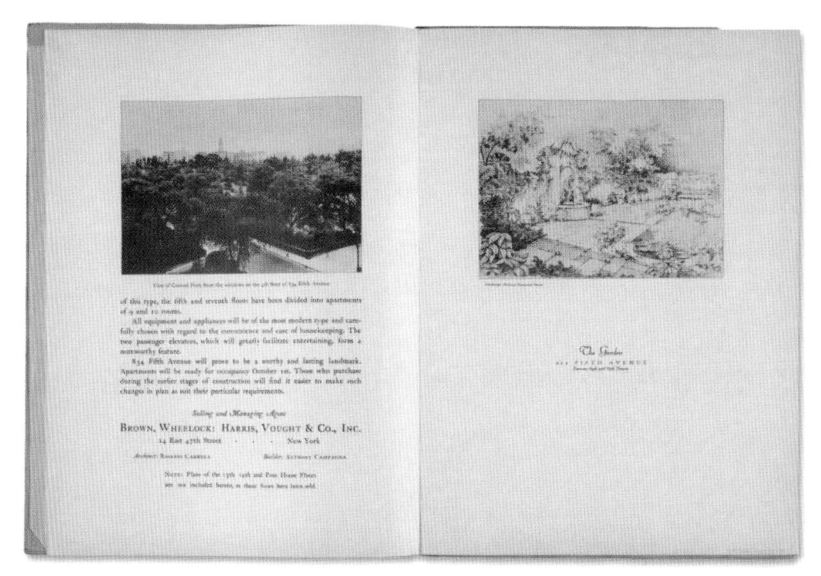

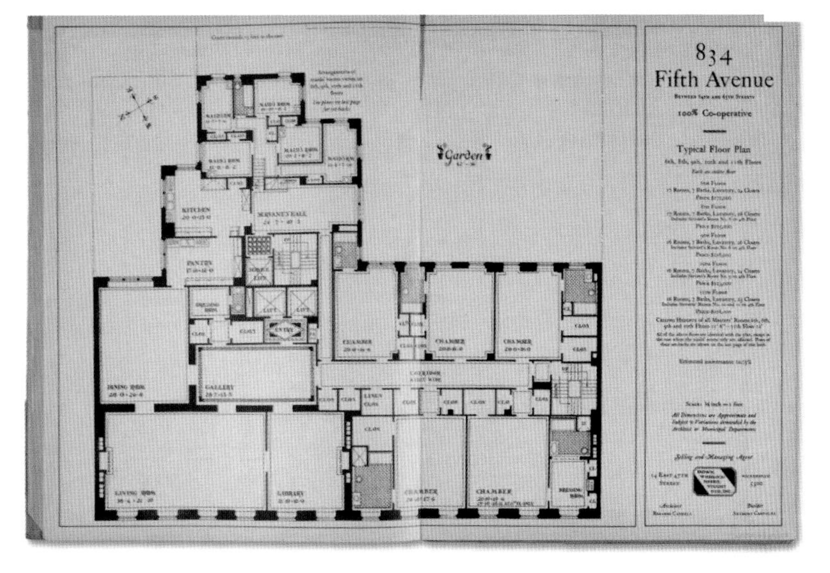

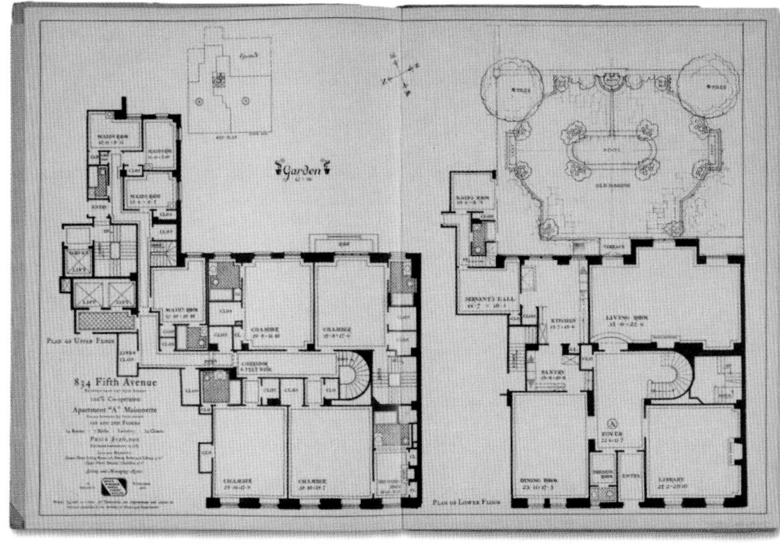

Marketed as a mid-block building, 834 features a water tower and front door centered majestically on the whole composition. With the acquisition of the townhouse at the corner of 64th Street, a line of duplexes was added (east in these plans), which threw off the external symmetry but created some of the most desirable apartments in the building, including those originally occupied by Carl Schmidlapp (6/7A) and Jessie Woolworth Donahue (11/12A). The garden as shown here exists, but the maisonette with projecting bay window was not built—when things shifted this space became occupied by the lobby.

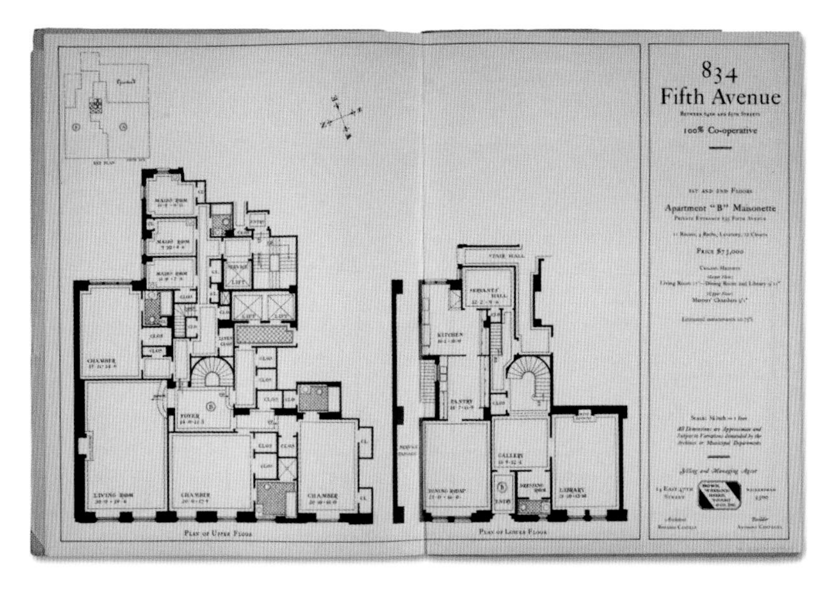
834
Fifth Avenue
100% Co-operative

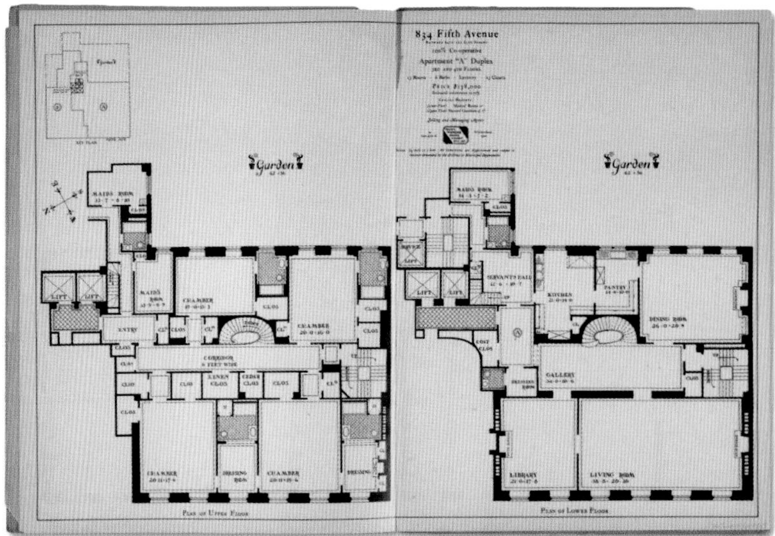
834 Fifth Avenue
Garden
Garden

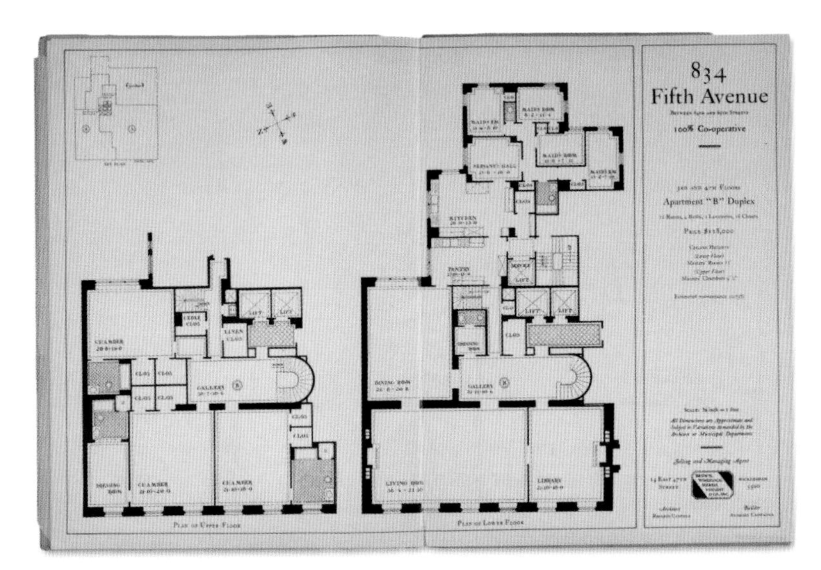
834
Fifth Avenue
100% Co-operative

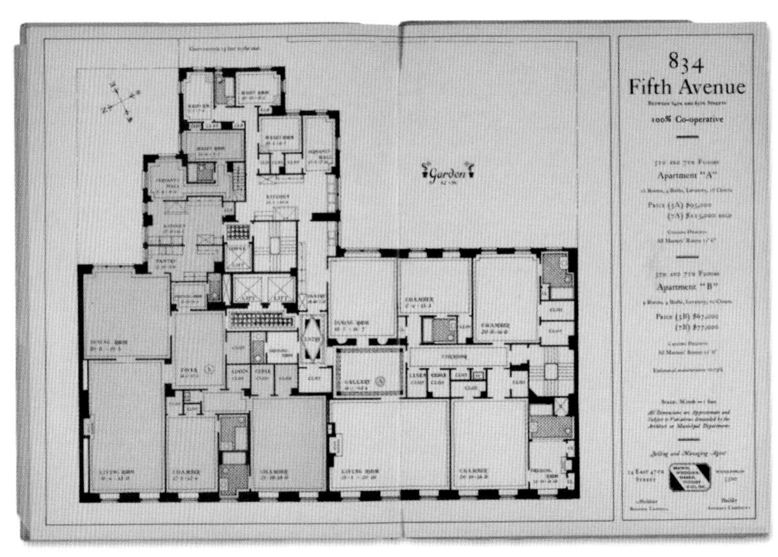
834
Fifth Avenue
100% Co-operative
Garden

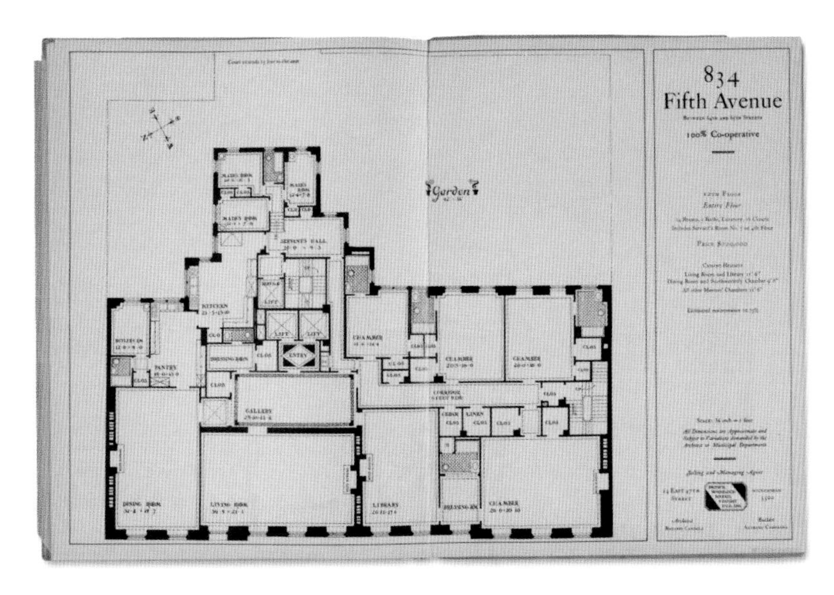
834
Fifth Avenue
100% Co-operative
Garden

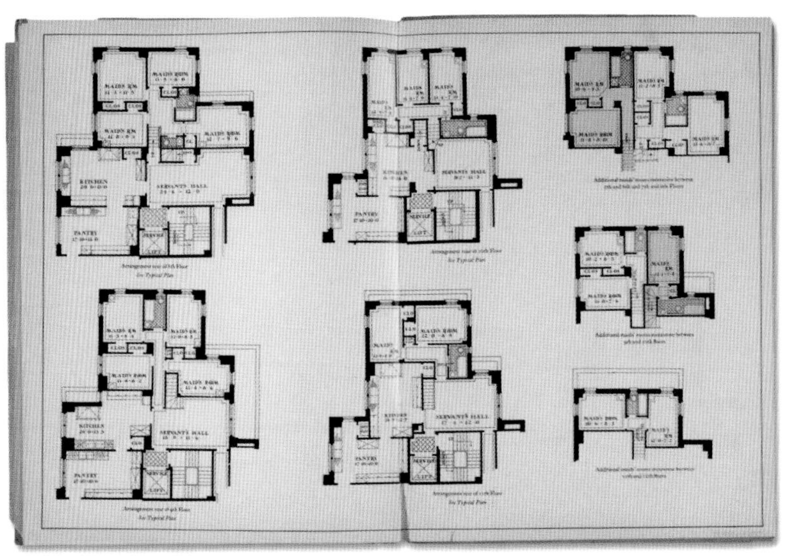

SELECT REGISTER OF APARTMENT HOUSE PLANS

100% Cooperative
Architect: Rosario Candela
Builder: Anthony Campagna
Plot: 150′ 4¼″ x 125′
13—New Law

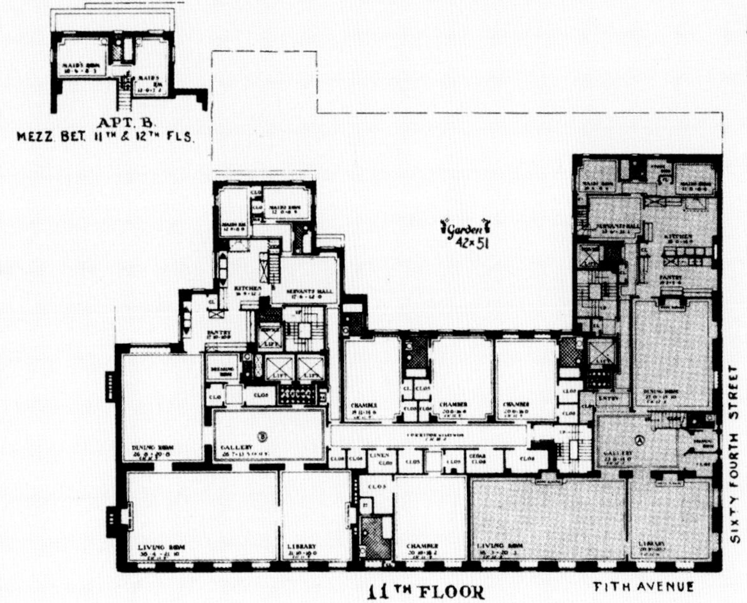

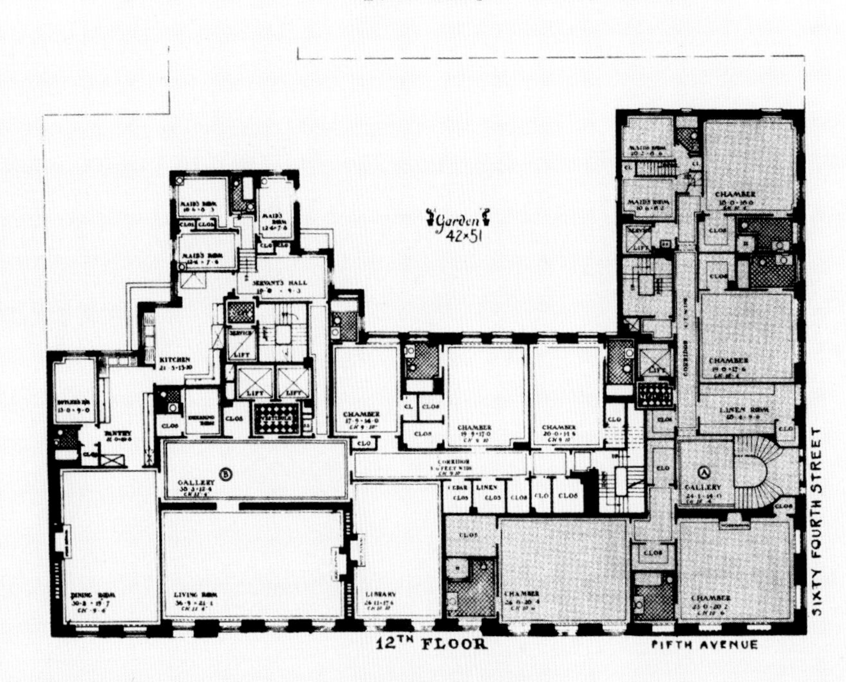

North Corner 64th Street **834 Fifth Avenue** 14 *Story and Pent House Building*

11th and 12th Floors

Duplex "A"	13 Rooms	6 Baths, Lavatory	4 Master's	4 Servants'
Apartment "B" (11th Floor)	15 Rooms	6 Baths, Lavatory	4 Master's	6 Servants'
(Includes Servants' Rooms Nos. 10 and 11 on 4th Floor)				
Apartment "B" (12th Floor)	13 Rooms	5 Baths, Lavatory	3 Master's	5 Servants'
(Includes Servant's Room No. 7 on 4th Floor)				

Apartment 11/12A has the second-largest staircase of any Candela designed—the largest is also in this building (6/7A).

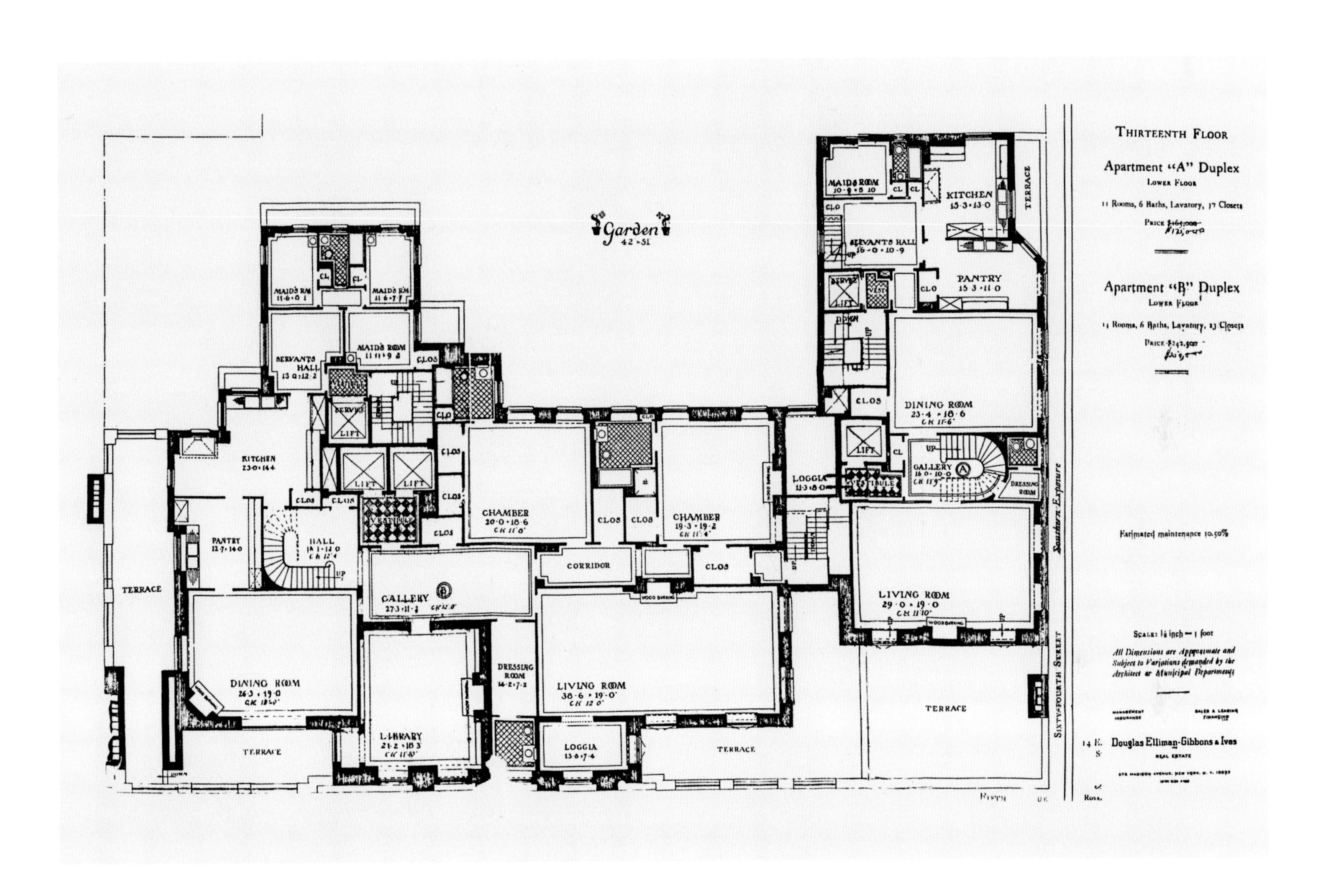

Lower floor of 13B, originally a four-bedroom duplex—two upstairs bedrooms were attached to the penthouse by Laurance Rockefeller at the time he owned the building. Originally occupied by Elizabeth Arden, 13/14A was until recently the home of Hal Prince.

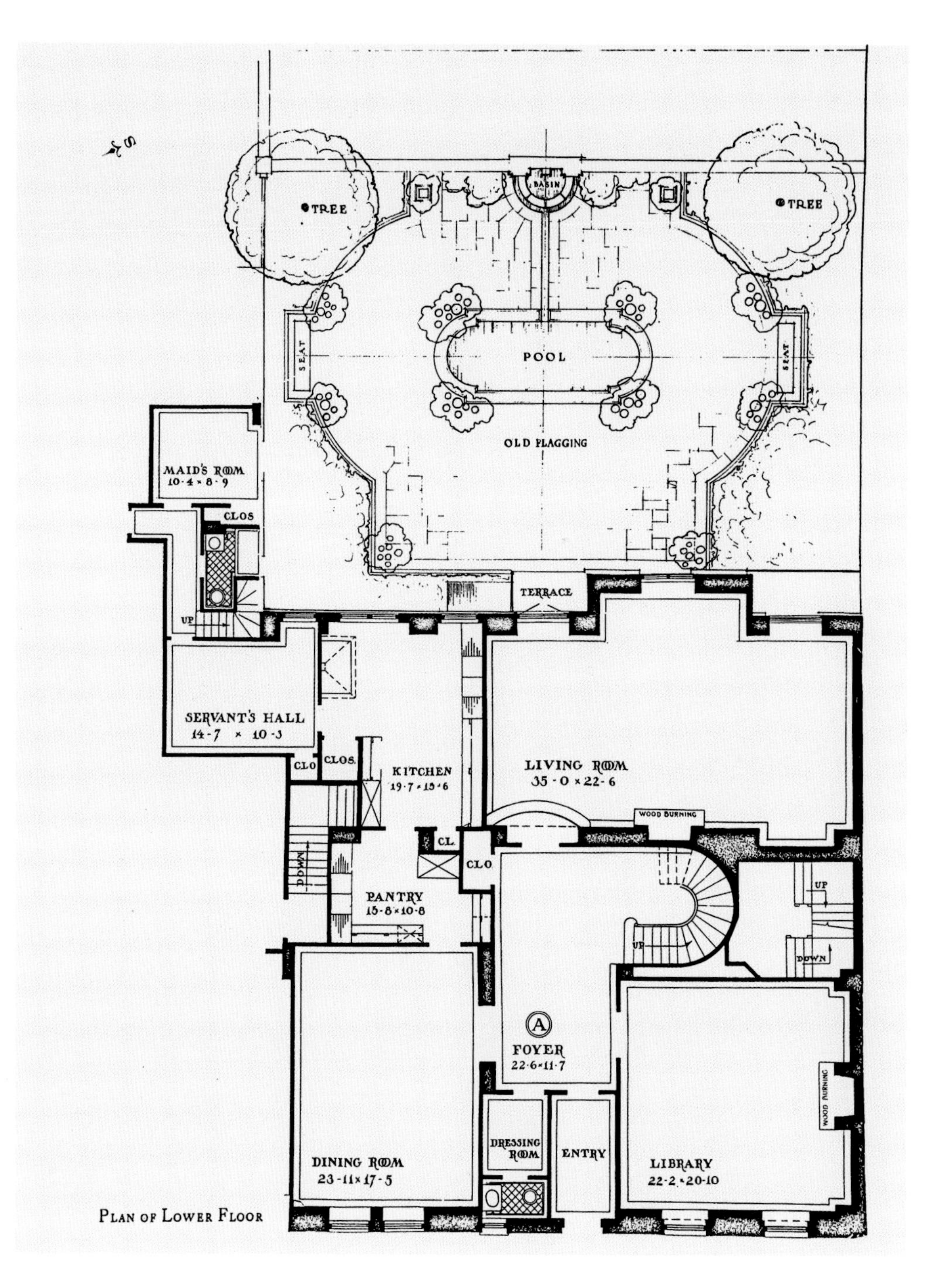

Above left: The pool in the garden originally belonged to this maisonette, not built.

Above right and opposite: The triplex penthouse as acquired by Laurance Rockefeller in 1944. The two bedrooms have yet to be added from 13/14B, but a children's playroom contains a theater with stairs leading to a stage.

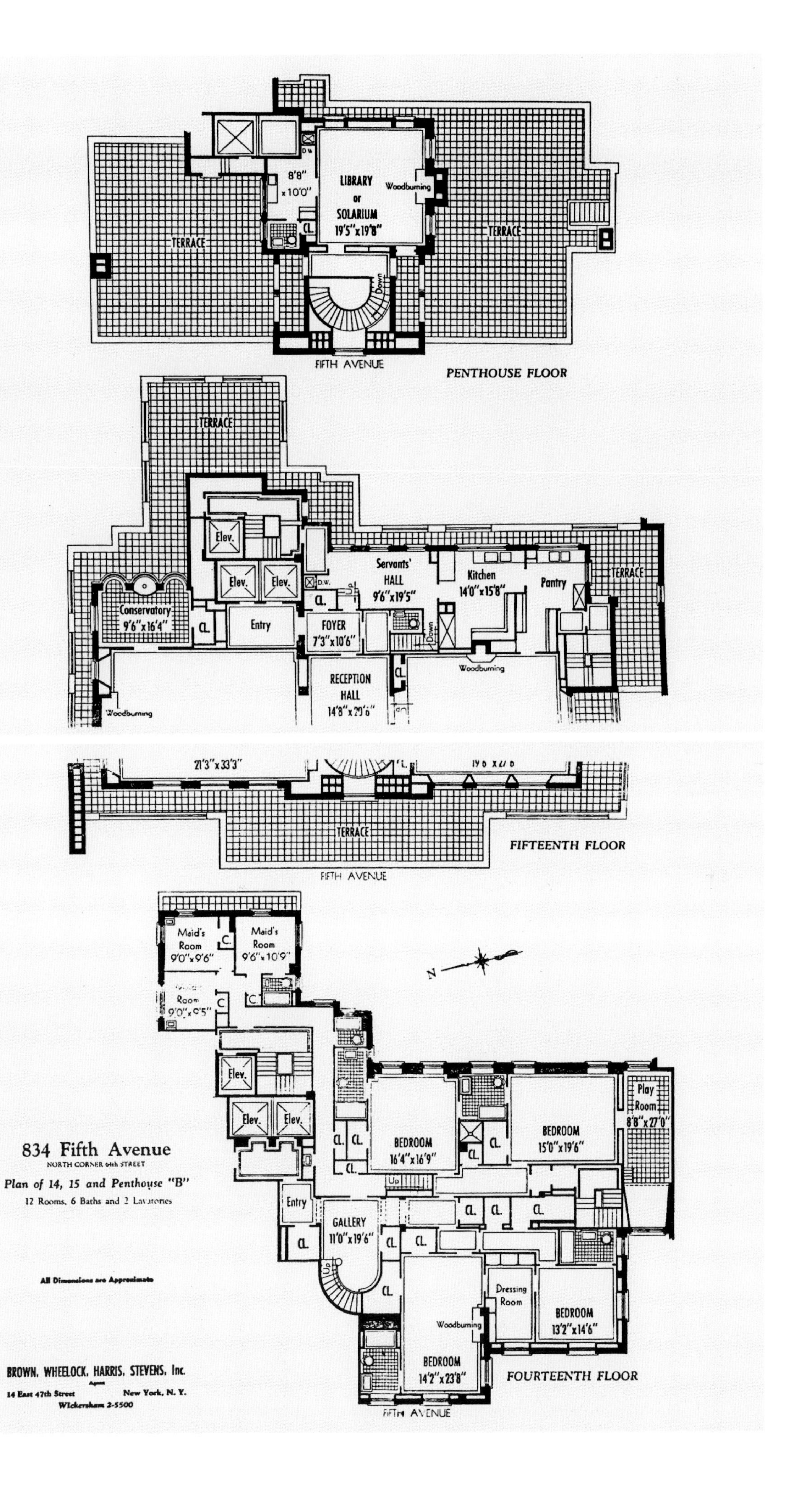

LIBRARY or SOLARIUM 19'5"x19'8"
Woodburning
8'8" x10'0"
CL.
TERRACE
TERRACE
Down
FIFTH AVENUE
PENTHOUSE FLOOR
TERRACE
Elev.
Elev.
Elev.
D.W.
Servants' HALL 9'6"x19'5"
Kitchen 14'0"x15'8"
Pantry
TERRACE
Conservatory 9'6"x16'4"
CL.
Entry
CL.
FOYER 7'3"x10'6"
Down
Woodburning
RECEPTION HALL 14'8"x29'6"
Woodburning
21'3"x33'3"
TERRACE
FIFTEENTH FLOOR
FIFTH AVENUE
Maid's Room 9'0"x9'6"
Maid's Room 9'6"x10'9"
Room 9'0"x9'5"
N
Elev.
Elev.
Elev.
Play Room 8'8"x27'0"
BEDROOM 16'4"x16'9"
BEDROOM 15'0"x19'6"
CL.
Up
Entry
GALLERY 11'0"x19'6"
CL.
Up
Dressing Room
Woodburning
BEDROOM 13'2"x14'6"
BEDROOM 14'2"x23'8"
FOURTEENTH FLOOR
FIFTH AVENUE
834 Fifth Avenue
NORTH CORNER 64th STREET
Plan of 14, 15 and Penthouse "B"
12 Rooms, 6 Baths and 2 Lavatories
All Dimensions are Approximate
BROWN, WHEELOCK, HARRIS, STEVENS, Inc.
Agent
14 East 47th Street
New York, N. Y.
Wickersham 2-5500

The trophy feature of 11/12A is the two-story staircase window.

Above, and following pages: This B-line apartment decorated by Stephen Sills became one of the most influential projects of the 1990s.

A masterpiece by Arshile Gorky hangs over the library fireplace amidst the kind of eclectic assemblage of eighteenth century, neoclassical, and contemporary furniture in a fresh plain envelope that characterized Sills's style at the time.

Dining room of the penthouse, containing panoramic windows installed by Wallace Harrison for Laurance Rockefeller. Originally this apartment was decorated in the Spanish/Italian style still popular in the 1930s for first occupant Hugh B. Baker; the present interior design is by Christian Liaigre.

One of the really successful renovations in a modernist idiom at 834 is by SheltonMindel. Georgian details are edited but not eliminated, with original elements like stair rail and crown moldings used to leverage the design. Photos ©Michael Moran/OTTO Archive

Entrance gallery of the Mr. and Mrs. Antenor Patiño apartment, decorated in the early 1980s by François Catroux

The auction of the contents of the Patiño apartment at Sotheby's in 1986 was a major event, eighteenth-century French decorative arts being the height of fashion at that time.

1040 FIFTH AVENUE, 1929

One of the most impactful of Candela's buildings—thanks in part to its site facing Central Park just below the reservoir and just north of the Metropolitan Museum of Art, but perhaps even more because of the influence of its dramatic silhouette on New York architectural history—is 1040 Fifth Avenue. The upper stories culminate in an enclosed water tower flanked by a loggia to the north and an unusual scooped "buttress" to the south—the latter a theatrical gesture rationalized by effecting the transference of chimney flues from the lower floors, specifically the A-line living room and library fireplaces, to exit through the top of the tower. It is one of the most appealing examples in any building of Candela's ability to take a practical problem, in this case the challenge of merging different chimney flues, and solve it in a way that is unusual, visually compelling, and yet in every way consistent with the overall architectural tone of the building.

It is not surprising, then, that Robert A. M. Stern, perhaps Candela's most accomplished follower, used the scooped buttress of 1040 as the inspiration for the top of his limestone apartment tower at 15 Central Park West, completed in 2008. Stern's tower calls to 1040 diagonally across Central Park, taller and bulkier than its progenitor, but nevertheless paying clear homage.

Always a society building, 1040 ascended into a unique position when the large simplex apartment on the fifteenth floor became home to the widowed Mrs. John F. Kennedy and her two children in 1964. Caroline and John Kennedy grew up in the apartment, and Jacqueline Kennedy Onassis lived at 1040 for thirty years, until her death in the apartment in 1994. She became very much a fixture in the neighborhood and took special pleasure in the running track around the Central Park Reservoir, visible from her windows,

"I just had Jackie O in my cab!" was a phrase heard frequently in 1970s New York daily life.

which was named in her memory after her death. During her years at 1040, the building occupied a special place in New York City folklore, and its front door showed up in numerous pictures by Ron Galella and other paparazzi. Other residents at 1040 have included Mr. and Mrs. Sheldon Whitehouse, parents of the present senator from Rhode Island; McGeorge Bundy during his tenure as President of the Ford Foundation; Mr. and Mrs. Dietrich von Bothmer; and KK Auchincloss.

As with the opulent 834 Fifth and 740 Park Avenues, 1040 is clad entirely in limestone—though a sharp eye can pick out that above the seventeenth floor the facade becomes buff-colored brick with limestone trim. It is hard to know whether this was Candela's way of giving the inventive top a slightly less formal air, or a cost-cutting measure imposed as the building rose and economic times darkened (1040 was begun on January 4 and completed October 8, 1930, an incredibly short ten-month period of construction). With two types of duplexes occupying the northern half and a stack of A-line simplexes at the corner, above the fourteenth floor the apartments enjoying setbacks become full floor, culminating in one of Candela's most intimate and romantic layouts: the duplex penthouse nestled among loggias and chimneys at the building's distinctive top.

Opposite: Offering plans for typical floors show the generous and symmetrical layout of C-line duplexes and—unusual for Candela—their paired living room windows.

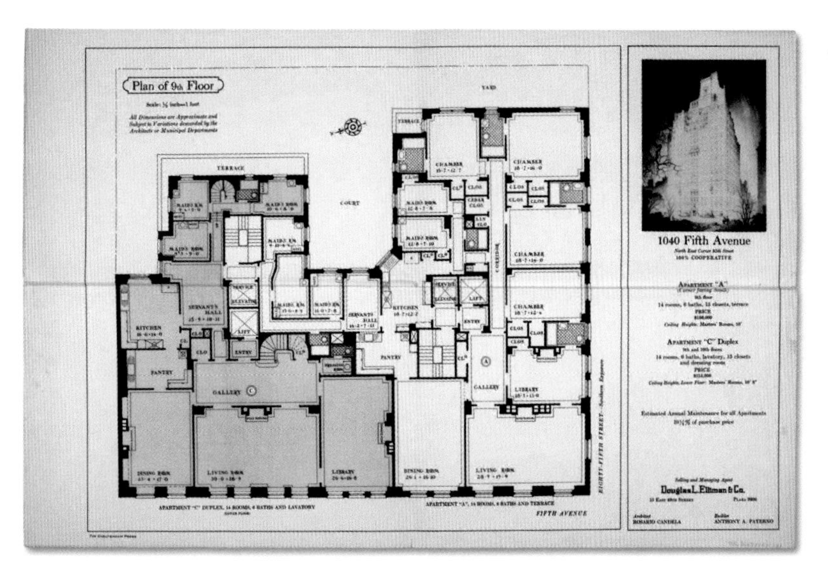

9th Floor, Apartment A

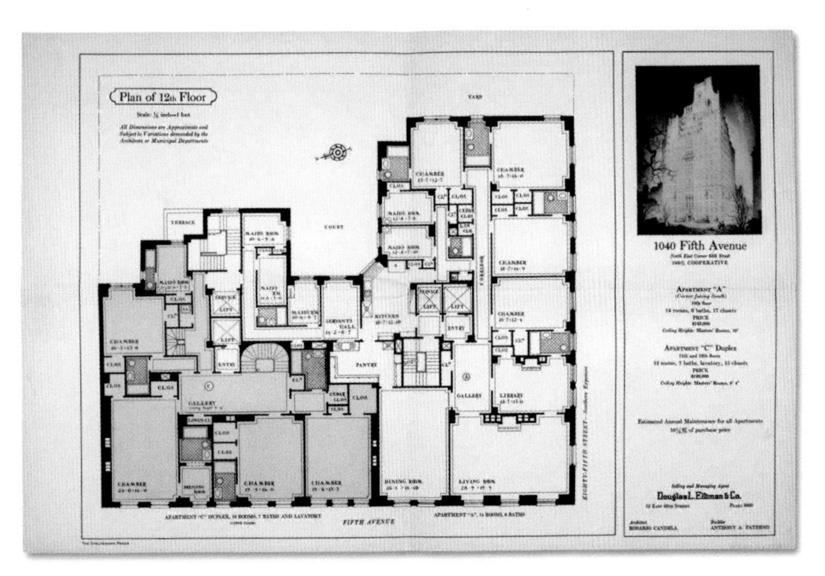

12th Floor, Apartment A

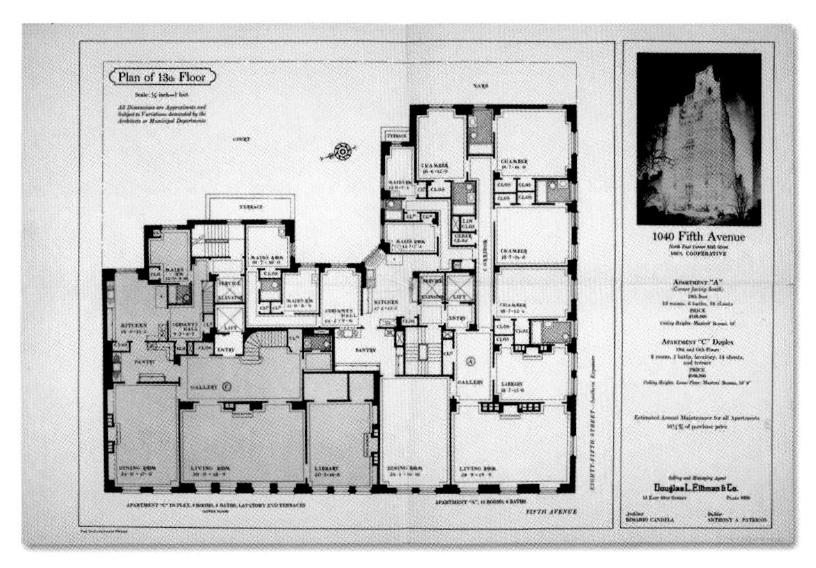

13th Floor, Apartment A

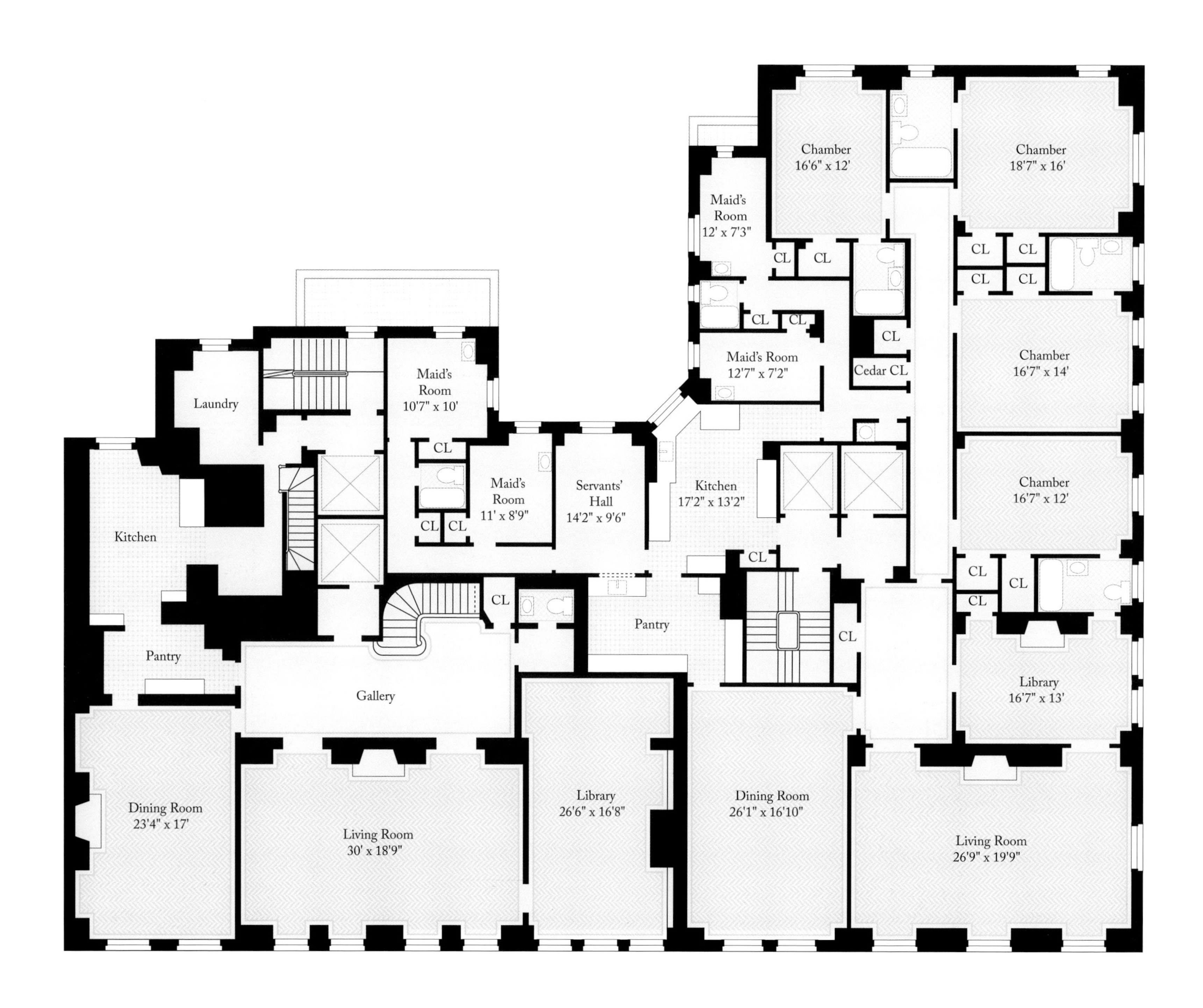

Apartment 13/14C is a unique plan in that two bedrooms have been forsaken for a luxurious master suite containing his and hers baths and dressing rooms—features incorporated in many renovations of later years.

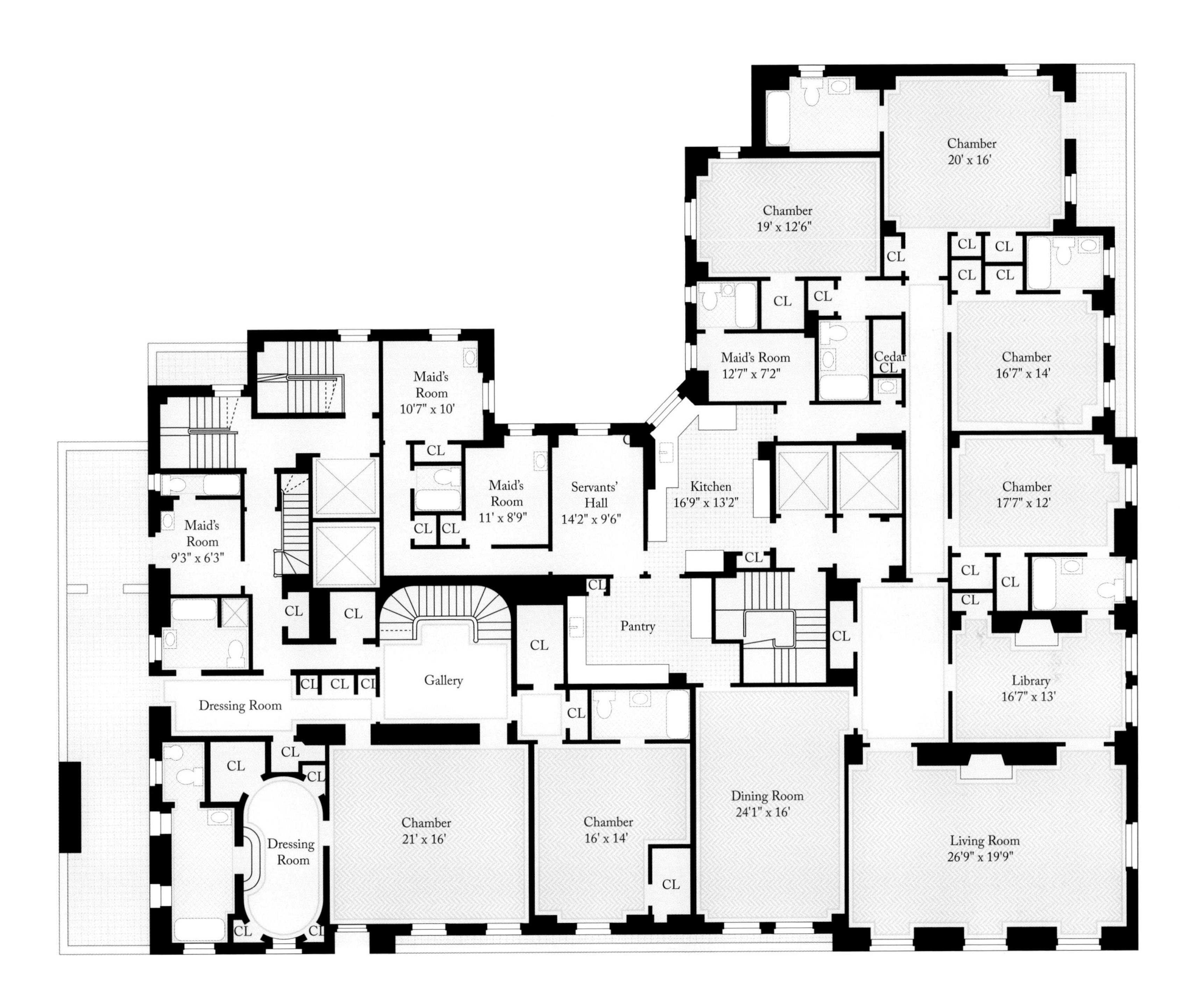
Chamber
20' x 16'
Chamber
19' x 12'6"
CL
CL
CL
CL
CL
CL
CL
Maid's Room
12'7" x 7'2"
Cedar
CL
Chamber
16'7" x 14'
Maid's
Room
10'7" x 10'
CL
Maid's
Room
11' x 8'9"
Servants'
Hall
14'2" x 9'6"
Kitchen
16'9" x 13'2"
Chamber
17'7" x 12'
CL
CL
Maid's
Room
9'3" x 6'3"
CL
CL
CL
CL
CL
Pantry
CL
CL
CL
CL
Gallery
Library
16'7" x 13'
CL
CL
CL
Dressing Room
CL
CL
CL
CL
Dressing
Room
Chamber
21' x 16'
Chamber
16' x 14'
CL
Dining Room
24'1" x 16'
Living Room
26'9" x 19'9"
CL
CL

Bought by Jacqueline Kennedy in 1964, the fifteenth floor remained her home for the rest of her life.

The room arrangement flips on the sixteenth floor, with bedrooms now in the north half—Candela the cryptographer knows that a big corner terrace should belong to the living room. Chimney flues from A-line apartments below obstruct what would have been a blockbuster view of Central Park from the library, but pay dividends on the facade.

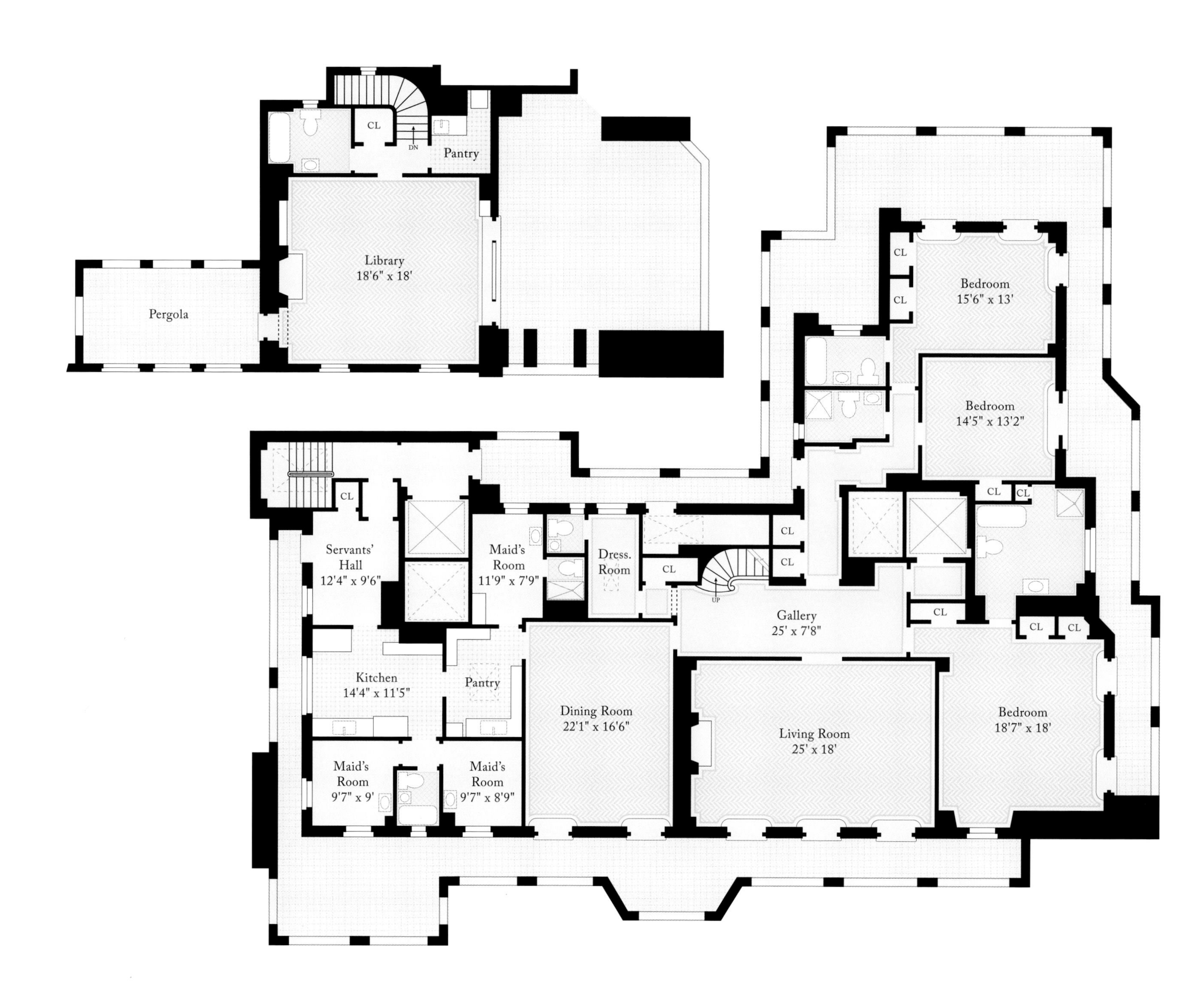

Penthouse with arched loggia off the solarium, now enclosed

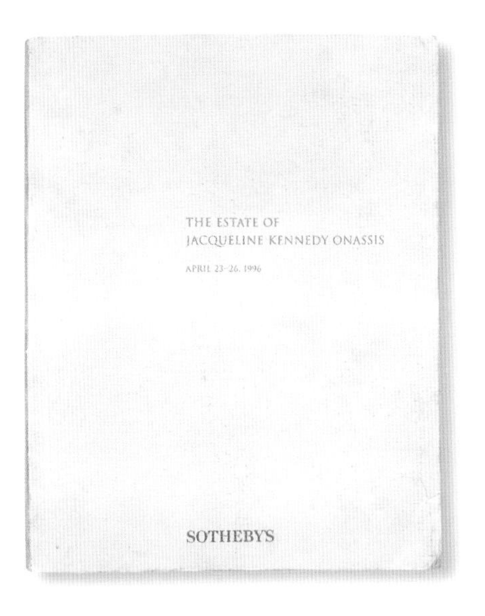

75

A Personal Reminiscence

My reminiscences of Jackie are as vivid today as ever. She was unique, unlike any other person I've known. There was this charismatic presence about her, made up in part by her intelligence, wit, and sense of the ridiculous. You never could be bored when you were with Jackie, because you never knew quite what to expect from her. She had this love of intrigue that often led to some sort of conspiritorial act. For instance, in 1964 when she decided to move from Washington to New York and we went apartment hunting, to avoid publicity she came up with the idea that I would play the part of the prospective buyer while she'd come along disguised as the children's nanny! She looked upon it as a game and she loved every moment of it. Jackie was a wonderful listener. When you told her a story that sparked her imagination, particularly if it included a dash of intrigue, she was not satisfied until you'd told her every last detail — and even then she'd ply you with all sorts of questions that were running through her mind.

I have countless memories of happy and fun times spent with Jackie; I only wish I could tell all of them. But, what I say here is written in the hope that for you who never knew her well - or not at all - it will give an indication of her captivating personality, her attributes and her accomplishments.

THE ESTATE OF
JACQUELINE KENNEDY ONASSIS

Auction:
Tuesday, April 23, 1996 at 7:30 pm
Wednesday, April 24, 1996 at 10 am, 2 pm and 6 pm
Thursday, April 25, 1996 at 10 am, 2 pm and 6 pm
Friday, April 26, 1996 at 10 am and 2 pm

Absentee Bids

Admission
Admission to the exhibition and auction will be limited to ticket holders. For further information, please call (212) 606-7000.

Catalogue

See special Copyright notice on page 7.

SOTHEBY'S

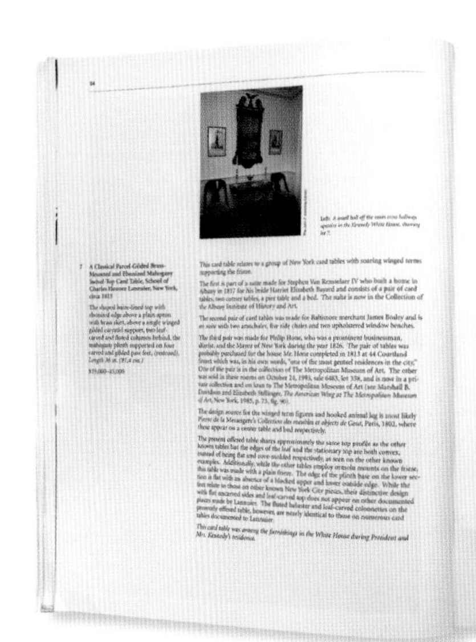

Left: A small hall off the main cross hallway upstairs in the Kennedy White House, showing lot 7.

7 A Classical Parcel-Gilded Brass-Mounted and Ebonized Mahogany Swivel-Top Card Table, School of Charles Honore Lannuier, New York, circa 1815

The shaped baize-lined top with ebonized edge above a plain apron with brass skirt, above a single winged gilded caryatid support, two leaf-carved and fluted columns behind, the mahogany plinth supported on four carved and gilded paw feet, (restored). Length 36 in. (91.4 cm.)

$35,000-45,000

This card table relates to a group of New York card tables with soaring winged terms supporting the frieze.

The first is part of a suite made for Stephen Van Rensselaer IV who built a home in Albany in 1817 for his bride Harriet Elizabeth Bayard and consists of a pair of card tables, two corner tables, a pier table and a bed. The suite is now in the Collection of the Albany Institute of History and Art.

The second pair of card tables was made for Baltimore merchant James Bosley and is en suite with two armchairs, five side chairs and two upholstered window benches.

The third pair was made for Philip Hone, who was a prominent businessman, diarist, and the Mayor of New York during the year 1826. The pair of tables was probably purchased for the house Mr. Hone completed in 1813 at 44 Courtland Street which was, in his own words, "one of the most genteel residences in the city." One of the pair is in the collection of The Metropolitan Museum of Art. The other was sold in these rooms on October 21, 1993, sale 6483, lot 358, and is now in a private collection and on loan to The Metropolitan Museum of Art (see Marshall B. Davidson and Elizabeth Stillinger, *The American Wing at The Metropolitan Museum of Art*, New York, 1985, p. 73, fig. 90).

The design source for the winged term figures and hooked animal leg is most likely Pierre de la Mesangere's *Collection des meubles et objects de Gout*, Paris, 1802, where these appear on a center table and bed respectively.

The present offered table shares approximately the same top profile as the other known tables but the edges of the leaf and the stationary top are both convex, instead of being flat and cove-molded respectively, as seen on the other known examples. Additionally, while the other tables employ ormolu mounts on the frieze, this table was made with a plain frieze. The edge of the plinth base on the lower section is flat with an absence of a blocked upper and lower outside edge. While the feet relate to those on other known New York City pieces, their distinctive design with flat uncarved sides and leaf-carved top does not appear on other documented pieces made by Lannuier. The fluted baluster and leaf-carved colonnettes on the presently offered table, however, are nearly identical to those on numerous card tables documented to Lannuier.

This card table was among the furnishings in the White House during President and Mrs. Kennedy's residence.

73

The Estate of Jacqueline Kennedy Onassis

In deciding what to do with our mother's possessions, we were guided first and foremost by her deep knowledge and love of history. She was proud to have played a part in the history of our country, and in accordance with her wishes, we have given objects and documents which help chronicle the Kennedy Administration and her role as First Lady to the John F. Kennedy Library Foundation which will make them available to the public.

Beyond that, our mother believed in individuals more than in institutions. She was able to evoke the lives and people of other times and places, describing to us the ancient pharaohs, court society at Versailles, or life on a Nantucket whaling ship so vividly that we felt we had visited these wondrous places. For our mother, history came alive through objects and paintings, as well as books. Because the things she collected link her with history, and because she cared about them, they represent more than just a record of her life and travels. As they go out into the world, we hope that they bring with them not only their own beauty and spirit, but some of hers as well.

Caroline Kennedy John Kennedy

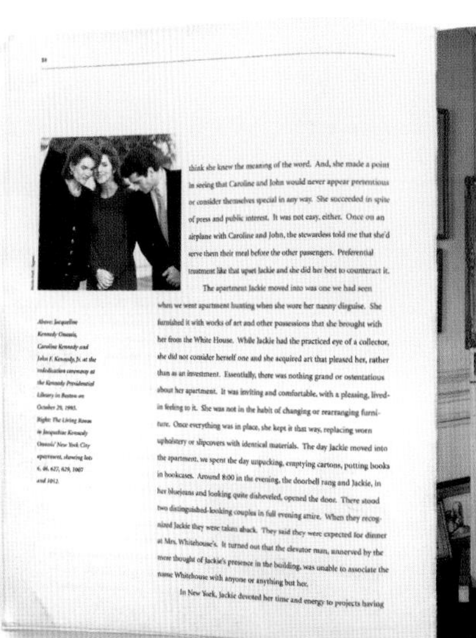

Above: Jacqueline Kennedy Onassis, Caroline Kennedy and John F. Kennedy, Jr. at the rededication ceremony at the Kennedy Presidential Library in Boston on October 29, 1993.
Right: The Living Room in Jacqueline Kennedy Onassis' New York City apartment, showing lots 6, 46, 627, 629, 1007 and 1012.

think she knew the meaning of the word. And, she made a point in seeing that Caroline and John would never appear pretentious or consider themselves special in any way. She succeeded in spite of press and public interest. It was not easy, either. Once on an airplane with Caroline and John, the stewardess told me that she'd serve them their meal before the other passengers. Preferential treatment like that upset Jackie and she did her best to counteract it.

The apartment Jackie moved into was one we had seen when we went apartment hunting when she wore her nanny disguise. She furnished it with works of art and other possessions that she brought with her from the White House. While Jackie had the practiced eye of a collector, she did not consider herself one and she acquired art that pleased her, rather than as an investment. Essentially, there was nothing grand or ostentatious about her apartment. It was inviting and comfortable, with a pleasing, lived-in feeling to it. She was not in the habit of changing or rearranging furniture. Once everything was in place, she kept it that way, replacing worn upholstery or slipcovers with identical materials. The day Jackie moved into the apartment, we spent the day unpacking, emptying cartons, putting books in bookcases. Around 8:00 in the evening, the doorbell rang and Jackie, in her bluejeans and looking quite disheveled, opened the door. There stood two distinguished-looking couples in full evening attire. When they recognized Jackie they were taken aback. They said they were expected for dinner at Mrs. Whitehouse's. It turned out that the elevator man, unnerved by the mere thought of Jackie's presence in the building, was unable to associate the name Whitehouse with anyone or anything but her.

In New York, Jackie devoted her time and energy to projects having

The Sotheby's catalogue for the sale of Mrs. Onassis's estate, shown above and on following pages, featured extensive photography of 1040, with an artist's easel in the living room, and a sophisticated and unconventional furniture plan in the dining room.

THE ESTATE OF JACQUELINE KENNEDY ONASSIS

SESSION ONE
TUESDAY, APRIL 23,
7:30 P.M.

The Living Room and Dining Room of Jacqueline Kennedy Onassis' New York City apartment, showing lots 3, 15, 72, 82, 94, 234, 239, 240, 246, 250, 263, 273, 309, 323, 341, 352 and 1003.

THE ESTATE OF JACQUELINE KENNEDY ONASSIS

SESSION TWO

WEDNESDAY, APRIL 24,

10:00 A.M.

The Living Room and Dining Room of Jacqueline Kennedy Onassis' New York City apartment, showing lots 12, 35, 40, 72, 120, 274, 308, 333, 341, 352 and 1002.

VANISHED CIVILIZATIONS
China
A TIME OF GODS
GODS, MEN & PHARAOHS
THE TAO OF PAINTING
FRANCE

THE ESTATE OF JACQUELINE KENNEDY ONASSIS

SESSION SEVEN
THURSDAY, APRIL 25,
6:00 P.M.

The Dining Room in Jacqueline Kennedy Onassis' New York City apartment, showing lots 14, 264, 265, 282, 303, 314, 332 and 968.

Onassis's library as decorated by Billy Baldwin and photographed by Horst for *Vogue* (June, 1973). Between the windows sits the desk on which JFK signed the 1963 Nuclear Test Ban Treaty.

The library and principal bathroom of the penthouse, flooded with sunlight and floating two hundred feet above Central Park, as decorated by KK Auchincloss and photographed by Derry Moore (1985)

The most romantic private space in New York? Quite possibly. Behind the Palladian arch that has such a prominent place in the skyline of Fifth Avenue is this intimate aerie, with Candela's picture window ensuring that Emery Roth's San Remo can be seen through the terrace and across the park.

19 EAST 72ND STREET, 1936

This is not only Candela's last "great" building—it was not finished until 1937—it is one of his most unusual, and his hardest shared design credit to decipher. Mott Schmidt was the associate architect, though it is difficult to figure out what the contribution of Candela's associate might actually have been. The plans are without question by Candela; the facade is pure Art Moderne—with a base motif taken from Josef Hoffmann's 1925 Austrian Pavilion. We are as far from Schmidt's signature Colonial Revival decorum as it is possible to get. Like Warren & Wetmore and Cross & Cross, Schmidt was better known than Candela and had the proper credentials of high Waspishness—but that last may have been the very point of the shared billing. A patrician tenant in 1930 could feel at home in a building with names of architects they knew because they had designed their friends' country houses connected to it.

Nineteen is singular in another way as well, since it was built not by a real estate developer but by John Thomas Smith, general counsel of General Motors. His wife wanted a townhouse, but Smith, conscious of the conspicuousness of such a dwelling during what was still the depths of the Depression, insisted they build an apartment building instead with the "house" embedded in it in the form of a special duplex on the fourteenth and fifteenth floors (Smith and his family ultimately occupied a total of three units). Mrs. Smith had admired the monumental, windowed stair of apartment 11/12 at 834 Fifth (see page 257), and requested Candela design one as similar as possible here.

The ghost at the banquet is the loss of McKim, Mead & White's extraordinary Tiffany house, which had occupied the site at 72nd Street and Madison Avenue since 1885; it was one of the Upper East Side's greatest houses, and a rare example of McKim, Mead & White working in a largely Romanesque style.

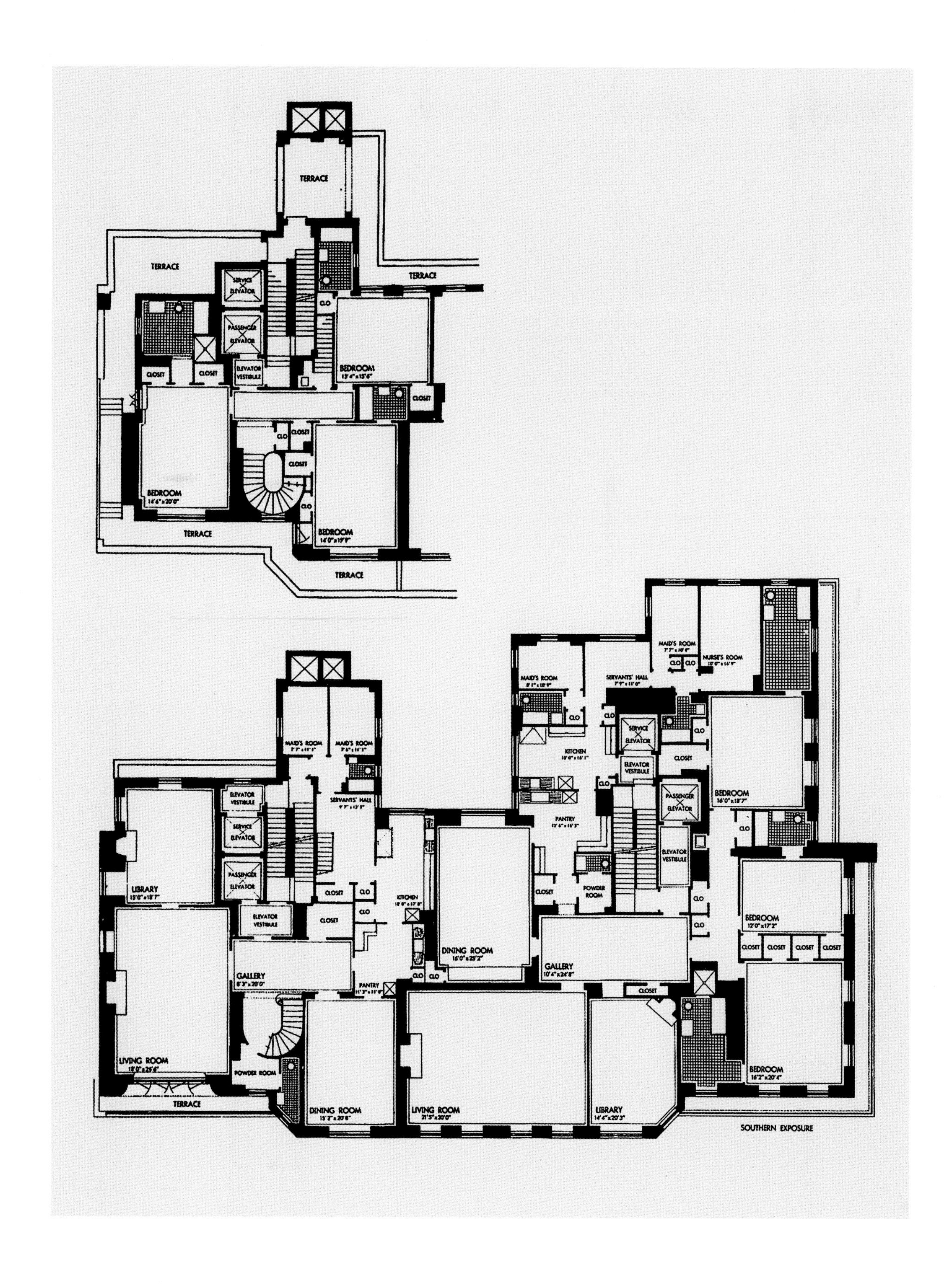

Above: The wide living room windows of a sixteenth-floor duplex are today augmented by a solarium that encloses the terrace.

Opposite: The deer sculpture in the entrance courtyard is by C. Paul Jennewein, who also did the bas-relief animals surrounding the entrance.

Sweeping stair in the entrance to a special duplex on the fourteenth and fifteenth floors. This apartment with its extraordinary staircase was constructed for the builder of apartment 19, John Thomas Smith, to resemble the one he admired in apartment 11/12A at 834 Fifth (see page 257).

Renovations by Richard Meier show the DNA of modernism making its way from the outside in. Candela's signature windows with their deep reveals are unchanged, giving a sense of heft and gravitas to the minimalist proceedings.

ACKNOWLEDGMENTS

This book began—for me—in 1987 as a research paper at Sarah Lawrence College with the support and encouragement of three professors: Tim Gilfoyle, Gil Perez, and Joe Forte. It continued with the help of Christopher Gray, Andrew Alpern, and Donald Wrobleski.

I would like to thank Edward Lee Cave, Mark Hampton, Joe Sulzberger, Slim Aarons, Pell James Burns, Serena Boardman, Anne Bass, Samantha and Hyatt Bass, Eric Boman, Louise Grunwald, Maria von Bothmer, Oberto Gili, Stephen Sills, and Bill Blass for showing me things there would have been no other way to see. Many others have told me things there would have been no other way to know; most would prefer not to be named. Thank you so very much for your trust.

Two books have shown the way: Michael Gross's *740 Park,* and Kirk Henckels and Anne Walker's *Life at the Top*. This book stands on their shoulders.

A very special thanks to Elisa Gallagher for saving the project at a crucial moment, in every way that a project can be saved. Thank you to Claudia Goldstein for your skill in drawing our magnificent new plans. Thank you Sam Cochran for helping us hit our marks, and to Helen Rice for a kitchen to hit them in. Thanks to my children for the best feeling in the world, being believed in. Thank you to Roger Lynch for the keys that opened the kingdom, which is the Conde Nast Photo Archive.

Lastly, thank you my co-authors Paul and Peter, to Aerin for contributing her unique perspective to our foreword, to our editor Douglas Curran, and to Takaaki Matsumoto and Amy Wilkins for their endless patience and ingenuity in designing this book.

—D. N.

First published in the United States of America in 2024 by
RIZZOLI INTERNATIONAL PUBLICATIONS, INC.
49 West 27th Street, New York, NY 10001
www.rizzoliusa.com

Photo Credits:
Front cover, pp. 42, 52, 55 top left, 58 top left, 62, 68, 69, 72–73, 80, 83, 86, 88, 98, 100 top left, 110, 116 top left, 138, 172, 173 top left, 234, 244, 246 top right, 256, 294: Wurts Brothers / Museum of the City of New York; p. 2: Courtesy of the Library of Congress, LC-USW3-014476-D; p. 7: Photo by Mark Lund; pp. 10, 18, 70, 139, 193: Kenneth Grant / Alamy Stock Photo; pp. 12 top left, 16 left, 16 right: Marc Wanamaker / Bison Archives; p. 12 top right: Album / Alamy Stock Photo; pp. 13 top left, 164: Courtesy Andrew Alpern; p. 13 top center: U.S. Army Signal Corps; p. 13 top right: Courtesy of www.peterharrington.co.uk; pp. 14–15: Archive Photos / Getty Images; pp. 17, 21, 39, 81, 84, 99, 216, 241 left, 241 right: Courtesy Joseph Candela; p. 18: NYC Parks Department Photo Archive; pp. 19, 150: Samuel H. Gottscho / Museum of the City of New York; p. 20 top left: © Oxford Publishing Limited. Reproduced with permission of the Licensor through PLSclear; p. 22: Photo by Brad Farwell; pp. 23, 36, 47 top left, 47 top right, 56 top left, 56 top right, 100 top right, 102, 112–113, 116 top right, 122, 124, 133, 166, 167, 174, 178, 239, 240, 250–251, 298–299: Avery Classics, Avery Architectural & Fine Arts Library, Columbia University; pp. 26, 132, 134–135, 136–137: Photo Oberto Gili; *The Three Sisters*, by Balthus (p. 134), © 2024 Balthus / Harumi Klossowska de Rola (Fonds Balthus); p. 27 top left: Zoom Historical / Alamy Stock Photo; p. 27 top right: Collection Center for Creative Photography, © Center for Creative Photography, Arizona Board of Regents; p. 28 top left: Ron Galella / Getty Images; p. 28 top right: WWD / Getty Images; p. 29 top left: Edward Steichen, *Vogue*, © Condé Nast; p. 29 top center: Constantin Alajalov, *The New Yorker*, © Condé Nast; p. 29 top right: Peter Arno / The New Yorker Collection / The Cartoon Bank; pp. 30 top left, 206–207, 208, 209, 210–211, 212–213, 214, 215: Eric Boman Archive; p. 30 top right: Cecil Beaton Archive © Condé Nast; pp. 31, 175: Slim Aarons / Getty Images; pp. 41 top left, 41 top center left, 41 top center right: © Peter Aaron / OTTO; p. 41 top right: Photo by Noe DeWitt; p. 44: Beecher Ogden / Museum of the City of New York; p. 45: From *The American Architect*, Volume 135, 2/5/1929, p. 168; p. 55 top right: Byron Collection / Museum of the City of New York; p. 57 top left: Irma and Paul Milstein Division of United States History, Local History and Genealogy, The New York Public Library. "No. 635 Park Avenue. Southeast Corner Sixty-sixth Street." The New York Public Library Digital Collections. 1913. https://digitalcollections.nypl.org/items/510d47da-d59e-a3d9-e040-e00a18064a99; p. 57 top right: Brown Brothers; p. 58 top right: Antiqua Print Gallery / Alamy Stock Photo; p. 64: MAK – Museum of Applied Arts, Vienna, Austria; pp. 65, 295: Kenneth Grant / NewYorkitecture.com; p. 71 bottom: Courtesy Lee Waldman; pp. 74–75, 76–77, 78–79: Fritz von der Schulenburg / Interior Archive; pp. 82 left, 82 right, 89, 119, 121, 123, 125, 142, 176, 177, 197, 224, 225, 252: From Select Realty Register, Inc. *The Select Register of Apartment House Plans, New York City*. New York: Select Realty Register, 1957–; pp. 87, 92, 93, 115, 140 top left, 235, 239: Gottscho-Schleisner / Museum of the City of New York; pp. 94, 95, 96–97: Durston Saylor, *Architectural Digest*, © Condé Nast; *Homme nu assis*, 1971, by Pablo Picasso (in background, p. 96) © 2024 Estate of Pablo Picasso / Artists Rights Society (ARS), New York; pp. 103, 104, 105: Photographs by François Halard; *Instruments de musique sur un gueridon*, 1914, by Pablo Picasso (in background, p. 103) © 2024 Estate of Pablo Picasso / Artists Rights Society (ARS), New York; pp. 106, 107, 108, 109: Photographs by Jonathan Becker; *Untitled XIV*, 1982, by Willem de Kooning (on side wall, p. 108) © 2024 The Willem de Kooning Foundation/Artists Rights Society (ARS), New York; *Peinture Murale*, (1932), by Ferdinand Léger (p. 109) © 2024 Artists Rights Society (ARS), New York / ADAGP, Paris; p. 111: Keystone-France / Getty Images; pp. 114, 165 top right, 190, 246 top left, 272: Courtesy of the New York Historical Society; p. 117: Drawing by Takaaki Matsumoto; pp. 126–127, 128, 129: Source unknown; pp. 130–131: Photo by Richard Averill Smith. Courtesy of the New-York Historical Society; pp. 140 top right, 194–195, 217: Photographs by Yoo Jean Han; p. 141: Source unknown; pp. 144, 145, 146, 147, 148, 149, 198, 199, 200–201, 226, 227, 228, 229, 230, 231, 276, 277, 278, 279, 280: Drawings by Claudia Goldstein; pp. 152, 153: Straus Historical Society; pp. 156, 157: Peter Vitale, *Architectural Digest*, © Condé Nast; pp. 158, 159, 160–161, 162–163: Photography by Michael Mundy; pp. 168–169, 297, 302: Museum of the City of New York; p. 170: Courtesy of Christopher Gray; p. 173 top right: Photo by Gea Elika, Principal Broker for ELIKA Real Estate; pp. 174 top right, 241, 243, 275 top, 275 center, 275 bottom: From Columbia Digital Library Collections; pp. 179, 180, 182, 184: Courtesy of Rockefeller Archive Center; pp. 181, 183, 185: Arnold Newman / Getty Images; pp. 186–187, 188, 189: Karen Radkai, *House & Garden*, © Condé Nast; pp. 191 top left, back cover: © Peter Aaron/OTTO (designed by Robert A.M. Stern Architects); pp. 191 top right, 218–219: Photograph by Rob Stephenson; p. 192: © Netflix; p. 196: From *Buildings and Building Management*, May 16, 1932. Courtesy Christopher Gray; p. 202: Courtesy of the Pittsburgh *Post Gazette;* p. 203: Rendering by Takaaki Matsumoto; pp. 204, 205: Richard Champion, *Architectural Digest*, © Condé Nast; p. 220 top left: WILLIAM E. SAURO / the *New York Times* / Redux; p. 220 top right: Courtesy of Mita Bland, Collection of Eric Cohler; pp. 222–223: Marco Ricca / Pavarini Design; pp. 232, 233: © Pieter Estersohn / Art Department; p. 242: Irma and Paul Milstein Division of United States History, Local History and Genealogy, The New York Public Library. (1908), Joseph Paterno. Retrieved from https://digitalcollections.nypl.org/items/510d47db-9eca-a3d9-e040-e00a18064a99; p. 245: From the *New York Times*, April 6, 1930, Section 12, p. 1; pp. 257 top left, 257 bottom right: Courtesy Pell James; pp. 258, 259, 260, 261, 262–263: Photo by Thibeault Johnson. Courtesy Steven Sills Associates; pp. 264–265: Photo by Sherry Griffin. Ceiling Installation by David Wiseman; pp. 266, 267: © Michael Moran/OTTO Archive; pp. 269–270, 271: Feliciano, *House & Garden*, © Condé Nast; p. 273: Source unknown; p. 274: Bettmann / Getty Images; pp. 281, 282–283, 284–285, 286–287: Photographs of Sotheby's catalogue cover and spreads by Takaaki Matsumoto; pp. 288, 289: Horst P. Horst, *Vogue*, © Condé Nast; pp. 290, 291, 292–293: Derry Moore, *Architectural Digest*, © Condé Nast; pp. 300–301: © Richard Meier. Courtesy MeierPartners

Publisher: Charles Miers
Editor: Douglas Curran
Production Manager: Rebecca Ambrose
Managing Editor: Lynn Scrabis
Copyeditor: Sarah Stump
Proofreader: Lars Dahlin Eckstrom and Kelli Rae Patton
Design Manager: Tim Biddick

Designed by Takaaki Matsumoto, Matsumoto Incorporated
Design assisted by Amy Wilkins and Robin Brunelle, Matsumoto Incorporated

Printed and bound in China

2025 2026 2027 2028 / 10 9 8 7 6 5 4 3 2

ISBN-13: 978-0-8478-6782-0
Library of Congress Control Number: 2024904750

Visit us online:
Instagram.com/RizzoliBooks
Facebook.com/RizzoliNewYork
X: @Rizzoli_Books
Youtube.com/user/RizzoliNY